THE RELEVANCE of the REVELATION

Vic Reasoner

3080 Brannon Rd
Nicholasville, KY 40356-9700

ISBN 979-8-9957589-0-7

Library of Congress Control Number:
2026940259

INTRODUCTION

2 Timothy 3:16 declares that *all* scripture is profitable. Nor should we hesitate to declare the whole counsel of God (Acts 20:27). Revelation 1:3 pronounces a twofold blessing for the one who reads, as well as the one who hears and keeps this book. While that promise could be made for all of God's Word, this is the only book containing a direct blessing — perhaps to invite us to overcome our reluctance toward its contents. This book is a revelation, not an attempt to obscure truth.

In 2005 I wrote *A Fundamental Wesleyan Commentary on Revelation*. It ran 592 pages. In 2023 a second, two-volume edition was published, running 726 pages. In both editions I attempted to interact with all the major literature on the book of Revelation. However, some readers found all of the various interpretations confusing.

Yet many people have only heard of one interpretation. For those who want to explore the range of options, see *Four Views on the Book of Revelation*, edited by C. Marvin Pate. The four views are preterist, idealist, historicist, and futurist. The two major options today are preterist and futurist. These options are debated by Thomas Ice and Kenneth L. Gentry, Jr. in *The Great Tribulation: Past or Future?* Another interpretative issue regards the nature and timing of the millennium. See *Three Views on the Millennium and Beyond*, edited by Darrell L. Bock. The three views are premillennialism, postmillennialism, and amillennialism.

I evaluate all of the positions in my larger commentary, but in this shorter version I advocate a preterist, postmillennial interpretation. I recommend *Revelation: Four Views, A Parallel Commentary* in which Steve Gregg puts the major interpretations in parallel columns going through the whole book of Revelation. In this edition I have also tried to keep footnotes to a minimum. However, I want to give credit where it is due. These footnotes also serve as references if you want to do more in-depth study.

Authorship

The author identifies himself as *John*. He uses his name four times (1:1, 4, 9; 22:8). No other person, other than the apostle, was so well known to the early church that he could identify himself simply as *John*. Since 22:6 implies that John held a specific prophetic office, he is claiming divine inspiration for his revelation.

This John further identifies himself as a servant (v 1) and a brother and companion in suffering (v 9). While the author does not exert the apostolic authority found in the letters of John, in this case John is the reporter and the authority comes from Christ, not John.

John wrote it some thirty to forty years earlier than his gospel and letters. Contrary to the Gospel of John, where the author never names himself, here John names himself. Yet there are similar concepts and expressions between the two writings. Jesus Christ is called the *logos* or Word only in John 1:1, 1 John 1:1, and Rev 19:13. John is the only evangelist who calls Jesus a lamb. He is called *the Lamb* only in John 1:29, 36 and twenty-eight times in Revelation. Both books promise the *water of life* (John 7:37; Rev 22:17), speak of the first resurrection (John 5:24-29; Rev 20:5), and refer to Satan being *cast out* (John 12:31; Rev 12:9,13). Furthermore, the concept of overcoming the world is addressed six times in 1 John and ten times in Revelation.

There is a similar style between the three letters of John and Revelation. In 1 John three tests are given by which the direct witness of the Spirit may be confirmed. The writer gives all three tests three times in succession in chapters 2-4. Finally, they are summarized in 1 John 5:1-5. This cyclical, as opposed to linear, presentation also is evident in Revelation 6-16 where John describes the great tribulation in terms of seven seals, seven trumpets, and seven bowls. Again, he covers the same event three times. Bob Emery described the seals, trumpets, and bowls as a three-ring circus. Acts are going on in each ring simultaneously. Sometimes one act spills over into another.[1] Both preterists and futurists see a telescopic interrelationship between the seals, trumpets, and bowls, all of which take place during the 3½

---

[1]Emery, *An Evening in Ephesus*, 59-60.

years of the Great Tribulation, not twenty-one consecutive judgments throughout history. Much like a video game, when the player reaches number six, he or she is bumped up to the next level.

Moses Stuart argued that John might have communicated the simple truth he wished to convey in a single chapter if he had written in prose with direct propositions, without the use of allegory and continued symbols. But John adapted the apocalyptic style of his day in order to make a deeper impression upon the mind and memory of his readers. Stuart also argued that the primary audience to which this book was written would have grasped the symbolism much more readily than we do and that the oriental mind preferred this style of communication.[2] He repeatedly emphasized that the prophetic style was essentially poetic.[3] Eugene Peterson wrote in *Reversed Thunder* that John utilized all five senses, engaging the imagination and emotions, as well as the intellect.[4]

While the Gospel of John moves in a more linear fashion, it is still sometimes even out of sequence with the three synoptic Gospels and thus less chronological in its presentation. John's Gospel is not a strict biography. While the synoptic gospels run more or less parallel, John devotes almost half of the book to cover one week. Like the book of Revelation, the Gospel of John is constructed around seven signs.

These apparent similarities seem to point to a common author. While he was capable of writing more than one style of literature and the genre of the Gospel of John, the letters of John, and Revelation are all different, yet the mode of presentation in each was not so much a logical sequence of ideas as the motivation to present and emphasize several key concepts.

Date

There is debate over when the book of Revelation was written.

---

[2]Stuart, Commentary, 1:34-35; 124-127.

[3]Stuart, Commentary, 1:125, 200,233, 374, 415.

[4]Peterson, *Reversed Thunder*, 13-17.

The early view, around AD 65-68, would be under Nero; the late date, AD 95-96, would be under Domitian. The date of the writing of the book will make a difference in how it is interpreted. J. Barton Payne concluded,

> Unless John's reference in 11:1 to the temple be taken figuratively, this structure's mere existence would require a date before 70; the writer's silence in respect to the course of the Jewish War, and his *predictions* of its devastation and 3½-year duration in 11:2; suggest a date prior to the winter of 66; and his symbolical specification in 17:10 of the currently reigning Roman emperor as the sixth of this line of rulers accords most easily with the historical position of Nero.[5]

According to 17:10 the sixth Roman king is reigning at the time John wrote and Nero was the sixth emperor. Nero is also the most natural solution to the meaning of 666 in Revelation 13:8. "John is telling us everything short of the name of the emperor he has in mind," wrote Bell, and according to his research, that is Nero.[6]

Philip Schaff argued for the early date since Jerusalem apparently was still standing (11:1), the twelve tribes had not yet disbursed (7:4-8), and Nero had just died (13:3). Nero died in AD 68. Schaff said that the early date of Revelation explained the fiery energy of this book as compared with the calm repose of John's Gospel, which was composed in extreme old age.[7] Thus, the early date best suits the nature and object of Revelation.[8]

---

[5]Payne, *Encyclopedia of Biblical Prophecy*, 592.

[6]Bell, "The Date of the Apocalypse," 99.

[7]Schaff, *History of the Christian Church*, 1:834-847.

[8]The most thorough research on this issue is by Gentry, *Before Jerusalem Fell*.

Genre

Although the entire Bible is authoritative, the proper interpretation of a given section must take into account the type of literature or *genre*. Daniel and Revelation are considered apocalyptic. This apocalyptic literature was considered "underground literature."[9] Ladd called it "tracts for hard times."[10]

Common traits of apocalyptic literature include the subject matter dealing with the suffering of the righteous and the apparent delay of the kingdom of God. The message came as a vision from a heavenly perspective which was symbolic. Greek verbs *to see, behold*, or *perceive* occur 140 times in this book, beginning with 1:11. The basis of the symbolism was the Old Testament prophecies. Thus, the book of Revelation must be interpreted from the Old Testament, not our newspaper.

Essentially apocalyptic literature is about the revelation of divine mysteries through visions or some other form of immediate disclosure of heavenly truths. In Daniel and Revelation the writer is brought up to the heavenly level to see full scope of what is happening on earth. It is as though he switches back and forth from heaven to earth at least seven times between two great cameras. The saints cope with trials on earth by joining the worship of heaven.

The entire Revelation also takes the form of a letter, with the salutation in 1:4 and the closing in 22:21. While the entire book of Revelation is framed as a *letter*, with a salutation in 1:4-5a and a concluding postscript in 22:21, the seven letters in chapters 2-3 constitute a separate category of genre.

---

[9]Boyer, *When Time Shall Be No More*, 22-23. It is significant both that Tolkien's *Lord of the Rings* is considered to be a modern apocalypse and that his purpose in writing was to smuggle the gospel past the barriers and biases of secularized readers.

[10]Ladd, *Commentary*, 10.

Method of Interpretation

John tells us in the first verse of Revelation that this is symbolic or figurative. *Semaino* means to give a sign or to express by signs or symbols. Throughout the book John reminds us of its symbolic nature — see 1:1; 12:1, 3; 15:1. In 11:8 the term "spiritually" is used. The term *mystery* used in 1:20; 10:7; 17:5, 7 also refers to a symbolic revelation; an equivalency or corresponding reality. Barclay said *mystery* meant "something which is meaningless to the outsider but meaningful to the initiate who possesses the key."[11]

John Wesley wrote,

> It is scarce needful to observe, that there is not in heaven any real book of parchment or paper, or that Christ does really stand there, in the shape of a lion or of a lamb. Neither is there on earth any monstrous beast, with seven heads and ten horns. But as there is upon earth something which, in its kind, answers such a representation, so there are in heaven Divine counsels and transactions answerable to these figurative expressions.[12]

Thus, Revelation should not be interpreted literally since we are told it was written symbolically. Eleven times John demonstrates how to interpret Revelation: 1:20; 4:5; 5:6; 5:8; 7:13, 14; 12:9; 17:9, 12, 15, 18. But why did John use figurative language?

- He is describing heavenly realities to earthly people. Therefore, he must use physical comparisons to describe spiritual truth. John often uses *as* or *like.* Two Greek particles, *hos* and *homoios*, occurs 87 times. They demonstrate how John works from the known to the unknown, describing what he has seen by comparing it with what his readers are familiar.

---

[11]Barclay, *The Revelation of John*, 1:53.

[12]Wesley, *Notes*, 668.

- Perhaps by using figurative language, John was able to avoid censorship by the Roman government. John never mentions Rome by name; however, his readers knew the identity of "the beast." While it could be considered an act of treason to speak openly, John described the fall of the Roman empire which was persecuting the church. In *Breaking the Code* Bruce Metzger described John as a prisoner writing in code from a concentration camp.

Some people object that if Revelation is interpreted figuratively then the book is open to the imagination of every person. However, no commentator takes every description literally.

Tenney categorized the symbols in Revelation under three headings. First, he gave ten examples of symbols which John himself explained. He then gave ten examples of symbols which had Old Testament parallels. Third, he gave eleven examples of symbols which are not interpreted by John and do not have Old Testament parallels. These symbols are to be interpreted on the basis of local custom or usage, which may be unknown to us, but was obvious to the initial readers. Tenney concluded, "The symbols as a whole are not taken from fanciful or imaginary sources, but are related to ideas that would be readily recognized by the readers. The Old Testament, which was their source of revelation, current religious literature embracing the apocryphal works, and the common phenomena of everyday life provided the backgrounds for the figures of the book."[13]

A working knowledge of the prophetic section of Scripture, Isaiah to Malachi, is a prerequisite for understanding all apocalyptic literature — and especially Revelation. There are 348 quotes and allusions in Revelation to the Old Testament.[14] Swete said 278 verses, of a total 404 verses, contained one or more allusions to an Old Testament passage.[15] William Barclay wrote, "He was so soaked in

---

[13]Tenney, *Interpreting Revelation*, 186-193.

[14]Tenney, *Interpreting Revelation*, 101.

[15]Swete, *Apocalypse*, cxl. The symbols are drawn most frequently from Daniel, Ezekiel, and Zechariah [Stuart, *Commentary*, 1:128].

the Old Testament that it was almost impossible for him to write a paragraph without quoting it."[16] Thus Eugene Peterson declared, "No one has any business reading the last book who has not read the previous sixty-five."[17]

Just as the archeologist may discover successive levels of civilization in the tells or mounds which he excavates, so the exegete of this book will, at times, discover that John is building his symbolism upon as many as five layers of biblical tradition. No other New Testament writer uses the Old Testament more. However, there is not one direct quote. Thus, the key to interpretation is not some secret code, occult knowledge, or personal opinion.

Revelation was not as difficult for the first century Jewish Christian as it is for us because it is based on their frame of reference. It is difficult for us because we do not have their mindset. When we come to a difficult passage, our first resource will be to turn to the prophets and see if the same phrase or image appears in their writings.

For example, the tree of life symbolizes eternal life. It is used literally in Genesis and symbolically in Revelation. While the Bible is really true, Genesis is a different genre than is Revelation. Revelation is reality presented in symbolism. It cannot be interpreted literally. The symbolic use is possible only because it builds upon this prior use in Genesis. The first chapters of Genesis describe a literal creation from nothing, while Revelation 21:1 symbolically describes a new heaven and a new earth. While the original creation took place in seven literal days, the number seven is used some fifty-four times in Revelation in the sense of completeness. In Genesis 2:10-14 four rivers water the garden of Eden. In Revelation 22:1-2 the river of life flows through the city of God. In Genesis 3 a literal serpent is used by Satan. In Revelation 20:2 Satan is symbolically called "the ancient serpent." Genesis 10:8-10 introduces Nimrod, the first rebel, while Genesis 11 records the rise of Babylon. In Revelation 13 the great rebel is symbolized as a beast and in Revelation 17-18 spiritual Babylon is destroyed. In Genesis 19, Sodom is described as a center

---

[16]Barclay, *The Revelation of John,* 1:35.

[17]Peterson, *Reversed Thunder,* 23.

of corruption and after the death of Joseph, Egypt becomes a place of oppression. Revelation 11:8 refers both to Sodom and Egypt in a symbolic sense. Genesis 35:23-26 supplies the basis for the twelve tribes of Israel which are named in Revelation 7:5-8. Joseph's dream in Genesis 37:5-11 provides the basis for the symbolism of Revelation 12:1. And although the prophecy of the lion of Judah in Genesis 49:9-10 is also symbolic, it is the basis for the revelation of Jesus as the Lion of the tribe of Judah in Revelation 5:5. While the curse is pronounced in Genesis 3, it is lifted in Rev 22:3. Paradise was lost in Gen 3:23-24 and regained in Rev 22:14.

Thus the book of Revelation must be interpreted from Old Testament precedent, not on the basis of newspaper current events. However, some people think that if Revelation is interpreted figuratively, I am explaining away its meaning. A symbol has meaning only because of the reality it represents. Symbolism is not a denial of the reality of the events predicted; it is a matter of the literary form used. Robert Mounce explained,

> That the language of prophecy is highly figurative has nothing to do with the reality of the events predicted. Symbolism is not a denial of historicity but a figurative method of communicating reality. Apocalyptic language has as one of its basic characteristics the cryptic and symbolic use of words and phrases.[18]

Time Frame

There are three major approaches to the time frame of the book of Revelation which attempt to set the prophecy in a period of time. In addition to the preterist, historicist, and futurist interpretations, the idealist or spiritual approach advocates no specific time frame, but emphasizes concepts, principles, and spiritual lessons from the book. While this approach can provide valid *applications*, it does not pay adequate attention to the time indicators:

---

[18]Mounce, *NICNT*, 212.

1:1 "what must soon take place"
1:3 the time is near
1:7 Christ is coming (present tense)
1:19 what he has seen, what is now, and what is about to occur
2:5 Christ will come to you (*quickly* in some mss)
2:10 they will have persecution for ten days
2:16 Christ will soon come to you
3:10 the hour of trial is about to come
3:11 Christ is coming soon
6:11 wait a little longer
11:14 the third woe is coming soon
22:6 things that must soon take place
22:7 Christ is coming soon
22:10 do not seal up the words of the prophecy of this book,
    because the time is near
22:12 Christ is coming soon
22:20 Christ is coming soon

Thus, there are some fifteen or sixteen time indicators within the book. However, John did not say that *all* the prophecies in his book will occur *soon*. Certainly, for Satan to be loosed after a thousand years (20:7) does not reflect a prophecy which would happen *soon*. Furthermore, the birth of Jesus, described in 12:1-6, reflects an event that was already past. Yet, "the overwhelming bulk of John's prophecies deal with near-term events."[19]

Theme

> Eugene Peterson wrote that the book of Revelation was a fitting conclusion to Scripture.
>
> Everything in the Revelation can be found in the previous sixty-five books of the Bible. The Revelation adds nothing of substance to what we already know. The truth of the gospel is already complete, revealed in Jesus Christ. There

---

[19]Gentry, *The Divorce of Israel*, 1:238-239.

> is nothing new to say on the subject. But there is a new way to say it. I read the Revelation not to get more information but to revive my imagination.[20]

Jesus Christ is the central character of this book. It is the Revelation of Jesus Christ. According to 19:10, "the testimony of Jesus is the spirit of prophecy." In John 11:24-25 Jesus declared that he was the resurrection. If the resurrection occurs at the last day, then *eschatology*, the study of last things, must center around him. In 1 Corinthians 15:45 Paul declares that Christ is the last (*eskatos*) Adam. Four times in Revelation he is declared to be *the first and the last*; the creator and the culmination of eschatology.

Christ assures his church that he knows their circumstances. In chapters 2-3 he declares *I know* a total of eleven times. This revelation of Christ portrays him as in control. The throne of God is mentioned forty-six times in this book, far more than any other book of the Bible. And Christ promises that he is coming some nine times.

The revelation was given in response to the question raised in 6:10-11, "How long until you judge the inhabitants of the earth and avenge our blood?" In response to the martyr's cry and the suffering church, God replies in this message to John that Christ is coming soon. It would provide little comfort for the early church to learn that *soon* actually means thousands of years later.

When we try to understand what God is saying through John, our biggest surprise is what is *not* emphasized. Most of Revelation deals with the period from Pentecost to the end of the old creation. The destruction of Jerusalem was the public vindication of Jesus, who had repeatedly predicted the destruction of Jerusalem as the event which would vindicate his claims. Wright acknowledged that Jesus did not proclaim the end of the space-time universe, he announced the end of the present evil age.[21] Thus, the book of Revelation does not mention the rapture and it contains surprisingly few details about the battle of Armageddon, the return of Christ, or the nature of heaven. This is not

---

[20]Peterson, *Reversed Thunder,* 22; xi-xii, 24.

[21]Wright, *Jesus and the Victory of God*, 594.

primarily a book about the future. The second coming of Christ is not a major theme. Some prophecy experts give the impression that we can decipher anything we want to know about the future from this book. The book is easier to understand if we do not read into it our own presuppositions. Once the theme is established. it ceases to be as fascinating to some as it once was when is was manipulated by the sensational prophecy teachers. Neither does it evoke the fear that many people have about the future. One of the most frequent comments I have heard is that we are no longer afraid of the book or the future. Yet, "You did not receive a spirit that makes you a slave again to fear" (Rom 8:15).

Moses Stuart wrote that the main theme of the book was "*the coming and completion of the kingdom of God or of Christ*, or in other words, *the final and complete triumph of Christianity over all opposition and all enemies, and the temporal and eternal glory and happiness to which this triumph leads the church.*"

The book of Revelation "is filled, from beginning to end, with encouragement and admonition and consolation to all who are engaged in the great contest then going on. Victory — victory — a final and universal and eternal victory of the church over all her enemies — is echoed at every pause."[22]

There is nothing in this book to frighten the followers of the Savior, but there is plenty in this revelation to empower us. We are not victims; we are victors. If God could take a group who were meeting behind locked doors after Jesus died and so transform their outlook that they turned their world upside down, then the lesson we are to learn is that the church of Jesus Christ cannot be stopped.

Something desperately wrong has happened when believers express fear and terror, even nightmares, regarding the book of Revelation. Satan has used carnal men, who do not understand the spiritual implications of this book, to totally pervert its basic theme. May God restore to his church a proper grasp of this message of triumph and may the day come soon when the church is no longer paralyzed with an unwarranted fear of the future which has largely been fed by a misunderstanding of this book. Ironically, the Chinese communist

---

[22]Stuart, *Commentary*, 1:9-26; 155.

government has banned the entire book of Revelation from being preached in their sanctioned Three-Self Churches.[23]

The early followers of Jesus could not fully grasp his deity, his majesty, his authority. They were surprised by the resurrection power they witnessed at Easter. Then they were overwhelmed by the baptism with the Holy Spirit at Pentecost. With their confidence based on the resurrection of Christ and the outpouring of the Spirit, they set out to evangelize the world. But now nearly a generation had passed since Pentecost and their confidence was waning. They had been scattered and hunted down. They had been betrayed by their Jewish brothers, persecuted by the Roman government, and many, like Stephen, had become martyrs. By now all of the original apostles had been executed except for John. It had cost them everything to identify with Jesus Christ. They had been rejected by their families, thrown out of the synagogues, barred from the trade guilds, counted as traitors by the Roman government because they would not say "Caesar is Lord." The Hebrew writer had to deal with the issue of discouragement. There was a temptation to go back to all they had left and give it up. Apparently some did renounce Christ and became apostates.

Not only was there the issue of disillusionment, but there was the question that if Jesus Christ is really Lord and has established a kingdom that will cover the earth, why were they beaten around like a band of renegades? The revelation was given to answer the question stated in 6:10, "How long, Sovereign Lord, holy and true, until you judge the inhabitants of the earth and avenge our blood?"

Apparently they were losing the battle. But John writes to explain that external opposition was not inconsistent with spiritual victory. Suffering does not indicate defeat, it indicates identification with Christ. This is simply an extension of the paradox of the cross. As Hilaire Belloc said, "The Church is a perpetually defeated thing that always survives her conquerors." Even today successful pastors must learn to expect opposition. "If you are not seeing any opposition and not getting any criticism, then God is not at work. The enemy always

---

[23]Yun, *The Heavenly Man*, 55.

opposes and criticizes what God is blessing."[24] Thus, in one sense, the entire book is an amplification and application of Psalm 73.

John who had heard him, and seen him, and touched him is now himself exiled on a lonely island called Patmos. Sunday was no day of rest for John. He came up out of the mines physically tired and spiritually troubled. Nearly forty years ago Christ had commissioned him and the other twelve to go into all the world. One by one the apostles have died for the faith and John is banished to a lonely isle. The church was under attack and Rome was preparing to lay siege to Jerusalem.

John must have noticed the high tide of the ocean and remembered Isaiah's description, "The wicked are like the tossing sea, which cannot rest, whose waves cast up mire and mud" (57:20). John's personal situation was typical of the entire church. He was their companion in tribulation (1:9). In this moment of despair God broke through with this message of hope for the church. John was caught up in the Spirit and catches a new vision of Christ. John must have remembered the time a storm arose on the Sea of Galilee. The boat was already beginning to fill with water and the disciples became fearful. But when Jesus spoke, the storm immediately subsided. It was that same voice which had spoken the world into existence. Now that Word was again speaking. "Do not be afraid," John heard, as he felt the touch of a familiar hand. "I am alive for ever and ever. And I hold the keys of death and hades." John was told to be patient. Once more that voice would speak and the storm of tribulation would cease. Satan would be chained. The enemies of the church would be judged. The gospel would be sounded like a trumpet throughout all the earth.

This is the revelation of Jesus Christ. In this revelation the curtains are parted and his followers see his deity, his majesty, and his authority like they have never seen him. They are assured that he is on the throne, he is in control, and everything is running right on schedule. They understand that in the spiritual realm there was a cosmic struggle taking place. Satan had usurped authority over this earth, but the legality of who owned this world and who was the

---

[24]Southerland, *Transitioning*, 153.

legitimate master of the human race was settled on the cross. Now the kingdom of God was rolling in like a mighty steam roller and these dejected followers of Christ were guaranteed victory. But it was explained to them that temporarily it would get worse before it got better. As the gospel was preached, strongholds were being brought down, Satan was being routed, the kingdom of God was becoming established — but not without one tremendous, final struggle from the forces of darkness.

They were in the middle of the great tribulation. Jesus had foretold that there had never been anything like it and it would never be equaled again. These early followers of Jesus Christ did not need to be told that the devil was trying to destroy them before they got the gospel seed planted. They knew they were under an all out assault. But the spiritual significance of this assault was explained to them in John's message through the use of symbolism. They were promised triumph through tribulation. Christ repeatedly assured them that he was coming soon to judge their oppressors. The struggle may be severe, but the victory of the Christ's kingdom "is at no time in doubt. The battle has already been won at Calvary."[25] This struggle, then, was the birth pangs of a new creation.

In that dark hour God gave John a fresh revelation of Jesus Christ to encourage the struggling church. The first word in Greek is *apokalupsis*, meaning unveiling. The reason Revelation is not an open book is that we use the wrong keys to open it. The word *apocalypse* does not mean a holocaust, a conflagration, or the end of the world. It means a revelation. When Hollywood produces movies with such titles, they are end of the world, run for your life, horror movies in which everything burns up. But this is a complete misuse of the word. It is not describing something fearful, but something wonderful. There is nothing we need any more greatly than an apocalypse, a fresh revelation of Jesus Christ.

Daniel and Revelation are considered apocalyptic. In apocalyptic literature the message is written as an encouragement for the faithful. In each case the subject matter is the suffering of the righteous and the apparent delay of the kingdom of God. The message came as a

---

[25]Bright, *The Kingdom of God*, 241.

vision from a heavenly perspective which was symbolic and the basis of the symbolism was the Old Testament prophecies.

Apocalyptic literature does not necessarily have reference to end times. Essentially it is about the revelation of divine mysteries through visions or some other form of immediate disclosure of heavenly truths. In Daniel and Revelation the writer is brought up to the heavenly level to see full scope of what is happening on earth.

So, John sees Jesus Christ as he is in heaven. He laid aside his glory when he came to earth, but John sees him in his full glory — as the ruler of the kings of the earth. The first three words in Greek are *the revelation of Jesus Christ*. The subject is not "Everything you ever wanted to know about the future." Be suspect of interpretations which do not glorify Christ (see 19:10). This book was not intended to scare the saints, but to bless them. John affirms that Jesus truly is Lord, that he has all things under his control, that his kingdom has come and those who keep the faith will overcome. In 2:10 the early church is promised that their persecution would last "ten days." Both the "ten days" of persecution and the "thousand years" of victory are figurative expressions, but there is a comparison made. Tribulation will be short, but victory will be long.

Our faith will be tested. "Everyone who wants to live a godly life in Christ Jesus will be persecuted" (2 Tim 3:12). We triumph through tribulation. When the way gets difficult and we are discouraged, we need a fresh revelation of Jesus Christ. While we await deliverance, we worship. Worship is spiritual warfare (see 2 Chr 20:15-23) and throughout this book the church overcomes through worship. John repeatedly pauses in his description of judgment to interject worship. In 4:8 and 5:9-10 the church sings. The book of Revelation contains sixteen hymns. In 4:11, 5:12-13, 7:10-12, 11:15, and 12:10-12 she lifts her voice in praise. In 11:17-18 she is on her face in worship. In 14:2-3 she sings a new song. In 15:3-4 she sings. In 16:7 she responds in praise. In 19:1-8 she shouts. Chapter 19 is the only place in the New Testament where *hallelujah* occurs four times.

Daniel's Seventy Sevens

The book of Revelation is built upon the foundation laid by

Daniel and the expansion of Jesus in his Olivet Discourse. Daniel prophesied in Jeremiah 25:11-12 and 29:10-13 that Judah would undergo seventy years of Babylonian captivity for failing to observe the seventh day as a Sabbath. Daniel was part of that captivity and he discovered that according to Jeremiah's prophesy, their seventy years are almost up (Dan 9:1-2). Then God gave Daniel a vision of seventy sevens (Dan 9:20-27). The text does not say *weeks*; it simply reads *sevens*. These *sevens* could be days, weeks, or years, but the context dictates that years are meant. In Daniel 10:2-3 *weeks* were specified.

Daniel also speaks of time, times, and half time (7:25; 12:7). If this *time* is taken to be a year and this formula represents 3½ years, then it coincides with the 1290 days of Daniel 12:11-12. Daniel saw this period of 490 years as a unit covering the span of time from the rebuilding of Jerusalem until its destruction. It begins with Artaxerxes and ends with the destruction of Jerusalem.

However, this is confused when a gap is inserted between the 69th and 70th week. This projects the termination point into the future and makes the subject of Daniel 9:27 a future antichrist who desecrates a rebuilt temple. This approach originated with John Darby who wrote in 1830 that the church was a "Gentile parenthesis" within Jewish history.[26] It was developed by Sir Robert Anderson in *The Coming Prince*[27] and popularized by the *Scofield Reference Bible*, which declared "the proof that this final week has not yet been fulfilled is seen in the fact that Christ definitely relates its main events to His second coming (Mt. 24:6, 15). Hence, during the interim between the sixty-ninth and seventieth weeks there must lie the whole period of the church set forth in the N. T. but not revealed in the O. T."[28]

Although the term *seventy weeks* is plural, the verb used is singular — seventy weeks is decreed (9:24). This is not borne out in the English translations, but the Hebrew verb *chathak* is singular. "This militates against the final week being separated from the others.

---

[26]Bass, *Backgrounds in Dispensationalism*, 129.

[27]Anderson, *The Coming Prince,* 149-170; 180; 288-290.

[28]Scofield, *The New Scofield Reference Bible,* 913.

Thus *sabuim* can only be rendered weeks, and the plural should be understood as a single period; "weeks" is an uninterrupted chronological period that cannot be made indefinite in historical time."[29] Daniel saw this period of 490 years as a unit or block of time. Yet this unit has three components:

1. From the decree of Artaxerxes in 457 BC to rebuild the walls (Ezra 7), to the actual completion of the walls under Nehemiah in 408 BC was a period of 49 years. While this decree was originally issued by Cyrus in Ezra 1, the work order was stopped. Jerusalem was rebuilt in "times of trouble" (Dan 9:25).

It can be established that the reign of Artaxerxes began around 464 BC. Ezra 7:8 specifies that Ezra arrived in Jerusalem in the seventh year of the king. This would confirm the starting point at around 457 BC. The actual completion of the walls, streets, and moats (Dan 9:25) was in 408 BC, a period of 49 years.

2. When we add 434 years (62 x 7) to 408 BC, we arrive at AD 26 (there is no year 0). It is commonly accepted that the birth of Christ was in 4 BC because of a miscalculation in the calendars. Thus, Jesus began his public ministry in AD 26 at thirty years of age.

3. At the middle point of the final seven years Jesus was cut off or crucified in AD 30. The Hebrew verb *karath* means cut off and "is used of the death penalty, Lev. 7:20; and refers to a violent death."[30]

Thus, the period of judgment is the 3½ remaining years. Nowhere in Scripture is the tribulation period said to be seven years.

Terry observed that the six statements in v 24 may be arranged in three lines of Hebrew parallelism with each line containing a double statement. The three lines represent (1) judgment, (2) redemption, and (3) completed revelation. They point to "the introduction of

---

[29]Konkel, "*Sabua*," *NIDOTT&E*, 4:21.

[30]Young, *The Prophecy of Daniel*, 206.

a new and glorious age."[31] According to Daniel 9:24, during this 490-year period span of time:

1. Israel's transgression would reach its full measure by rejecting their Messiah (Dan 9:11; Matt 23:32).

2. To put an end to sin, Jerusalem would be destroyed (Dan 9:26-27). The destruction referred to in this passage is a reference to the destruction of Jerusalem. The Jewish nation sealed their doom by rejecting the Messiah. According to v 26 this desolation was decreed, but not necessarily fulfilled, within the 490-year unit. While the sentence was pronounced, it was not executed until forty years later. There was a delayed response. The destruction of the temple is a consequence of the events which transpired within the seventy weeks. Clarke put the latter parts of vv 26-27 *after* the completion of these seventy weeks.[32] Thus, God in his mercy gave Israel one generation to repent.

Jerusalem was under siege from Nero, the Roman emperor, for 3½ years, from AD 67-70. According to Daniel 12:11 the abomination, described in the last phrase of Daniel 9:27, would last 1290 days or 3½ years. Josephus, the Jewish historian, wrote

> And indeed it so came to pass, that our nation suffered these things under Antiochus Epiphanes, according to Daniel's vision, and what he wrote many years before they came to pass. In the very same manner Daniel also wrote concerning the Roman government, and that our country should be made desolate by them.[33]

Gentry wrote, "The events involving the destruction of the city and the sanctuary with war and desolation are the *consequences* of the cutting off of the Messiah. They do not necessarily occur in the

---

[31]Terry, *The Prophecies of Daniel Expounded*, 78.

[32]Clarke, *Commentary*, 4:603.

[33]Josephus, *The Antiquities of the Jews*, 10.11.7.

seventy weeks time-frame — they are an *addendum* to the point of the prophecy stated in verse 24."[34]

Jesus warned the Jews, "Your house is left to you desolate" (Matt 23:38). The last phrase of Daniel 9:27 refers to the destruction of the temple as described in Matthew 24:15 (compare with Luke 21:20).

3. Atonement would be made. This is a reference to the mediatorial work of the Messiah.

4. The kingdom of everlasting righteousness would be brought in. John Wesley said, "To bring in justification by the free grace of God in Christ, and sanctification by his Spirit; called everlasting, because Christ is eternal, and so are the acceptance and holiness purchased for us."[35]

5. Revelation would be sealed up. While Daniel was told to seal up the words of the scroll until the time of the end (12:4), the seals were broken open in Revelation 5. Daniel foresaw the end of the kingdoms of men and John saw the establishment of Christ's kingdom.

6. The most holy would be anointed. The emphasis in this passage is on the Holy One. Daniel calls him the "anointed one" in vv 25-26. At his baptism, the anointing of the Spirit came upon him (Mark 1:9-11) and three verses later he declared "the time is fulfilled." Thus, the seventieth week had begun.

7. According to Daniel 9:27 the new covenant would be established which would cause the covenant sacrifices and offerings to cease. According to Wesley, "Christ confirmed the new covenant."[36] The pronoun *he* in v 27 cannot refer back to "the people of the prince" in v 26 because *people* is plural and *he* is singular. It must refer to "the Anointed One."

---

[34]Gentry, *Perilous Times*, 25; see also *He Shall Have Dominion*, 320-322.

[35]Wesley, *Notes*, 3:2456.

[36]Wesley, *Notes*, 3:2456.

The subject of this entire section is the Anointed One and he is clearly the ruler or king in v 25. His kingdom would destroy the kingdoms of man (Dan 2:24-45; 7:1-27). Thus, Daniel pinpoints the generation in which the Messiah would be born. If the Messiah was to come within 483 years of 457 BC, if we realize that a priest began his duties at the age of 30, and if we realize that Christ began his ministry at 26 AD, that pushes the date of his birth back to a very narrow time frame or window of opportunity.

Christ also came as king. Daniel pinpoints the time this kingdom would begin as the time of Christ's first advent. But can he be king if he has no kingdom? This prophecy of Daniel also pinpoints the coming of the kingdom. But the dispensational school of thought believes that the kingdom was rejected by the Jews and not established. They were expecting a Jewish kingdom while the kingdom which came was a spiritual kingdom. Because dispensationalists see the establishment of Christ's kingdom as a future event, they are forced to put a gap between the 69th and 70th week of at least two thousand years duration. This is unlikely since there was no gap between the first seven weeks and the next 62 weeks. Again, there is nothing in the text to indicate a gap; the gap is a necessity because of their assumptions. Therefore, they have projected into the future events which have already been fulfilled. This seven-year gap is then transferred to the book of Revelation and they teach that it constitutes chapters 4-19.

The burden of proof is theirs to explain why there would be an undetermined period of time within a determined period of time. The unmeasured gap is at least four times as long as the measured period. This entire system is a house of cards.

John McLean noted eight literary motifs from Daniel which were incorporated in the Olivet Discourse. These include the rebuilding of Jerusalem and the temple, the coming of Jesus the Anointed One, who died as the Messiah, a foreign invader, the abomination of desolation, this abomination coming as the midpoint or major event, the destruction of Jerusalem, and the destruction of the desolater.[37]

---

[37]McLean, *The Seventieth Week of Daniel 9:27*, 160-167; 278-279.

The Olivet Discourse

On Tuesday of Holy Week Jesus spent much of the day in the temple debating. As he and his disciples left, the disciples were more impressed with the building than the Teacher. This was not Solomon's temple, but the rebuilt temple under Ezra, which had been recently reconstructed by Herod. While work on this temple was still going on, most of it had been completed for about 39 years. It was relatively new and the Jews thought that the rebuilt temple was a sign of their security; that God was in their midst. Jesus knew, however, that because the nation had rejected him they had no future and this symbol of their security would soon be torn down.

The disciples were shocked when he announced the soon-coming destruction of the temple and Matthew recorded their three questions:

1. When will the temple be destroyed?
2. What will be the sign of your coming?
3. What will be the sign of the end of the age?

The last two questions belong together, for Christ had taught them in Matthew 13:39-40 that at the end of the age, he would send his angels to separate sinners from those in the kingdom. The sinners would be cast into hell and the righteous would shine like the sun in the kingdom of their Father. Through further revelation Paul would expand upon this great judgment, teaching that Christ himself would return to raise the dead and judge the world. Thus, the disciples were correct in associating the coming of Christ with the end of the world.

But the disciples also made an inference which was not valid. They assumed that if the temple was destroyed, it would be the end of the world. However, the temple had been previously destroyed twice and the world had not ended. Neither would it end when the temple was destroyed the third time. The rest of the Olivet Discourse records the answer Jesus gave to these questions. However, the account by Luke focuses only on the first question. Mark also records only one question and focuses on the immediate crisis, at least up to v 32. While we may have relatively little interest in the historical circumstances surrounding the destruction of the temple, we must realize that all three questions were future for the disciples and that of the three questions, the first was the most important to them because Jesus warned them that it would happen in their lifetime (Matt 24:34).

Matthew does not shift from the first century to the future until v 36. Jesus began answering the first question in v 4 and his answer is very specific. This specificity continues all the way to v 36. Eight times the events are connected with *then* as Jesus describes concurrent events. And at v 29 *immediately after* does not allow a huge gap in time. This linking together of the discourse of Jesus means that events cannot be randomly pigeonholed first under one heading, then the other. But at v 36 there is an abrupt shift. The Greek text reads *but concerning*. This phrase, at the beginning of a sentence, is connected with the verb that follows. This usage "marks a deliberate change of subject."[38]

There are two demonstrative pronouns: *this* and *that*. *This* indicates something is nearer; *that* indicates something more remote. There is no mention of "this generation" after Matthew 24:34. In contrast to *this* generation, v 36 turns to *that* day. *This* refers to something comparatively near at hand, just as *that* refers to something comparatively farther away.

Although Jesus said he did not know the time of *that* day nor hour, he was very specific about the impending siege of Jerusalem. Although certain signs would come, *the end is still to come* (v 6). He warns the disciples in advance (v 25) and declares that their generation will live to see it (v 34). The tribulation of *those days* (plural) is the subject of the first section of Jesus' reply. But when Jesus refers to his second advent, he speaks of *that day* (singular).

Jesus picks up the last two questions regarding the end of the world at v 36. And immediately he shifts from precise information, to very general statements — even to the statement that he did not know when the end of the world would happen. Without attempting a verse-by-verse exegesis of all the events described in vv 4-35, there are several indicators of a specific time and culture, and not a future,

---

[38]France, *TNTC*, 1:347.

worldwide tribulation:

- v 16 those in Judea
- v 17 those on their roofs
- v 20 whenever half of the world is having summer, the other half is having winter
- v 20 the Sabbath
- v 21 “never equaled before; never to be equaled again” does not indicate the end of the world. This is a clear statement that the great tribulation would not occur at the end of time. Jesus clearly taught that war, famine, pestilence, earthquake — the events of the seals, trumpets, and bowls — were not the end, but the beginning (Matt 24:6-8; Luke 21:9-10).
- v 34 this generation. This Greek word *genea* is never used of *race*; the context is speaking of time, not race

The greatest difficulty with this view is found within vv 29-31. While Jesus had been describing an event which would literally happen, the destruction of the temple, the catastrophic events of v 29 — sun darkened, moon ceases to give light, stars fall, heavenly bodies shaken did not literally happen in the first century. But the phrase *immediately after* will not allow a shift to the end of the world.

However, that these words in v 29 are a quote from Isaiah 13:10; 34:4. The context of these statements by Isaiah is figurative. Jesus has been speaking literally, but it is as though he quotes a bit of poetry. Therefore, while this chapter is literal, this verse is not. The key is Genesis 37. There Joseph dreamed that his father, Jacob was the sun, his mother, Rachel was the moon, and his eleven brothers were stars. This was the origin of the Jewish nation. For Jesus to say that the sun, moon, and stars will go out, means the Jewish light will be extinguished. They have rejected Jesus, the light of the world, and they will be plunged into darkness.

Verses 30-31 do not describe the second coming of Christ if they are set in the first century. The phrase *at that time* will not allow a leap into the future. This is describing an event in heaven, not on earth. It connects with Daniel 7:13-14 which describes his ascension to heaven, not his return to earth. It is those in heaven who see him coming with the power and glory described in Daniel 7:14. France wrote that the "coming" of v 13 was a coming *to* God to receive power, *not* a "descent" to earth.[39] In v 31 the word *angel* simply means messenger, whether human or supernatural. This verse describes the great commission given to the church to sound the gospel trumpet.

Thus, it is possible to interpret this section, from vv 4-35, consistently as the answer of Jesus to the first question. It also means, then, that the tribulation, mentioned in Matthew 24:21, is past. This conclusion, that the great tribulation was a first-century event, will be the interpretation of the only other two passages which refer, by name, to the great tribulation: Revelation 2:22; 7:14. The phrase *great tribulation* is found in Revelation 2:22; 7:14, but the judgments of the seals, trumpets, and bowls depict, in symbolic language this time of great tribulation. This is not a study of tribulation in a generic sense. Jesus taught, "In the world you will have trouble or tribulation" (John 6:33) and 2 Timothy 3:12 warns that all who want to live a godly life in Christ Jesus will be persecuted. The focus, instead, is on a specific term *the great tribulation*. This specific time is described by Jesus in the parallel accounts of Matthew 24, Mark 13, and Luke 21, but this specific term is used only in Matthew 24:21.

Thus, the Great Tribulation was that period of time when the old covenant came to an end and the temple was left in desolation, when the apostate Jewish nation was punished for its rejection of Christ; it was the days of vengeance. It was the holocaust which came to those who did not embrace Pentecost. It was the demolition of the old, in order to make way for the construction of the new. The Great Tribulation was the time of struggle between the two kingdoms in which Satan attempted to stop the establishment of Christ's kingdom — the very struggle in which the first century church found itself and to whom the book of Revelation was written to encourage.

The Book of Revelation

The only Gospel of the four which does not contain the Olivet

---

[39]France, *Jesus and the Old Testament*, 235-236.

Discourse is John's Gospel. John's Revelation is his exposition of the Olivet Discourse. Terry concluded, "We thus find that John's Apocalypse is but an enlargement of our Lord's eschatological sermon on the Mount of Olives."[40]

- Matthew 24:3-5; 9-13 and Revelation 2-3 deal with false apostles, persecution, lawlessness, love grown cold, and the need to persevere.
- Matthew 24:6-8 and Revelation 4-7 deal with wars, famine, and earthquakes.
- Matthew 24:14-27 and Revelation 8-14 tell of the church's witness to the world, her flight into the wilderness, the Great Tribulation, and the False Prophet.
- Matthew 24:28-31 and Revelation 15-22 describe the beast's kingdom, the destruction of the harlot, the gathering of eagles over Jerusalem's corpse, and the gathering of the church into the Kingdom.[41]

McLean argued that John, in Revelation 4-19, gives an expanded apocalypse of Daniel's seventieth week, especially the abomination of desolation, and that the Olivet Discourse provides the historical link between Daniel 9:27 and Revelation. In the Olivet Discourse Jesus gave several general indicators, but "the abomination of desolation is the principal sign that warns the people that the destruction of Jerusalem and then end times are drawing near."[42]

While the seventy weeks of Daniel span the entire period from the rebuilding of Jerusalem until its destruction, Revelation focuses primarily on the end. John identified the abomination as the beasts he describes in chapters 12-13 and more specifically, the harlot in 17:4-5.

In Revelation 12, the church flees from the dragon and is protected for 1260 days (12:6) or "time, times and half a time" (12:14).

---

[40]Terry, *Biblical Apocalyptics*, 269. See also pp. 276, 283, 309.

[41]Chilton, *Days of Vengeance,* 20.

[42]McLean, *The Seventieth Week of Daniel 9:27*, 141.

In the Olivet Discourse the Christians fled to Pella (Matt 24:16-20; Mark 13:14-19; Luke 21:20-24). In Daniel 7:25 and 12:7 the period of persecution is "time, times and half a time."

In Revelation 13 the beast represents the final mutation of the four beasts Daniel described in 7:4-8. This beast makes war against the saints for forty-two months. According to McLean, "John portrays the abomination of desolation under the symbolism of the beast that rises up out of the sea." John's language parallels the emphasis of Luke who warned of captivity, death by the sword, and the necessity to persevere in faith (Luke 21:19, 24).

McLean also observed that in the Olivet Discourse it is the city of Jerusalem and the people of God who are tormented. "The Apocalypse is almost a reversal of the synoptic gospels as it proclaims the destruction of Babylon, the city of the enemy of Israel, and the torment of the people of the beast, who have persecuted the followers of the Lamb." In Revelation 17-18, "John amplifies the abomination of desolation under the symbolism of the Great Harlot."[43] She sits on the beast, which was introduced in Revelation 13, and has become a dwelling place of demons and a prison of every unclean spirit (Rev 18:2). This means that Jerusalem has committed spiritual adultery against God and now worships Babylon, the enemy of God. Not only have the heathen defiled God's temple, but the Jews have corrupted their worship by rejecting God's Son. Therefore, Jerusalem will be destroyed.

Clearly John's Revelation was connected to the prophecy of Jesus and the original vision of Daniel. Daniel gave the pronouncement of God's seventy week decree. Jesus warned of the coming destruction at the end of the seventieth week. John provided hope to the early church going through that time of judgment.

If Revelation 6-19 is an expansion of the Olivet Discourse, which was fulfilled in the first century, and if the Olivet Discourse is an expansion of Daniel's seventy weeks, which were completed in the first century, then Revelation 6-19 was also fulfilled in the first century.

---

[43]McLean, *The Seventieth Week of Daniel 9:27*, 201-204; 206

Introduction Summary

The Apostle John wrote the book of Revelation first. Later he wrote his Gospel. His three letters were some of the last books of the New Testament to be written. Jerusalem and the temple fell in AD 70. John wrote the Revelation before this fall. Revelation is apocalyptic literature. It was written in symbolism in order to capture the imagination. John might have communicated the simple truth he wished to convey in a single chapter, but instead he created a literary masterpiece that engages the imagination and the emotions, as well as the intellect. It should produce commitment and lead to worship. It contains sixteen hymns. Those who are bored with worship will be uninterested in what this book actually teaches.

However, it was based on a working understanding of Daniel's seventy weeks and the teaching of Jesus Christ in the Olivet Discourse. Too often the book of Revelation is interpreted under the assumption that it discloses events which are future in the twenty-first century. Most of the book deals with first century events. If it was written to encourage the early church, twenty-first century fulfillment would be irrelevant.

Too often it is interpreted with an overactive imagination which does not have a biblical foundation. Any true believer who is frightened by its message has misunderstood it. Ultimately, this is the revelation of Jesus Christ as victorious.

REVELATION 1

Introduction 1:1-11

1.Title, theme, and blessing 1:1-3

The first word in the Greek text is *apokalupsis*, which is the basis for our word *apocalypse*. This word means to take away a cover, to unveil, or to reveal. It is used eighteen times in the New Testament and usually designates "the supernatural revelation of divine truths unknown to men and incapable of being discovered by them."[44]

Verses 3; 22:7, 10, 18 also call this book a prophecy. Scholars categorize Revelation as apocalyptic literature — based on the first word of the text. But it is also prophetic literature. The work of the Spirit emphasized in this book is his ministry as the Spirit of prophecy. The Spirit speaks through the Christian prophets bringing the word of the exalted Christ to his people on earth. The purpose of prophecy was not so much to foresee the future as to enable them to see the present from the perspective of the future. The Spirit speaks through the prophets to the churches and through the churches to the world. This Spirit of prophecy has life-giving and life-changing effects.

Only God knows the future (see Isa 41:21-26). This is the biblical doctrine of God's foreknowledge. God alone controls the future. This is the biblical doctrine of predestination. John writes about events which *must* occur. They will occur because God has determined that they shall happen. This phrase "what must soon take place," expresses the sure fulfillment of the purpose of God.

It is significant that Daniel was commanded to "close up and seal the words of the scroll until the time of the end" (12:4, 9). While Daniel's revelation concerned what would happen in the latter days (2:28), John's revelation concerned "what must soon take place." Thus, the book of Revelation is the opening and unsealing of what had not been previously disclosed — the revelation of God through Jesus Christ.

---

[44]Ladd, *Commentary*, 19.

The last days began with the first advent of Christ (Acts 2:16-17; 3:24; Rom 16:20; 1 Cor 10:11; Heb 1:2; 9:26; 1 Pet 1:20, 4:7; 1 John 2:8,18) and John is living in the time of the end, the time when Jesus Christ is fully disclosed (22:10). Thus, the "end" described in Revelation is not primarily the end of time, but the end of the old covenant.

God, who had promised to exalt his Son (Phil 2:9-11), gave this revelation about Jesus Christ to his Son, and Christ sent it to John through an angel, who is not named. It was given to John, the servant of Christ, on behalf of all who serve Christ. The church is referred to as servants of Christ in 2:20, 22:3,6. Thus the message was *from* God, *about* Jesus, *through* the angel, *to* John, *for* God's servants.

John was in the Spirit and recorded everything he saw and heard. While *in the Spirit* commonly means "in the Spirit's control," in each case (v 10; 4:2; 17:3; 21:10) the reference is to John's reception of the prophetic vision. This, then, "was a theological claim as much as a psychological statement."[45] This message of God concerning Jesus consists of everything that John saw in his vision and that revelation constitutes the contents of this book. John, like the rest of the prophets, was carried along by the inspiration of the Holy Spirit (Num 11:25; 2 Sam 23:2; Ezek 2:2; 3:24; 2 Pet 1:20-21). Thus, this revelation of God came to the church through the agencies of Christ, the Holy Spirit, the angel, and John.

The first three words of the Greek text clearly indicate that the subject of the book is the *revelation* of *Jesus Christ.*
Does this mean "the revelation *which is* Jesus Christ" or "the revelation *from* Jesus Christ?" While the grammatical construction indicates that the phrase is in the genitive case, it does not indicate whether the phrase is to be interpreted as objective or subjective. Both meanings are probably implied.

The fact that Jesus Christ is the central character of this book comes as a disappointment to carnal readers who are more fascinated with antichrist than with Christ, with violence and destruction than with the kingdom of Christ, with monsters and hideous creatures than

---

[45]Bauckham, *The Climax of Prophecy*, 158.

with the bride of Christ, and with speculation than with adoration. According to 19:10 "the testimony of Jesus is the spirit of prophecy." Since the purpose of prophecy is to testify to the identity of Jesus, all interpretations of prophetic passages which do not make Christ central should be considered suspect.

This revelation to John is the word of God, which is also the testimony given about Jesus Christ. The phrase the *word of God* is joined by the conjunction *and* to the phrase "the testimony of Jesus Christ." Here the conjunction *and* gives additional explanation that the contents of this book is the word of God, which is the testimony given about Jesus Christ. The same, or similar, constructions exist in v 9, 6:9; 12:17; 20:4. The "testimony of Jesus" occurs twice in 19:10. Again, the question is whether John's revelation came *from* or *by* Jesus Christ.

John was exiled to Patmos because he preached the testimony of God's Word *about* Jesus before he received this revelation *from* Jesus. Again, in 20:4 saints were martyred because of their testimony *about* Jesus (see 6:9).

The Old Testament prophecies were about a coming Messiah who was both a suffering servant and a reigning king. When Jesus came into the world through the incarnation, he came in disguise. Many who rejected him only saw a suffering servant. John's vision pulls back the curtains revealing Jesus as the King of kings and Lord of Lords.

The time frame of this vision is also established in the first verse. John is shown things which *must occur soon*. This phrase *dei genesthai* also occurs in Matthew 24:6, Mark 13:7, Luke 21:9 — which are all accounts of the Olivet Discourse. There Jesus anticipated what he would later show John in greater detail. This phrase is also used in Revelation 4:1, 22:6 (see also Matt 16:28; 26:64; Rom 13:11-12; 1 Cor 7:31; Heb 10:37; Jas 5:8-9).

The adverbial phrase *en tachei* is also used in 22:6. It means with speed, quickly, speedily, soon, shortly, or to place in order. While Daniel predicted events which were future, John described them as imminent. According to v 3 the time is near. Beale wrote that John deliberately substituted *en taches* for Daniel's "in the latter days." Therefore, John is not referring to the speedy manner in which the Daniel prophecy is to be fulfilled nor the possibility that it could be fulfilled at any time, but "the definite, imminent time of fulfillment, which likely has already begun in the present . . . in his own generation, and, indeed that it had already begun to happen."[46] Bruce Metzger wrote, "The word *soon* indicates that John intended his message for his own generation."[47] It was necessary that these things *come to pass shortly*, for Jesus had repeatedly declared that the consummation of that age and his coming in his kingdom would take place before that generation passed away (Matt 16:28; 24:34)

We are also told in v 1 that this vision is communicated through the use of symbolism. The verb *semaino* means to give a sign. The subject of the verb could be either God or Jesus Christ; it is not stated. In the Gospel of John this verb is used three times, in 12:33 the symbol of the brazen serpent pointed to the crucifixion, in 18:32 the Jewish appeal for a Roman execution implied crucifixion, not stoning; in 21:19 Peter's outstretched hands symbolized his own crucifixion. Here it is used to indicate that the entire revelation is symbolic.

Tenney wrote, "This term evidently meant a kind of communication that is neither plain statement nor an attempt at concealment. It is figurative, symbolic, or imaginative, and is intended to convey truth by picture rather than by definition."[48]

While all scripture is profitable (2 Tim 3:16), this is the only book which promises a blessing. All three participles are in the present tense, indicating that we are to continue to read, hear, and keep what is written. Six more blessings follow: 14:13, 16:15, 19:9, 20:6, 22:7, 14.

At that time not many copies of John's Revelation were avail-

---

[46]Beale, *NIGNTC,* 181-182.

[47]Metzger, *Breaking the Code,* 21.

[48]Tenney, *Interpreting Revelation,* 186.

able. Therefore, the reader served an important function in the liturgy of the service. The fact that this book was read alongside the Old Testament Scriptures, during the first four centuries of the Christian era, was acknowledgment that it was recognized as inspired Scripture. The blessing is pronounced upon the one who reads (singular) and those (plural) who both hear and obey. The Hebrew verb for *hear* (*shama*) also means to *obey*. In Revelation 2-3 each of the seven letters contains an admonition to hear, but a promise only to those who overcome. There is no blessing promised for those who merely hear and do not obey. Obedience is the ground of blessing. This theme of both hearing and heeding is emphasized in 1:3 and 3:3. Perseverance in obedience is found, as well, in 2:26: 3:8, 10; 12:17; 14:12; 16:15; 22:7, 9. Thus, the focus of this book is not just on eschatology, but also on ethics.

2. John's Salutation 1:4-6

The salutation *grace and peace* occur in seventeen books of the New Testament. Although the book of Revelation is in a category by itself, it still retains this common salutation. This greeting embodies the promise and fulfillment theme of early Christian preaching. The age of peace promised to restored Israel has been inaugurated by the transforming grace of God through Jesus Christ. These blessings are now granted to a restored Israel, the church, which includes not only believing Jews, who are characteristically greeted with the Hebrew *shalom* or peace, but also believing Gentiles, who are characteristically greeted with the Greek salutation *grace*.

The seven churches of v 4 are listed in v 11. John addresses the seven churches collectively in v 4. They will be addressed individually in chapters 2-3. It was common to seal an agreement by using seven tokens. The Hebrew word for *swear* (*shaba*) literally means to seven oneself or bind oneself by seven things. These seven congregations represent the whole church in God's covenant with his people.

John conveys grace and peace from God the Father in v 4. God's eternity is expressed as him who is, and who was, and who is to come. *Ho on* (the one who is) occurs in 1:4, 8; 11:17; 16:5. John avoided the concept of process theology, that God himself is evolving, by writing literally "the one who is and that which was and the one who is coming." Nor did John use the future tense. There is no *will be* with an eternal God. With Him all *is.* He does not change (Mal 3:6).

This reference to God's eternity is a paraphrase of God's name *Yahweh*, which is based upon the verb *I am* (Exod 3:14-15; 6:2-3). He will be worshiped for ever and ever (v 6). Yet we might expect John to write of him who is, and who was, and *who will be.* The fact that John uses a present participle (the one coming), instead of the future tense (the one who will be) emphasizes an imminent coming, not a coming in the distant future. John writes of him who is coming, in both vv 4 and 8, to correspond to the theme of v 7.

As Lord of time, God who lives in eternity, comes in salvation and judgment. He establishes times and seasons. He defines the beginning of the end time longed for in the Old Testament by sending his Son (12:5). Not only does he reveal himself through that redemptive act, but he comes to the believer through the Spirit in partial realization and in an anticipation of the consummation.

Reference is also made in v 4 to the sevenfold Spirit (see also 3:1; 4:5; 5:6). The one Holy Spirit is described in his completeness in Isaiah 11:2-3: the Spirit of the Lord, the Spirit of wisdom and of understanding, the Spirit of counsel and of power, the Spirit of knowledge and of the fear of the Lord.[49] He is the Messiah, the one anointed by the Spirit.

Grace and peace come from the throne[50] of God *and* from the Holy Spirit *and* from Jesus Christ (v 5). Thus, all three members of

---

[49]It is sometimes objected that the Hebrew text only contain a sixfold description. It is the Greek translation, the Septuagint, that adds the final clause.

[50]The word *throne* is used forty-six times in this book, far more than in any other book of the Bible. In all but five chapters of Revelation there is reference to the throne.

the Trinity are named in vv 4-5. Yet the normal order is not followed. By placing Jesus Christ last, John establishes his subject through v 8. Jesus Christ is then given three titles. This is a comprehensive portrait of Jesus Christ as prophet, priest, and king.

As our prophet, Jesus Christ is the faithful witness (v 5; 3:14; Ps 89:37). He testifies concerning himself (John 8:14, 18; 18:37) and is the trustworthy representation of the Father. The description of Jesus Christ in vv 13-16 looks the same as descriptions given elsewhere of the Father. According to John 14:9 anyone who has seen Jesus has seen the Father. He is the image of the invisible God (Col 1:15), the exact representation of God's being (Heb 1:3). Christ has made God known (John 1:18; 3:32; 5:36). He is the greatest and final prophet because he manifests God to us (John 17:4). "In these last days he has spoken once for all by his Son" (Heb 1:2).

As our priest, Jesus Christ is the firstborn from the dead. *Firstborn* speaks not of his creation, but of his resurrection (Col 1:18; Acts 13:33; see also Ps 89:27; Rom 8:29). He is the first to rise from the dead (v 18; 1 Cor 15:23) and he is sovereign over the realm of death; he is first in time and in importance. As *firstborn*, Christ inherited all of creation and can rightfully claim, "All authority has been given to me" (Matt 28:19). He freed us from our sins with his own blood, functioning as both the high priest and the sacrifice. He offered himself as the atoning sacrifice because of his love for us. This participle is in the present tense. His love for us is ongoing. According to Peter, the church in its entirety is a holy priesthood (1 Pet 2:5). Corporately, believers are a kingdom and a priesthood. This priesthood is always spoken of corporately, never individually. Christianity does not *have* a priesthood; it *is* a priesthood.

In Exodus 19:6 God said "you will be for me a kingdom." Here John declares that "he has made us to be a kingdom." According to Ladd, 1:6 and 5:10 "are the clearest references in the New Testament where the church is called a kingdom."[51] A. T. Robertson wrote the idea in v 6 is that "Christians are the true spiritual Israel in God's

---

[51]Ladd, *Commentary*, 27.

promise to Abraham as explained by Paul in Gal 3 and Rom 9."[52]

We are also priests unto God, the Father of Christ, and our ministry, in the words of the Westminster Catechism, is to glorify him and to enjoy him forever. As our king, Jesus Christ is the ruler of the kings of the earth (Ps 89:27). When did his rule begin? When John wrote this description in the first century, Christ was then already the ruler of the earth. The declaration in 11:15, that the kingdom of the world has become the kingdom of our Lord and of his Christ, is in the past tense.

According to Daniel 7:13-14 his reign began at his ascension and once begun, it will never end. The *son of man* whom John saw in 1:13; 14:14 is the same *son of man* in Daniel 7:13-14 and his reign is forever.[53] Jude wrote, "To the only God our Savior be glory and majesty, dominion and power, before all ages, *now*, and forevermore" (v 25). He is now King of kings and Lord of lords (19:16). He holds the keys of death and hades (v 18). Death describes the condition and hades describes the place. To have these keys is to possess authority over their domain.

He has freed us from our sins which held us in bondage. Since we have been redeemed, Satan has no authority over us because we are seated with Christ (Eph 2:6). If Christ has all authority (Matt 28:18) and we are "in Christ" we are overcomers through his blood (Rev 12:11) which has loosed us from Satan. This is the new exodus.

Bauckham concluded that this doxology in vv 5-6 is evidence enough that John's churches offered praise to Christ comparable with that offered by the angels in heaven. Doxologies were a Jewish form of praise to the one God. "There could be no clearer way of ascribing to Jesus the worship due to God."[54]

---

[52]Robertson, *Word Pictures,* 6:287.

[53]In John's Gospel he uses the phrase *Son of Man* thirteen times. Jesus applies Dan 7:13 to himself in Mark 13:26. Whether in Daniel, the Gospels, or Revelation the *Son of Man* title is Messianic.

[54]Bauckham, *The Climax of Prophecy*, 140.

Amen occurs nine times in Revelation. It is a transliteration from Hebrew (*amen*) into Greek (*amen*) and from Greek into English. While it is used as a name for Christ in 3:14, it occurs in 1:6 and 7 as *so be it*, a liturgical word expressing emphatic agreement with God's plan (1 Cor 14:16; 2 Cor 1:20).

3. John's Declaration 1:7

John announced in v 7 that Christ is coming. This is the theme of his vision. While the Bible teaches the second advent, it is not necessarily promised in this verse. Every reference to the coming of the Lord is not a reference to the second advent.[55] Passages such as Psalm 18:7-15; 104:3; Isaiah 19:1; Ezekiel 30:3-4; 32:7-8; Joel 2:1-2; Micah 1:3-4; Nahum 1:2; Zephaniah 1:14-15 describe the Lord coming with clouds, but these historic judgments were not the end of the world. Jesus placed the time of his "coming with the clouds" within the lifetime of his audience in Matthew 16:28; 24:30, 34; 26:64. He also warned that judgment would come upon that generation in Matthew 23:32-38 and that it would not pass away until all these things have happened. Thus, he came in judgment.

"Those who pierced him" refer the Jewish people (see Acts 2:22-23, 36; 3:13-15; 7:52; 1 Thess 2:14-15). The Greek word *phule* usually refers to the tribes of Israel and would be better translated "tribes."[56] Gentry observed,

> This coming will be especially directed against 'those who pierced him,' that is, the first-century Jews who demanded his crucifixion. . . . John's reference to Christ's piercing demands a first-century focus if the theme is to be relevant and true, for those who pierced him are now long since

---

[55]Deut 33:2; Isa 19:1; Zech 1:16; Mal 3:1-2; Matt 10:23; Rev 2:5; 3:20. See the discussion by Loraine Boettner of eight different ways in which Christ comes [*The Millennium,* 252-262].

[56]Maurer, "φυλή," *TDNT*, 9:246.

deceased.[57]

The Greek word for *earth* may also be understood as referring to *the land*, the land of Palestine. Thus, this verse describes the judgment of Christ upon that generation of Jews who crucified him.

R. C. Sproul wrote that

> The coming of Christ in A.D. 70 was a coming in judgement on the Jewish nation, indicating the end of the Jewish age and the fulfillment of a day of the Lord. Jesus really did come in judgement at this time, fulfilling his prophecy in the Olivet Discourse. But this was not the final or ultimate coming of Christ. The parousia, in its fullness, will extend far beyond the Jewish nation and will be universal in its scope and significance. It will come, not at the end of the Jewish age, but at the end of human history, as we know it. It will be, not merely a day of the Lord, but the final and ultimate day of the Lord.[58]

The Greek word *nai (* yes) and the Hebrew *amen* corresponds to the Greek salutation *grace* and the Hebrew *peace* in v 4. They are also the response of the church to God's righteous judgment. To the *amen* of the church is added the direct voice of Christ.

4. Christ's Declaration 1:8

In v 8 Christ declares, "I am the Alpha and Omega." There are five "I am" declarations in Revelation: 1:8, 17; 2:23; 21:6; 22:16. There are seven in John's Gospel. This is a statement of eternity using the first and last letters of the Greek alphabet, ΑΩ, and implying all the letters in between. We would say he is from A to Z. Only God is

---

[57]Gentry, "A Preterist View of Revelation," 45-49.

[58]Sproul, *The Last Days According to Jesus*, 158.

eternal (Isa 44:6; 48:12); created beings are not eternal. God the Father was declared eternal in v 4, but the subject changes in v 5 to Jesus Christ. After all, this is the revelation of Jesus Christ; he is the subject of this book. Every pronoun which follows from vv 5-8 refers to the stated subject, Jesus Christ, until vv 9-10 where John makes it clear that he is now referring to himself. The same speaker in v 8 resumes his message in v 11. The eternity of Jesus Christ is reaffirmed in v 17, "I am the First and Last" and in 22:13. If Christ is the one coming in v 7, he must also be the one who is to come in v 8.

Alfred Plummer wrote that the Lord who utters the words found in v 8 is surely the Christ. This seems clear from v 17, 2:8, 22:13.

> To attribute them to the Father robs the words of their special appropriateness in this context, where they form a prelude to "the Revelation of *Jesus Christ*" as God and as the Almighty "Ruler of the kings of the earth." Yet the fact that similar language is also used of the Father (6:6; 21:6) shows how clearly St. John teaches that Jesus Christ is "equal to the Father as touching his Godhead."[59]

Therefore, in v 8 Jesus Christ is called "the Lord God." He not only utilizes divine titles, but he describes himself with divine attributes. At the close of v 8 he declares that he is Almighty or omnipotent. There is one God, composed of Father, Son, and Spirit. The Son is equal with the Father in his attributes and his acts. He is the object, as well as the source of this revelation.

5. John's Circumstances 1:9-11

After this burst of worship, which summarizes the theme of the entire book, John returned to the task of introducing himself. John's circumstances mirrored the first century church. He was their companion who shared in the tribulation and patient endurance (v 9). John

[59]Plummer, *The Pulpit Commentary*, 51:4-5.

was also a partner in the *kingdom*, but at this time it was hard to see much of a future for the kingdom. However, the people of God were not to share or fellowship (same word, used as a verb) in the sins of Babylon (18:4). Barclay wrote that there was only one way from affliction to the glory of the kingdom, and it was through endurance.[60]

It was a time of persecution under Nero and John himself was exiled to the island of Patmos, a rocky island about ten miles long and six miles wide, in the Aegean Sea about 60 miles from Ephesus, perhaps to work in the mines. He was there because he had preached the Word of God and because of his testimony to Jesus (v 9; 19:10). Here the word *martus* (witness) finds its third use in this chapter. Jesus Christ is the faithful *martur* (v 5; 3:14) who bears testimony of the Father. This revelation which John received from Jesus, is the *marturia* concerning Jesus (v 2; 19:10). John bore *martureo* of the message of Jesus (vv 2, 9). As Christians, we can only bear witness to Christ as effectively as we have received the testimony from Christ (6:9; 20:4).

John's circumstances were bleak, shut off from friends and fellowship, but he, like all who serve Christ, must persevere. The Greek word *hupomone* means to abide under or to endure. Jesus warned that only he who endures (same word) to the end will be saved (Matt 24:13). While all Christians will be tested (2 Tim 3:12), John refers to endurance of the Great Tribulation (7:14). Those who keep the command to endure (same word) the hour of testing coming upon the whole world (3:10), will be kept from falling (Jude 24; compare to Matt 24:10-12).

John was in the Spirit on the Lord's Day, when this revelation came and along with it, the command to write what he saw. "The whole of the book between prologue and epilogue is recounted as a single visionary experience which took place on Patmos on the Lord's Day."[61] The early church called Sunday the Lord's Day and met on

---

[60]Barclay, *The Revelation of John*, 1:40. See Acts 14:22; 2 Tim 2:12.

[61]Bauckham, *The Climax of Prophecy*, 3.

Sunday for worship (Acts 20:7; 1 Cor 16:2).

I. The Revelation of Jesus Christ 1:12-20

John now turns from his circumstances to a description of his vision. According to v 12 John turned to *see* the voice. The Greek word for voice is *phone.* In v 15 it is used twice, for voice and for sound. John may be connecting with the words of Exod 20:18. Voice and personhood are closely related. John the Baptist was called a voice in the wilderness. When John turned to see who was speaking to him, he saw Christ depicted in the midst of the lampstands (v 13). According to v 20 the lampstands are churches giving forth light. Clarke wrote,

> A lamp is not *light in itself,* it is only the *instrument* of dispensing light, and it must receive both *oil* and *fire* before it can dispense any; so no Church has in itself either *grace* or *glory, it must receive all from Christ its head, else it can dispense neither light nor life.*[62]

John Bunyan incorporated this image in *Pilgrim's Progress,*

> Then I saw in my dream that the Interpreter took Christian by the hand, and led him into a place where was a fire burning against a wall, and one standing by it, always casting much water upon it, to quench it; yet did the fire burn higher and hotter.
> Then said Christian, "What means this?"
> The Interpreter answered, "This fire is the work of grace that is wrought in the heart: he that casts water upon it, to extinguish and put it out, is the Devil; but in that thou seest the fire notwithstanding burn higher and hotter, thou shalt also see the reason of that." So he had him about to the backside

[62]Clarke, *Commentary*, 6:974.

> of the wall, where he saw a man with a vessel of oil in his hand, of the which he did also continually cast, but secretly into the fire.[63]

This image of the lampstand comes first from Exodus 37:17-23, the basis for the Jewish menorah later used in the temple. Zechariah 4:1-6 also describes a lampstand with seven lights. A pipeline of olive oil supplied the lampstand. As long as the oil flows the light will not go out. “Not by might nor by power, but by my Spirit” (v 6).

When we assemble to hear his Word taught, light emanates from us, we become a lampstand or a lighthouse, a city set on a hill, the light of the world and he is in our midst (Matt 18:20).

In 2:1 Christ is pictured as walking among these seven lampstands. Metzger wrote, “Therefore when John says he saw Christ in the midst of the lampstands, he wants to let us know that Christ is not an absentee landlord. On the contrary, he is in the midst of his churches, supporting them during trials and persecutions.”[64] And Peterson wrote, “Christ is not seen apart from the gathered, listening, praying, believing, worshiping people to whom he is Lord and Savior. It is not possible to have Christ apart from the church. . . The only way from Christ to heaven and the battles against sin is through the church.”[65]

John describes Jesus in vv 13-16, using the same language Daniel used of the Ancient of Days in 7:9-10; 10:5-6.

---

[63]Bunyan, *Pilgrim's Progress,* 37.

[64]Metzger, *Breaking the Code*, 26.

[65]Peterson, *Reversed Thunder*, 44-45.

DANIEL	REVELATION
clothing white as snow; linen	robed to his feet
golden belt around waist	golden sash around chest
hair white like wool	hair white like wool
eyes like flaming torches	eyes like blazing fire
arms and legs like burnished bronze	feet like glowing brass
voice like the sound of a multitude	voice like many waters
face like lightning	face like the sun shining

Jesus is the "faithful witness." Anyone who has seen him has seen the Father. John is teaching that the Son and the Father are of the same substance. The description of Jesus is chiastic.

A head like wool, as white as snow
  B hair like wool, as white as snow
    C eyes like fire
      D feet like bronze
        E voice like waters
      D′ hand with stars
    C′ mouth with sword
BA′ face like sun

Thus, because it is his voice which is emphasized in the chiasm, Jordan pointed out that it is the Word of God that is central. "The central aspect of Jesus is His voice. That is what does not change. His appearance changes in history; His Word does not."[66]

In each of the seven church letters of Revelation 2-3, one aspect of this portrait is emphasized as being the quality each congregation needs most to be reminded of. Most of the attributes are taken up in reverse order in chapters 2-3. All seven descriptions put together form the composite portrait. Each church had its own problem, but Christ revealed himself to each situation in just the aspect they needed. We may know him in some capacities, but no one has ever seen him in

---

[66]Jordan, *The Revelation of Jesus in Revelation 1:12b-16*, 4.

his fullness. Christ is dressed in a robe reaching down to his feet and with a golden sash around his chest. This was the garb worn by the high priest (Exod 28:4; 29:5; 39:27-29; Lev 16:4). According to Edersheim it was worn only during the actual ministry of the priest and then taken off. Therefore, we should understand from this depiction of Christ that "our heavenly High Priest is there engaged in actual ministry for us."[67]

His head and hair were white like wool, as white as snow. This is an obvious reference to Daniel 7:9. White hair does not symbolize age and infirmity, but holiness, wisdom, and maturity.

His eyes were like blazing fire signifying that Christ is all-knowing (see also 19:12). Each letter begins with the words *I know*. Here the hair and the eyes of Christ portray him as the wise judge of the world.

His feet were like brass glowing in a furnace. The kingdoms of man were described as having feet of iron and clay mixed (Dan 2:33). They have a flawed foundation. Most rulers who lose power do so because of internal weaknesses. He will never be toppled from power. There are not inconsistencies with him. His kingdom is built upon a firm foundation.

His voice was like the sound of rushing waters. But this voice can sound like a trumpet (see Exod 19:16, 19) to awaken or like many waters to sooth (Ezek 43:2). The ocean is a continual roar. It is loud and awe-inspiring, but it is also peaceful. Out of his mouth came a sharp double-edged sword (v 16; 2:12, 16; 19:15, 21, see also Isa 11:4; 49:2; Eph 6:17; Heb 4:12). This symbolizes the divine inspiration of Scripture. No carnal weapons are needed (2 Cor 10:4; Isa 11:4; 2 Thess 2:8; Rev 2:12, 16; 19:15, 21). This Word first penetrates, then makes alive. It is this word that first incites fear, then peace (see Deut 32:39-41; 2 Kgs 5:7).

In v 16 Christ holds seven stars. He himself is the star of Numbers 24:17. In Genesis 37:9 the eleven patriarchs are called "stars." According to Philippians 2:15, the people of God are to shine like

---

[67]Edersheim, *The Temple*, 98.

stars (see also Dan 12:3). The man whom Isaiah describes in 14:12 was called a *morning star*. In Revelation 22:16, Christ himself is the morning star. False teachers are called wandering stars (Jude 13). The term is used of demons in 12:4. Revelation 1:20 interprets these stars in v 16 to be messengers.

His face was like the sun shining in all its brilliance. The shining of God's face upon his children is blessing (Judg 5:31). Paul saw that brilliance on the Damascus Road (Acts 26:13). The world once sat in darkness, but they saw a great light at his coming. That darkness turned to dawn and dawning will turn to noonday brightness. That brilliance will destroy all rebellion (2 Thess 2:8).

John worshiped Jesus in v 17. John knew Jesus. Their mothers were sisters. But some thirty years pass and now Jesus appears before John. John, who had leaned against Jesus (John 13:25; 21:20), now falls before him. John had never seen the full glory of Christ until now.

In vv 17-18, Christ asserts his supremacy and his eternal existence as the Son of God. But this living One became incarnate in Jesus. He took on the substantial nature of humanity. He thus became the Second Adam. In this human personality he tasted death for every man.

With absolute authority Christ proclaims that he has obtained the government and taken possession of the earth, the underworld, and heaven. Of these he holds the keys and maintains the dominion.

The resurrection of Christ forms the central point of the world's history. The text contains the assurance that as Christ is eternally linked to the fortunes of the race he died to redeem, so the august powers of an *endless life* are now and shall forever be engaged in the work of completing and eternally perpetuating the salvation of his people. He is alive forever more to consummate his redeeming work though all the ages of the world's future.

In 19:10 and 22:8-9 John fell to the ground in the presence of an angel and told to get up because it is idolatry to worship anyone other than God. But Jesus is God and received John's worship. John said the Living One died and the one who was dead is alive forever. He is the source of life (Luke 9:24; John 1:4; 14:6; 1 Tim 6:16).

The early church was reassured that Jesus Christ is God; coequal with the Father. Jesus Christ is in control; his kingdom is established. He has authority over the kings of the earth, over Satan — freeing us from his demonic kingdom, over the church — holding the pastors in his right hand and walking in the midst of the congregations, and over death. Therefore, we are not alone. He is not only over us, but he is with us. The early church, as well as believers of all times, was comforted with the vision of Christ's transcendence and immanence.

John is commanded to write both what he has just seen and what will be shown him afterward. This final phrase describes the things which are about to happen and connects with v 1, describing things which would happen "soon." John simply could not see everything at once. Therefore, throughout this book, John introduces new visions with the phrase *after this* (4:1; 7:1, 9; 9:12; 15:5; 18:1; 19:1; 20:3). It is a mistake to use v 19 as a threefold outline of the book.

In v 20 the word *angelos* means *messenger* and the same word is used whether the reference is to natural or supernatural messengers. The Hebrew word *malak* is also used both of human messengers and angelic messengers.

If the mystery or symbol is the star, the interpretation of the symbol, the *angel*, cannot also be symbolic. But the word *angel* means messenger and does not necessarily refer to a messenger who has come down from heaven. Thus, the *angel* can be the human leader of each congregation. The fact that he is called a *messenger* of the church reveals that this man is not called to exercise his own authority or teach his own doctrine and will. He is a "steward of God" and must teach and manage the church according to the Word of God.

There are 67 references in this book to angels, and all but the eight references in the first three chapters definitely refer to supernatural angels. Strong wrote that angels in the widest sense are agents of God's providence, natural and supernatural. Psalm 104:4 calls the servant of God an angel (see Heb 1:7). The term is applied to ordinary messengers in Job 1:14; 1 Samuel 11:3. It is applied to prophets in Isaiah 43:19, Haggai 1:13, Malachi 3, and to ministers of the New

Testament (Rev 1:20).[68]

Since these *angels* are charged with the deficiencies of the congregations, addressed in Revelation 2-3, they could hardly be heavenly angels. While supernatural angels are present in the congregation (1 Cor 11:10), they can hardly be held responsible for the actions of the congregation. Nor would they need to repent, along with their congregation. Furthermore, if these angels were heavenly beings, Christ would hardly need to send them a message through John, an earthly agent, so that they then could take that message to earthly congregations. Clarke considered "the angel of the Church as signifying the messenger, the pastor, sent by Christ and his apostles to teach and edify that Church."[69] When believers assemble for worship, supernatural angels are present, Christ anoints his human messengers, and Christ himself is in their midst.

John could have used the term pastor, bishop, or elder. By using the term angel he emphasizes the pastor is God's *messenger*. This means that he must not speak his own mind or agenda. He has not been given the place of leadership to present his own opinions. He must study to show himself approved unto God. He must preach the Word. There is, therefore, a link between prophets of old and New Testament pastors. Like the prophet of old, the New Testament pastor of a local church must not be afraid to speak God's truth. He must not speak to be praised by men.

Notice that each letter to the seven churches is addressed to the messenger of the church — the pastor. Christ holds pastors and congregations in his hand. He holds the whole world in his hands, but in a special sense he upholds those who lift him up.

---

[68]McClintock and Strong, *Cyclopedia*, 1:225-227.

[69]Clarke, *Commentary*, 6:975.

Chapter One Summary

Introduction 1:1-11
1. Title, theme, and blessing 1:1-3
2. John's salutation 1:4-6
3. John's declaration 1:7
4. Christ's declaration 1:8
5. John's circumstances 1:9-11
I. The revelation of Jesus Christ 1:12-20

The first three words of the Greek text clearly indicate that the subject of the book is the *revelation* of *Jesus Christ*. The time frame of this vision is also established in the first verse. John is shown things which *must occur soon*. The word *soon* indicates that John intended his message for his own generation. We are also told in v 1 that this vision is communicated through the use of symbolism.

A comprehensive portrait of Jesus Christ as prophet, priest, and king is given in vv 5-8. In vv 12-16 John describes Jesus Christ as walking among his churches. Seven specific descriptors are given. Each descriptor had been used in the Old Testament to describe God the Father. They are deliberately appropriated to describe God the Son in order to declare his deity. But rather than a logical argument regarding the deity of Christ, the doctrine is given in visual form. He is coequal with the Father. He has established his authority. He has authority over the kings of the earth, over Satan — freeing us from his demonic kingdom, over the church — holding the pastors in his right hand and walking in the midst of the congregations, and over death. Therefore, we are not alone. He is not only over us, but he is with us.

REVELATION 2

In 1:19 John was told to write about what he had seen — the vision of Christ recorded in chapter 1. Now we move to "the things which are now"— the state of the seven representative congregations in chapters 2-3.

Christ sent a message to seven congregations all within a radius of 180 miles. According to William Ramsay the sequence of the letters indicates the route to be followed by a courier.[70] These congregations are located in Asia Minor, which today is Turkey.

The message from Christ always begins with *I know*. In fact, five times Jesus said specifically, "I know your works." The Greek verb *oida* carries the idea of discernment and full knowledge. The fact that Christ knows all things is either comforting or frightening.

The five deficient congregations are warned that Christ will come to judge them. These *comings* are not the second Advent. If these are promises of Christ's imminent return and the church letters are taken chronologically, then Christ would have already returned three times prior to our age (2:5; 2:16; 3:3). Caird argued that Christ was preparing them for persecution and not his second advent.[71]

Eugene Peterson concluded, "A random selection of seven churches in any century, including our own, would turn up something very much like the seven churches to which St. John was pastor."[72]

II. Seven letters from Jesus Christ 2:1-3:22
A. Ephesus 2:1-7

Twenty years after Paul's conversion he had one of his most successful ministries, preaching in Ephesus from AD 52-55 (Acts

---

[70]Ramsey, *Letters to the Seven Churches*, 132-141.

[71]Caird, *The Revelation of St. John,* 27-28.

[72]Peterson, *Reversed Thunder*, 56.

19:1-41, 20:31). Upon his arrival there he met with about twelve men and found that they only knew John's baptism. They were baptized into the Lord Jesus and received the Holy Spirit. Paul ministered night and day for three years. The whole town was shaken and occult books were burned.

After Paul left Ephesus he was eventually arrested in Jerusalem and five years after leaving Ephesus he arrived in Rome. While held in a Roman prison Paul remembered the congregation in Ephesus and wrote the Ephesian letter in AD 61. The Ephesian letter reveals little about the condition of the congregation at that time, but Paul does pray that they will know Christ in the fullest sense and that they will get their eyes open to their glorious privileges (Eph 1:17-18).

Onesiphorus ministered in Ephesus (2 Tim 1:18). Tychicus was sent by Paul to minister in Ephesus (Eph 6:21; 2 Tim 4:12). Following his release, Paul and Timothy passed through Ephesus and Paul left Timothy in Ephesus (1 Tim 1:3). John may have followed Timothy as pastor of Ephesus. After his return from Patmos, John spent his last years in Ephesus and was buried there.

This letter from Christ is written to the Ephesian congregation about six years after Paul wrote his Ephesian letter and some twelve years after the revival in Ephesus. Jesus said they were out of balance. There must always be a balance between faith and works; between doctrinal purity and devoted love. They had left their first love — the love they had during the days of Paul's revival, which had been poured into their hearts through the Holy Spirit (Rom 5:5).

Therefore, Jesus is portrayed to the Ephesian church as holding the stars or messengers and walking among the congregations. We must maintain this balance, that Christ is over us and, at the same time, in our midst. This congregation had lost its balance and thus Christ is depicted to them as both transcendent and immanent. A proper concept of Christ will help us maintain our balance. If we lose this balance we are in danger of eventually losing love for Christ, losing light as he removes our candlestick, and losing life as we are barred from the tree of life.

Jesus acknowledged their works, their labor, and their endurance (v 2). The Greek word for *endurance* (*hupomone*) means patience in trying circumstances, in contrast to *makrothumia*, which describes patience with people. Labor and endurance are two aspects of their deeds which are singled out for approval. Although they had labored hard, they had not grown weary (v 3). While the same three words are found in 1 Thessalonians 1:3, yet in the case of the Thessalonians their work was motivated by faith, their labor prompted by love, and their endurance inspired by hope.

The church at Ephesus could not tolerate false apostles. Paul said he was the least of the apostles and the last of the true apostles (1 Cor 15:7-9). Because he was not one of the original twelve, Paul had to defend his apostleship. He argued, "Am I not an apostle? Have I not seen Jesus our Lord?" (1 Cor 9:1). Again he argued, "The things that mark an apostle — signs, wonders and miracles — were done among you with great perseverance" (2 Cor 12:12).

The Ephesian church also hated the deeds of the Nicolaitans (this will come up again in v 15). While love is a Christian virtue, we cannot love indiscriminately. We must love what is good and hate what is wrong.

Nicolas of Antioch was a convert to Judaism and according to Acts 6:5 he was ordained as one of the seven original deacons. But he had become apostate and as a false apostle he taught heresy and compromise, advocating complete freedom to participate in heathen feasts and free love. Nicolas said a Christian is so free he can do whatever he desires; he was indifferent to matters of adultery and idolatry.

Gnosticism held that all evil resides in matter, two opposite inferences could be drawn—that all material indulgence must be avoided or that all material sins could be indulged and yet the spirit would be pure. Apparently, Nicolas took the second option, which would amount to antinomianism. Christ says in v 6 that he hates this doctrine and practice.

They failed to maintain devoted love. Jesus says in v 4, "I hold this against you: You have forsaken your first love." How serious is this charge? Is this merely a loss of enthusiasm or excitement? John also wrote, "Love comes from God. Everyone who loves has been born of God and knows God. Whoever does not love does not know God" (1 John 4:7-8). Is it possible to lose our love without losing our salvation?

Jesus does not say that their love had waned, he said they had left and they had fallen. The Greek word *aphiemi* means let go, send away, leave, give up, abandon. This is a warning against apostasy. Paul taught that, despite all we might be doing, without this love we are nothing and our works profit us nothing (1 Cor 13:2-3). If we do not recover this love, we cannot please God or grow in grace, and the Lord will come and remove our candlestick. To remove the candlestick is for the light to go out, resulting in a loss of witness. While the warning is serious, Clarke insisted that we must preach a message of hope and not a message of desolation and death.

> God still strives with you, still loves you, still waits to be gracious to you; take courage, set out afresh, come to God through Christ; believe, love, obey, and you will soon find days more blessed than you have ever yet experienced.[73]

When Christ promised to give from the tree of life, he referred back to Genesis 3:22, where Adam and Eve were barred from the tree of life in the Garden of Eden. In a similar way the church at Ephesus not only left their first love, they lost their light and their life. Three times in Proverbs wisdom is called a tree of life; a fourth reference calls the fruit of the righteous a tree of life. While in a secondary sense a righteous man has a life-giving influence, the more profound truth is that the personification of wisdom in Proverbs points to the *Logos*, the Son of God. Thus, Christ is the wisdom of God (1 Cor 1:24, 30; Col 2:3). The tree of life is alluded to in Ezekiel 47:12 and mentioned four times in Revelation (2:7; 22:2, 14, 19).

Eternal life is not promised to the one who merely makes an initial decision for Christ, but to the one who overcomes. The fact

---

[73]Clarke, *Commentary*, 6:976.

that Adam and Eve had previously eaten from the tree of life, then were barred from continuing to partake of it, indicates they had to continue in obedience in order to maintain life. One bite would not suffice.

The city of Ephesus had a population of about 250,000 in the first century. The Goths destroyed it in AD 263 and while it was rebuilt, it never recovered its former glory. The third general church council, the Council of Ephesus convened there in AD 431, but it declined in importance after that. The darkness of Islam swept that region in the thirteenth century and by the fourteenth century the city no longer existed.

Ephesus was located at the mouth of the Cayster River as it emptied into the Mediterranean Sea. Even then the harbor was beginning to accumulate silt. This accumulation of silt stopped up the harbor and today the ruins of Ephesus is eight miles from the sea; the old harbor is now a grassy, windswept plain. Thus, the town left the sea, just as the church left Christ. Today Ephesus, now a small Turkish village known as Ayasaluk,[74] is a ruin with no church remaining. The tomb of John was under the Basilica of St. John, now in ruins; an Islamic mosque stands nearby. If any repentance was produced by this solemn warning, its effects were not permanent.

B. Smyrna 2:8-11

Forty miles north of Ephesus was the town of Smyrna, with a population of 100,000. It had a good harbor and was a major trade center. It was a beautiful city and the citizens were proud of five pagan temples, a famous stadium, library, and the largest public theater in Asia Minor. There was also a monument to Homer who was born in Smyrna.

While the church at Ephesus had internal problems, the problem at Smyrna was external. The Christian community was under pressure

---

[74]*Ayasoluk* is the Turkish adaptation of two Greek words meaning "holy theologian," a reference to the Apostle John the theologian or "divine."

from two sources: Smyrna was a center of emperor worship and Smyrna had a large Jewish population which opposed the church. Rome sought to hold its vast empire together by requiring every citizen to burn a pinch of incense on the altar to Caesar and say "Caesar is Lord." They were then given a certificate to verify that they had performed their religious duty. In practical terms this act was a test of political loyalty.

But Christians refused to compromise at this point because they believed Jesus alone was Lord. Their refusal to comply branded them as outlaws and made them liable to persecution at any time. By bringing Christian principles into the business world, they were in danger of losing their job. Alan Johnson speculated that their refusal to participate in emperor worship lead to economic sanctions against them. They were also poor because their property was vandalized and destroyed since they had no rights. Jesus acknowledged their extreme poverty (v 9), but they had their priorities in order. Of two Greek words for poverty, one meant having nothing extra while the other word meant having nothing at all. John used the more intense term which carried the meaning of destitution.

The worship of Caesar was not as big an issue in every region, but Smyrna was an enthusiastic center of Caesar worship. In Smyrna a person took his life in his hands to declare his loyalty to Jesus Christ. The church was encouraged not to be fearful, but to be faithful. They would triumph through tribulation.

Jesus wrote a letter of encouragement to the pastor at Smyrna. There is not one word of rebuke in this letter. He said, "I know your afflictions." Literally this word means pressure or crushing weight. They lived under stress and strain. This is addressed in v 10; you will suffer, you will be tested, be faithful even to the point of death. Why would anyone want to follow Jesus Christ to their death?

- Christ has conquered death - v 8. He became dead and yet came to life.
- Christ will give the crown of life to those who keep on being faithful. This is not a special crown for martyrs, but all who

belong to Christ will receive the crown of life (Jas 1:12). While death is the retribution of sin, eternal life is not a wage that is earned. It is a gift (Rom 6:23).

The Greek language has two words for *crown*. *Stephanos* is the victor's crown and *diadema* is a royal crown. Five times in Revelation the church is described as wearing a *stephanos*, never a diadem.[75] Christ wears the diadem in 19:12, while the dragon and the beast have a diadem in 12:3, 13:1, representing usurped authority. Here the crown of life is an epexegetical genitive, meaning that *life* is an additional explanation that the crown is, or consists of, eternal life. Therefore we cannot hold that the crown may be lost, but not salvation. The crown of life is contrasted with the second death in v 11. Thus, the crown is not a special reward, it is eternal life.

- Those who persevere will absolutely never be hurt by the second death. According to 20:14, 21:8 the second death is the lake of fire. "The *first death* consists in the separation of the soul from the body for a season; the *second death* is the separation from God's favor forever."[76] Thus, John reminded the church it was better to suffer "ten days," even if that suffering brought death, than to suffer the second death "day and night for ever and ever" (20:10).

Therefore, the church at Smyrna was told to stop being afraid. Jesus also told them that they would only live under this pressure for ten days (v 10). This anticipates the question, "How long?" (6:10) He is saying that the trials they face would be short in comparison with eternal life they would gain and the eternal death they would avoid.

While their opposition at this time was primarily from the Jews,

---

[75]The five references in Revelation are 2:10; 3:11; 4:4, 10; 12:1. Compare to 9:7.

[76]Binney, *People's Commentary,* 674.

it would soon shift to Rome. Just as there were ten plagues on Egypt and then God's people were liberated, so the church would be persecuted by ten Roman emperors, then Christianity would conquer the Roman Empire.

The first emperor to persecute the church was Nero, following the fire that destroyed half of Rome in AD 64. He was the prototype for what was to follow. Jesus may have meant that they would have nine more brief periods of persecution. After the great tribulation which they were about to suffer under Nero, the next persecution occurred under

Domitian around (c.) 95
Trajan c. 108
Marcus Aurelius c. 162
Septimius Severus c. 202
Maximinus c. 235
Decius c. 249
Valerian c. 257
Aurelian c. 274

Then a forty-year period of peace followed by the most intense persecution under Diocletian (303-313). This persecution lasted eight years under Diocletian and then continued two more years under his two sons for a total of ten years. Then his successor, Constantine, converted to Christianity.[77] Ten days of tribulation in exchange for one thousand years of victory!

The Jews were very jealous of their special privileges in the Roman Empire. The Christian movement, as depicted in the book of Acts, threatened to upset the delicate balance between the Jewish and Gentile communities. Therefore, the Jews in their attempt to dissociate themselves from the Christian movement were willing to enlist

---

[77]*Foxe's Book of Martyrs* covered this three hundred year period under the heading "A Description of the Ten First Persecutions in the Primitive Church" [1:99-304].

Roman persecution of the Christians.

Perhaps the Romans would have not persecuted the church if they had not been encouraged by the Jews. As we seek to follow the Lord Jesus Christ, we will find our greatest opposition often comes from religious people. The strong statements made by Jesus through John about the "synagogue of Satan" are not anti-Semitic (based on race), but based upon their rejection of Jesus as Messiah and their subsequent persecution of the true church. These people could trace their ancestry to Abraham and racially they were Jews, but they had rejected their Messiah and had developed their own legalism. Jesus told the Jews of his day that if Abraham was really their father they would recognize and rejoice in him (John 8:39-47).

Just as the Christians were poor by the standards of the world, but in the spiritual realm they were actually rich, so the Jews, who enjoyed status in Smyrna, were in the spiritual realm actually the "synagogue of Satan."

The name *Smyrna* means myrrh or bitter. Myrrh is a resinous gum used as an ointment, for embalming or perfume. If there is any significance in the name it would be that although the church was under tremendous pressure, they were not crushed. Instead they gave off a fragrance or ointment which gave honor to Christ. We may not avoid the pressure, but we can give off the fragrance of Christ. "But thanks be to God, who always leads us in triumphal procession in Christ and through us spreads everywhere the fragrance of the knowledge of him. For we are to God the aroma of Christ" (2 Cor 2:14-15).

The entire church could not be put to death. There was a strong Christian influence in Smyrna, now called Izmir, with Christians outnumbering Muslims three to one, until 1922 when the Turks took control. Today Izmir is the third largest city in Turkey, with a population of over two and a half million in 1990. It is the only city of the original seven that still exists as a major city.

C. Pergamum 2:12-17

Pergamum laid north of Smyrna sixty-five miles, with an estimated population of 120,000. Today Pergamum is a small village of about 48,000 named Bergama. Pergamum was a provincial capital and had been granted the authority to execute by Rome. The Romans called the "right of the sword" *ius gladii*; only they had the right to carry out the death penalty. For Jesus Christ to describe himself as having a sword was to set himself above Roman authority. Capital punishment is symbolized by the sword (Rom 13:4). Yet the sword *machaira* of Rome is short in comparison with the sword *rhomphaia* of the Lord. The *machaira* was a short sword or dagger six to eighteen inches long. The *rhomphaia* was a large broad sword three to four feet long. *Machaira* occurs 27 times in the New Testament, while *rhomphaia* is used only seven times. It is significant that six of seven occurrences are found in Revelation and that in five of these occurrences this *rhomphaia* proceeds from the mouth of Christ. Both words are found together in 6:4, 8.

Christ revealed himself to the church at Pergamum as having the sharp, double-edged sword. In 1:16 this was depicted as proceeding from his mouth. The significance of the double-edged sword (Heb 4:12) is that Christ not only pronounces judgment, but the same Word which convicts us, laying us open also brings comfort and healing (see Deut 32:39, 41; Hos 6:1; Eph 6:17).

God rules this world (Ps 24:1). "Heaven is my throne, and the earth is my footstool" (Isa 66:1). Christ is seated on the throne of heaven and he will not get up until his enemies have been conquered (Ps 110:1). "Yet at present we do not see everything subject to him" (Heb 2:8). Satan still walks around looking for someone to devour (1 Pet 5:8). Wherever he can establish a foothold (Eph 4:27) he will set up a rebel government. He had established a *seat* or *throne* in the seat of civil government. "You live where Satan has his throne" (v 13).

Pergamum had a temple of healing to the god of healing, Asklepios. He was called Askelepios the Savior, the god of Pergamum. In this temple tamed snakes were allowed to crawl. The sick were left to spend the night in the darkness of the temple. If the sick were touched by a snake as it glided over the person, the touch of the snake was regarded as the touch of god.

A second temple, high on a hill overlooking Pergamum, was a temple to Zeus. Smoke rose continually from this altar. There were also temples to the patron goddess, Athene and to Dionysos. More importantly, there was a temple to the Roman emperor. Built in 29 BC, this was the first such Asian temple. In time, a second and third temple were added in honor of the emperor. Thus, the state also usurped the role of God. The church in Pergamum felt the tension between the claim of Caesar and Christ. Jesus knew where they lived (v 13); they lived in a center of Satanic power and influence.

In the face of this paganism the church had remained true — even when Antipas was martyred during an outburst of persecution. They had refused to say Caesar is Lord, continuing instead to confess Jesus as Lord. While the church had witnessed the Roman sword of execution against Antipas, they needed a vision of the sword of the Lord.

We do not know much about Antipas. While that name means "against all," other people had this name as well. It is also claimed that "Antipas" was a shortened form of "Antipatros," which may or may not make the meaning of "Antipas" significant. Terry wrote that the mention of Nicolaitans (v 6), Antipas (v 13), and Jezebel (v 20), "is evidence that the epistles deal with actual persons and events, though the names employed are probably symbolical."[78]

The overcomer was promised three things in v 17.

- Hidden manna

The original reference to *manna* is Exodus 16:31. However, in Psalm 78:24-25 it is called "the grain of heaven" and "the bread of angels." Therefore, the emphasis is that those who deny themselves the pleasures of the world feast on heavenly food. See also Hebrews 9:4.

Verse 14 refers to the lure of eating food sacrificed to idols. Nearly all the meat in Pergamum had been offered to idols. While

---

[78]Terry, *Biblical Hermeneutics*, 469.

Paul instructed the Corinthians that they could not become demon possessed through eating food (1 Cor 8:4-13; 10:25-33), the Christian in Pergamum could not go to the pagan temples to eat because of the immoral rituals which followed the meal. Notice that v 14 connects eating and committing immorality (see also the connection in Acts 15:20, 29). To those who refuse the banquets of pagan gods, Christ will give them the bread from heaven (John 6:47-58 says Jesus himself is the bread of life). In John 4:32 Jesus himself declared that he had food to eat that his disciples knew nothing about. Those who do not banquet with the world feast on heavenly food and will eat at the marriage supper. Both meals are hidden from the world.

- A white stone

In Roman culture these *tessera* were tokens or symbols of recognition, privilege, and admittance. *Tessera* is a Latin word describing a small tablet of wood, bone, or ivory which was used as a ticket, tally, voucher, or means of identification. Such was also presented to the winner in the Olympic games. The Greek word used by John was *psephos*. It is significant that this word came to mean *vote*. In secret societies voting was done with white and black balls. We still have an idiom about *black balling* someone. To *blackball* means to exclude or ostracize. In courts the jury voted with a white pebble for innocent and a black pebble for guilty. Thus, the white stone would represent acquittal.

While Pergamum had the authority to execute, Christ not only claims an authority which overrules Rome, he also has the authority to justify, as well as the authority to judge. To have the white stone, according to Adam Clarke, is to have the earnest of the Spirit. "He then who has received and retains the witness of the Spirit that he is *adopted* into the *heavenly family*, may humbly claim, in virtue of it, his support of the bread and water of life."[79]

---

[79]Clarke, *Commentary*, 6:980.

- A new name written on the white stone

When Jacob overcame, he received the new name, *Israel.* After we overcome we, too, will receive a new name. A name reflects character. If we remain true to his name (v 13), and do not deny the faith, we will be transformed and will need a new identity. Notice Jesus is called "the faithful witness" in 1:5 and 3:14.

After Antipas overcame, he was called "my faithful witness." As overcomers, we take on the image of Christ (Isa 62:2; 65:15; Rev 19:12-16). Compare to 3:12, where Christ promises to write on the overcomer the name of God.

Christ accepts responsibility to maintain them in hostile surrounding. He explains that the resistance will improve and transform their character and he assures them of his acceptance. While Pergamum was promised strength to resist the external pressure, they also had internal weakness.

"But I have a few things against you," Jesus declared (v 14). Within the church a minority was in error. The first teaching, that of Balaam, led to immorality; the second teaching, the teaching of the Nicolaitans justified immorality. Some commentators hold that they are the same group, but the words *also* and *likewise* in v 15 seem to indicate two separate groups.

In Numbers 22-24 Balak, king of Moab, hired Balaam, a heathen fortune teller, to curse Israel. There is no mention of any doctrine in the account. After Balaam failed to stop Israel, in chapter 25 it is recorded that the men of God were seduced by Moabite women who invited them to worship pagan gods.

We do not learn until Numbers 31:16 that Balaam had advised this tactic. In 2 Peter 2:15, Balaam is described as one who would do anything to make money. Jude 11 also reveals that Balaam's motive was profit. Not until Revelation 2:14 is the doctrine of Balaam explained. Apparently some within the church advised conformity to pagan customs to avoid persecution. While the church at Pergamum could not be cursed externally, it could be compromised from within by people who were indifferent to and intermingling with the lifestyle of the world. We must remain separate from the world. Beware of the social life and entertainment of the world; be careful about gaining status and acceptance by the enemy. Sinful man has perverted everything good that God has provided. Our goal is to enjoy the good things God has provided without getting trapped by temptation to sin.

Pergamum means marriage. The church at Pergamum was in danger of becoming yoked with unbelievers. There is no neutrality. Either we win them or they weaken us. Yes, we are to infiltrate the world system until the leaven of the gospel permeates every stratum of society (Matt 13:33), but we must remember our task is to influence them without having them influence us.

As mentioned at 2:6 Nicolas had taught that our lifestyle is not an issue. This perversion of the doctrine of grace justified the church in their adaptation of the practices of the world. The Lord will not lead people to do things his Word condemns. We must steer clear of anything involving occult practices (Eph 4:27) or immorality (Eph 5:3). The message was that the church must not trade their white stone of justification by God for acceptance by their society and thus face the sword of Christ. "Be not overcome with evil, but overcome evil with good" (Rom 12:21). The danger was that all their suffering and self denial would be forfeited; that after standing alone for Jesus, the Lord would become their enemy. The sword of the Lord cuts both ways. Balaam was also threatened with being killed by the sword (Num 22:23, 31). Christ has a message for us today. We must either remain true and overcome or repent before he comes to make war against us and cut us off (Rom 11:22). Notice the call to repent (v 16) was directed toward the whole church. Both those members who indulged and those who tolerated such indulgence needed to repent. However, the threat of the sword was directed only against *them* —the followers of Balaam and Nicholas.

D. Thyatira 2:18-29

We move forty miles southeast of Pergamum to the town of Thyatira. Now the modern town of Akhisar, it has a population of 82,000. Founded by Seleucus I, a successor to Alexander the Great, in the third century BC, it was not a center of political power. The local deity was Apollo Tyrimnos, who was a composite of Lydian, Macedonian, and Greek mythology. Both he and the Roman emperor were considered sons of Zeus. This tendency to syncretism, the mixing of different beliefs, also found its way into the church. However, Christ declared to the church that *he* was the Son of God (v 18). He would come and so deal with the situation that all the churches will know he is opposed to antinomianism.

Thyatira was an obscure city except that it was prosperous, having more trade guilds than in any other Asian city. It was also known for the manufacture of purple dye. Purple dye was expensive and one major source for it was from the madder root which grew plentifully around Thyatira.

The only other mention of Thyatira is found in Acts 16:14-15. Paul had been led to bypass the region of Asia he was in and to cross over to Europe. While in Philippi on the Sabbath, he went out of the city to the river to find a place of prayer. Philippi did not have a Jewish synagogue, but he found some women gathered and among them was Lydia, a God-fearer. She was not raised Jewish, but had become a proselyte to Judaism in her search after God. When Paul discovered her, she was practicing the Jewish traditions. She had moved there from Thyatira or else maintained a house in both locations. She was a dealer in purple cloth. As she heard Paul, the Lord opened her heart and she responded, making her the first European convert. She was baptized and through her influence the servants and other dependents were also baptized.

She is an example of hospitality, inviting Paul and his company to her home. When Paul and Silas got out of jail, they went to Lydia's house, which had become the location where the Philippian church met (Acts 16:40). She apparently was a widow, for Acts 16:15 refers to members of her household, but not her husband. She had crossed the Aegean Sea and was about 200 miles from home. She had set up a business in her home and had become a woman of some financial means. Other commentators describe Lydia as an overseas agent or a manufacturer from Thyatira. It is possible that at some later point in time she moved back to Thyatira and helped Paul establish a church (Acts 19:10) in the very area that Paul had previously been led to pass over.

At least fifteen years have now elapsed since the conversion of Lydia and Christ sends this message to the church in Thyatira. "I know all your activities" (v 19), he acknowledges. But busyness is not godliness. They were doing more than they did at first, but accomplishing less. Activity alone does not indicate spiritual growth. Christ was not impressed because his eyes are as a flaming fire piercing through the appearance of success. He searches hearts and minds (v 23; see Jer 17:10), sees past the facade and says, "I have this against you: You are allowing a woman to destroy the church." If Lydia had helped build it; Jezebel is now tearing it down.

Just as the teaching of Balaam lived on centuries after Balaam died, so the spirit of Jezebel was present in Thytira nine hundred years after the historical woman by that name died. Therefore we know John was speaking figuratively, not literally. The woman Satan used is unnamed, but there is some evidence to suggest that it was the pastor's wife.

This reference to Jezebel draws from the historical account in 1 Kings 16:31-21:25; 2 Kings 9. Jezebel was the daughter of Ethbaal, a pagan priest-king. She married Ahab to effect a political alliance between two nations, Tyre and Israel, in direct contradiction to God's Word. This illustrates the intermixture of the church and the world.

Jezebel encouraged idolatry in Israel. The first reference in the Bible to Jezebel is that she introduced Asherah poles, an obscene phallic symbol into Israel (1 Kgs 16:33). In 2 Kings 9:22 she is accused of whoredom and witchcraft. Through her the ten northern tribes forsook the covenant, destroyed the sacred altars, and killed the prophets. One person corrupted an entire nation, except for the seven thousand who refused to bow to Baal. This remnant compares to the remnant mentioned in Rev 2:24.

Just as Nimrod, the founder of Babylon, was the first man to openly rebel against God, so Jezebel was the first woman to do so. Thus, Jezebel becomes a prototype or the mother of rebellion. According to the Hebrew, rebellion *is* the sin of divination (1 Sam 15:23). The mother of harlots (Rev 17:5) also has offspring (Rev 2:23). Jezebel was haughty and proud. She outlived her husband Ahaz by ten years. He was followed to the throne by their two sons. Jehu assassinated her sons and came riding into Jezreel. Customarily a widow who had just lost her son would put on the veil of mourning, but 2 Kings 9:30 says she painted her eyes and arranged her hair. When Jehu arrived, she taunted him (v 31). But she was thrown down to her death and the dogs ate her bones. This characteristic is portrayed in 18:7, "In her heart she boasts, I sit as queen; I am not a widow, and I will never mourn." Yet according to 17:16 her flesh will be eaten, just as the dogs did Jezebel.

The woman of Thyatira brought this spirit of Jezebel into the church. She also encouraged idolatry in the church. In Thyatira all the industry and commerce were regulated by trade guilds. Thyatira was known for its strong "unions." The guild itself was not necessarily wrong, but they combined business and pagan rituals — food sacrificed to idols and immorality (v 20) until Christians could not belong in good conscience. Thus, their pressure did not come from political fanaticism or religious bigotry, but from economic concerns.

This created an economic hardship for them, but they had resisted. To those who excused the fact that they made their living by making idols, claiming they must live and had no other way of making a living, Tertullian, writing at the end of the second century, replied, "Must you live?" Physical survival is not the ultimate priority.

Jezebel encouraged lawlessness, teaching that sexual immorality and idolatry did not matter. God was gracious and the more they sinned the more they would be forgiven. The more they experienced the deep things of Satan, the better they could witness to the unsaved. Perhaps her teaching was a perversion of Paul's words in 1 Corinthians 8:4-8. Since an idol is nothing, no harm will come from participating in the immoral rituals of the guild.

The idol she introduced was money. She was willing to compromise principle for material prosperity. Wall wrote, "Jezebel's heresy is the ancient equivalent of the current 'gospel of prosperity' that equates the gospel with present, material blessings."[80]

Yet, Jezebel's teaching was considered *deep*. These idolaters justified themselves by saying, "The more we know of sin, the more we can appreciate grace" (Rom 6:1, 15). But it is better not to know "Satan's deep secrets" (v 24). This should be read as a sarcastic statement; "You have not known 'the deep things' of Satan — as they say." There is nothing intellectually profound about filthiness and obscenity or about paganism and the occult. "I want you to be wise about what is good, and innocent about what is evil" (Rom 16:19). It is better not to know some things. The message from Jesus is that if the church is willing to get in bed with the world, he will cause it to be a bed of suffering. Just as Jezebel was thrown down to her death, so this "Jezebel" will be *cast* or thrown in a bed. The word for *bed* in v 22 refers to a banqueting couch. As she reclines in the pagan atmosphere she is committing spiritual adultery; she is being unfaithful to Christ. Quite possibly she was also involved in the sexual immorality with which she was surrounded. In this case, her illegitimate children will die, as did David's child by Bathsheba (2 Sam 12). If Christ is speaking symbolically, the children would represent those who were influenced by her teaching and followed it to their own spiritual destruction. According to 2 John 1, the true church also has *children*.

The great tribulation was about to begin (v 22; see also 1:9; 2:10; 3:10). Just as Jezebel brought three and a half years of drought on Israel, so the great tribulation was the days of vengeance when Jehu destroyed the house of Ahab.

Jezebel usurped her husband's role. When God's law forbid the king from taking Naboth's vineyard, she announced that she would get it. She wrote letters in his name and used his seal to take charge (1 Kgs 21:7-8).

She influenced or "stirred up" her husband to serve Baal (1 Kgs 21:25). Likewise, Eve usurped her husband's authority, eating of the forbidden fruit. It is the characteristic of carnal women to control their

---

[80]Wall, *NIBC*, 18:78.

husbands (Gen 3:16; 4:7). According to 17:3, this Jezebel controls governments.

Jesus rebuked the *angel* or pastor for allowing her to prophesy, teach, and mislead the congregation. But is it wrong for a woman to have a ministry or to have spiritual influence? Lydia's ministry exemplified a proper influence. Yet the same Apostle Paul who worked with Lydia in founding congregations in Philippi and Thyatira wrote, "I do not permit a woman to teach or to have authority over a man" (1 Tim 2:12). And the pastor of Thyatira was told "you permit Jezebel to teach and deceive my own servants" (v 20). Love cannot allow toleration of sin (vv 19-20).

Jezebel is haughty and proud. "I have given her time to repent of her immorality, but she is unwilling" (v 21). She had been given time to repent, but her time was up. She and her "children," her "hard core" converts will be judged. However, there seems to be another group of people who tolerated her. They are accused of committing adultery with her. This is a reference to the spiritual adultery of those who are unfaithful to Christ in their toleration of heresy. While Christ had given her time to repent, they had permitted her to have a platform through which she deceived others. They still have an opportunity to repent (v 22). A third group will be introduced in v 24, who never have known or believed the teachings of "Jezebel" and who still do not accept them. Everyone at Thyatira did not go along with the new program. In vv 24-25 the *you* is plural, referring to the "rest." This group is genuinely saved. Christ is aware of their love and faithfulness, their service and perseverance. Barclay noted that their love led to service and their faith led to endurance.[81]

Jesus revealed himself to them as the one with feet like burnished brass. This term, *chalkolibanos*, occurs only in Revelation 1:15 and 2:18. It is not found anywhere else in ancient Greek literature. While the translation *polished* or *burnished* refers to the finished product, the process involves refining the metal in a furnace until it becomes

---

[81]Barclay, *Letters to the Seven Churches,* 73.

liquid.[82] He still walks in the furnace to protect the righteous (Dan 3:25; 10:6). These two passages in Daniel connect the concepts of "furnace" and "feet." The feet glowed because they had been in a furnace (Rev 1:15). Beale also noted that in Daniel 3:25 the three Hebrews were protected by the Son of God and in Revelation 2:18 it is the Son of God who has feet like burnished brass.[83] This is the only time in Revelation that the phrase *Son of God* is used.

He instructs them to hold on until he intervenes (v 25). Christ will come in judgment, just as he has promised the other congregations. According to v 23, Christ will judge them according to their works. While we are saved by faith, genuine faith will produce good works. Some forty-two times the Scriptures declare that at the judgment we will be judged by our works (see Rev 2:3; 18:3-6; 20:12-13; 22:12).

In the meantime, he promised, "I will not put more on you" (see Acts 15:28). The answer to compromise is not the opposite extreme of legalism, but faithfulness. Jesus made two promises the overcomer, that is the one keeping or his works or commands to the end. For the first time this phrase is added, which defines the overcomer as the one who perseveres.

- I will give him authority (v 26). Even though it has been challenged and usurped in this congregation, the overcomer will rule over the nations. While this is a reference to the rule of Christ in Psalm 2:9, here the overcomer shares that dominion with Christ.

- I will give him the morning star. While the pastor is called a "star" in 1:20, Venus is the morning star which appears before sunrise. To those who have just about been worn down by the attack of Satan, Jesus says hold on. Things may look hopeless, but the sign of the times is not the evening star, but the morning

---

[82]Hemer, *Letters to the Seven Churches*, 114-117.

[83]Beale, *NIGNTC*, 259.

star. A new day is about to dawn.

Jesus is our morning star (Num 24:17, Mal 4:2, 2 Pet 1:19; Rev 22:16), not the king of Babylon (Isa 14:12). Hold on. Help is on the way. A lost battle does not mean a lost war (v 25). The kingdom of Christ will shine more and more unto the perfect day (Prov 4:18).

REVELATION 3

E. Sardis 3:1-6

Thirty-five miles southeast of Thyatira, Sardis was a city of commerce. Five roads junctioned at Sardis. It seemed to be an ideal place to live. The population was probably about 100,000. There was no persecution from the Roman government nor Jewish opposition. The church was not accused of false doctrine. In fact the church had a good reputation (v 1). The word *name* occurs four times in this message (vv 1, 4, twice in v 5).

> This word-play on "name" emphasizes the problem at Sardis. They have become a church in name only. They have a name for being alive, but their name or reputation is false. Because of their faithlessness, they will lose even their names when they are blotted out of the Book of Life.[84]

Yet in spite of a good reputation Christ was not impressed with this congregation. Nothing good was said about them. The small village of Sart now occupies the ancient site. This congregation had people in three different conditions:

Some were lifeless. Cybele, the local goddess was supposed to be able to restore the dead to life. Her worship included wild dancing, revelry, and self-mutilation. Yet Christ held the sevenfold fullness of the Spirit of God and promised to give the life-giving Spirit to this dead church. Christ also held the seven stars, the pastors of the seven churches, and they must give account to him.

Some were careless. Sardis was built on a steep hill. On three sides, the north, east, and west, there was a 1500 foot elevation. From these vantage points, the city was imposing. On the south side there was an isthmus, a narrow neck of land, which was steep and winding. The citizens felt no one could overtake their city. Croesus, the king, had been warned by Solon, when he visited Sardis to beware of self-satisfaction. In 547 BC Cyrus the Persian overtook Sardis. Cyrus had

---

[84]Reddish, *Revelation*, 72-73.

announced a special reward would be given to any soldier who worked out a way to get into Sardis. A soldier inside the city was on guard when he accidently dropped his helmet and it rolled down the cliff. The enemy watched as the soldier went down the path to recover his helmet and that night the enemy climbed up the same path to the top and found the city unguarded. Croesus awakened one morning to find the enemy was in control of the city and that all was lost. While the narrow neck of land on the south was guarded, the enemy had made its ascent on a side which was considered inaccessible. Cyrus had come as a thief (v 3).

Again, 320 years later Antiochus the Great conquered the city. The isthmus was guarded, but there was no one on guard on the other three sides. This careless attitude had crept into the church. Some were weak in faith and about to die spiritually. This implies, however, that they had been awakened and did have a degree of spiritual life. Christ warned them that unless they woke up he would come unexpectedly to judge them. Christ would be ashamed to own them and would erase their names from the book of life.

Christ rebuked them in v 2, "I have not found your deeds perfect." In other words their deeds were incomplete. They had been given white garments, but had not kept them clean (see Rev 19:8; 7:14; 22:14; Jude 23). They had not maintained the fullness of the Spirit. Their careless attitude was represented by soiled clothing. In vv 2-3 there are five commands: be watchful, strengthen, remember, keep, repent. They are admonished, "Remember what God has done for you, hold on to what you have, repent for your carelessness" (v 3). They were to remember what they had received and heard when they were first saved. They had received the Spirit and Christ, who holds the Spirit (v 1), can pour out that Spirit in revival.

Jesus says they will not remain in this gray zone. They will either wake up (v 3) and repent or else they will fall soundly asleep and lose out. Half asleep and half awake is a miserable position in which to be. We are made in such a way that we cannot long stand the tension of indecision. We will either wake up or go sound asleep.

And yet some were blameless. A few had kept their white garments pure. They were the overcomers. Christ was not ashamed to own them (Matt 10:32-33) and as long as they continued to walk in holiness there was no danger that their names would be erased (Matt 10:22b).

Ramsay also noted that Roman citizens wore a pure white toga especially to celebrate a triumph.[85] Paul referred to such a triumph for the Christian in Colossians 2:15 and developed the concept in 2 Corinthians 2:14-16. These overcomers will march with Christ in his final victory. We are to walk in white in this life (3:4, 8) and we shall be clothed in white in the next life (3:5; 4:4).

He who overcomes will never have his name erased from the book of life (v 5). Death can never separate us from life in Christ. However, this promise is hollow if the doctrine of unconditional security is true. Reddish wrote,

> The converse of this assurance to the faithful, though not stated, is certainly implied — those who are not faithful will have their names expunged from the Book of Life and will lose their place in God's fellowship. This is a sobering wake-up call to those who take their relationship to God for granted. As Wilfrid Harrington has noted, "While one cannot earn the right to have one's name in this book, one can forfeit it."[86]

The church at Sardis had many who had grown careless and were about to die. Their names were about to be erased. Only a few were overcomers. Benson wrote,

> This passage plainly implies, that some names shall be blotted out from the book of life: this is, some who, in consequence of their adoption and regeneration, were entitled to and fitted for eternal life, shall, through falling from grace, lose these blessings, and come again under guilt, condemna-

---

[85]Ramsey, *Letters to the Seven Churches*, 282-283.

[86]Reddish, *Revelation*, 72-73.

tion, and wrath.[87]

What is *the book of life*? The Old Testament declared that the righteous are written in God's book. In the New Testament this expresses the idea of assurance of salvation. The Lord knows those who are his (2 Tim 2:19). The book is the book of the crucified Lamb of God and the phrase serves as a metaphor for God's memory.

What does it mean to have your name removed from the book of life? In ancient times city registers contained the names of its citizens. There were two reasons why a name could be erased: committing a capital offense or death. Howard Marshall wrote,

> The possibility of failure to endure is mentioned. Christians who fail to persevere will come under judgment and their names will be blotted out of the book of life. There is no reason to suppose that these warnings are purely hypothetical, directed against non-existent dangers; the reverse is the case. Moreover, the reference to the book of life indicates that John is addressing his warning to believers.[88]

F. Philadelphia 3:7-13

Twenty-eight miles southeast of Sardis we come to Philadelphia. The name is a compound word made up of *phileo* (to love) and *adelphos* (brother). Thus, *Philadelphia* means brotherly love. It was named for its founder, Attalus II, who loved his brother Eumenes.

Philadelphia was a border town where three countries met. The highway which connected Europe and Asia also passed through it. The church there was strategically located and had an open door of opportunity for missionary work (1 Cor 16:9; 2 Cor 2:12; Col 4:3).

Ramsay wrote that several characteristics distinguished Philadel-

---

[87]Benson, *Notes*, 5:713.

[88]Marshall, *Kept by the Power of God*, 175.

phia from other cities. It was a missionary city, founded to promote unity of spirit, customs, and loyalty between Greek and Asian culture. Its people always lived in dread of a disaster. It had been destroyed by earthquake in AD 17 and Jesus spoke about the "hour of trial" (v 10). Many of its people went out of the city to live because of the panic created by aftershocks. These earthquakes were an everyday occurrence for several years. It was considered unsafe to enter Philadelphia. Taxes were remitted for five years.[89] Because of kindness shown by the emperor in rebuilding the city, it was given a new name — Neocaesarea.[90] Today it is the Muslim town of Alasehir, with a population of 44,000.

Jesus said this church had little strength. They were small in number, poor in wealth, and weak in influence. Jesus said he knew their works. We would probably not have been impressed, but Jesus offered no word of rebuke to this church. Christ knows what our capabilities are and he knows when we have done our best.

In spite of their weakness they had kept his word and acknowledged his name (v 8). To keep his word meant that they had kept the commandments of Christ (compare to 2:26—keep his works). Again in v 10, they had kept the command of Christ to endure. The *word of my patience* literally means they had followed the same kind of endurance that Christ displayed (see Heb 12:1-3). In v 11 Jesus gave his only command to them, encouraging them to keep on doing what they are doing; "hold on to what you have."

The phrase *to take away someone's wreath or crown* is a metaphor for being disqualified in a contest. In 2:10 the crown signified future reward; here it represents their present state. However, they must maintain their present victory. "If they failed to maintain their walk, they too could lose their reward." Therefore, they must perse-

---

[89]Hemer, *Letters to the Seven Churches*, 156.

[90]Ramsey, *Letters to the Seven Churches*, 292. This name was dropped after 25-30 years.

vere.[91] Despite their perseverance to this point, they must continue to hold fast what they have. Losing their crown means roughly the same as the warning to the preceding church: exclusion from the kingdom (v 5). It is not enough to start the Christian race; we must finish it.

Consistency and dependability are virtues which reflect the nature of God. This principle is illustrated in Isaiah 22:20-25. Shebna was once a leader in Judah and he had failed to carry out his obligations. Instead, he sought to build a memorial for himself. Isaiah declared that God would depose Shebna from office and replace him with Eliakim.

Shebna was a disappointment. He was like a peg driven into a firm place which was meant to bear the weight of a load hung upon it. Instead, the peg was sheared off and the load fell. Eliakim, on the other hand, was dependable. He was a peg driven into a firm place. All the glory of his family hung on him and he did not let them down.

Christ is the door (John 10:9). He is the door that controls the circumstances of life. The man who seeks to promote himself by opening his own doors will find them shut. The man who trusts God finds God will open the door and put him in a position of influence.

The reason this congregation had a great future is not because of their abilities, but because they had submitted to Christ. Here Christ is depicted as holy and true; this description is given of God the Father in 6:10. All holiness is derived from him and all truth proceeds from him. Although they have little authority or influence, Christ holds the key, or authority, of David. Therefore, he is sovereign. This is the first time his description is not drawn from 1:13-16. However, keys are mentioned in v 18.

In order to understand the significance of this statement, we must turn again to Isaiah 22. God speaks through Isaiah and says he will place on the shoulder of Eliakim the key to the house of David or authority over the royal treasury. "What he opens no one can shut, and what he shuts no one can open." Only Christ can determine for

---

[91]Osborne, *BECNT*, 195. Osborne connected this warning with 2:5; 21:8; 22:18-19.

whom the door is opened and shut. The Scriptures teach that faith and obedience unlock the door of God's blessing. God is sovereign and he will put us where he wants us. He opens the doors. Yet he also closes doors. After Noah entered the ark, God shut the door and no one else could enter (Gen 7:16). Jesus said at his second coming the door would be shut (Matt 25:10) and there would be no second chance. He holds the keys of death and hell (Rev 1:18). He holds the key to our future. The door of opportunity stands open because Christ holds the key. God will prosper his cause. If we are on his side, we will share in the victory. Our success is not based upon our works, but upon his finished work. Christ has promised:

- I will turn your opposition into support (v 9; Isa 49:23; 60:14). The Jews were once God's chosen people, but they rejected their Messiah. For the second time Jesus called them the "synagogue of Satan" (2:9). Christians were locked out of the Jewish synagogue, but Christ said not to worry. Since he holds the keys, they were only banned from the synagogue of Satan. He holds open the door of salvation and even the Jews will be drawn to Christ and will acknowledge that this little congregation is the true Israel of God and the inheritor of the promises to Abraham and Moses. Clarke wrote, "The love which was formerly fixed on the Jews is now removed, and transferred to the Gentiles."[92]

- I will protect my own; "I will keep you from the hour of trial coming upon the whole world." John did not use *kosmos*, but *oikoumene*, which probably means the whole Roman empire. It was used in this sense in Luke 2:1. Therefore, this prophecy of general persecution was written before the first general persecution began under Nero in AD 64. This is a reference to the great tribulation.

  The emphasis is that we are kept. What did this promise mean to the first century congregation at Philadelphia? Nero would send Titus

---

[92]Clarke, *Commentary,* 6:984.

to lay siege to Jerusalem. Nero would also unleash the first wave of persecution against Christians. The pressure was already being felt in some areas such as Symrna and Pergamos. In fact the Greek text literally says that hour "is about to come upon the whole inhabited world." It was about to happen at any moment. But God knew the church at Philadelphia could not take any more and he promised them exemption. Therefore, he was coming quickly (v 11) and would keep them. *Taxos* means quickly, speedily, soon, or shortly.

- I will claim the overcomer as my own. "I will make him a pillar" (v 12). In Philadelphia famous citizens were remembered by putting their name on the pillar of the heathen temple. About fifty years prior to this letter, Philadelphia had been leveled by an earthquake and Ramsay felt that the temple was still in a state of dilapidation and decay when this letter was written.[93] Yet the church is the pillar and foundation of the truth (1 Tim 3:15; Gal 2:9). We are part of a kingdom that cannot be shaken (Heb 12:28). When all the self-sufficient have fallen, we can stand in his mighty power. God will honor his own. He has established us and we will never again go out or be dislocated because of instability.

They will stand as monuments of grace. The one who does not deny his name (v 8) is promised: I will write on him the name and nature of my God (Exod 28:36-38), making him a priest, the name of the city of my God (we have a heavenly citizenship - Phil 3:20), and my new name ("King of Kings"- Rev 19:12, 16). These promises are assurances of stability and security that God acknowledges his own.

G. Laodicea 3:14-22

[93]Ramsey, *Letters to the Seven Churches*, 301.

REVELATION 3:14-22

Forty-three miles southeast of Philadelphia was the town of Laodicea. It was established by Antiochus II and named for his wife Laodice, whom he later divorced in 253 BC. This was a prosperous town, famous for its medical school, especially its "Phrygian powder," which was mixed with oil to make eye salve, and ear ointment. Phrygia was the region, Laodicea the city. Phrygia is mentioned in Acts 2:10; 16:6; 18:23.

Laodicea also produced glossy black wool. They bred sheep to get a certain color of wool. It was also a banking center. The town was destroyed three times by earthquakes. The last time it was rebuilt in AD 60 without government aid because of wool revenues. It was proud and self-sufficient. Of the seven cities, only Laodicea is today uninhabited.

Writing around AD 60, Paul referred to this church and its pastor, Archippus, in Colossians 2:1; 4:13-17. Only a few years have passed and Jesus had nothing good said about this church. Jesus denounced the attitudes which make him sick: apathy, complacency, pride, materialism, and presumption. "You are neither cold nor hot, I wish you were either one or the other!"(v 15).

A stream flowed through Laodicea. The waters came from Hierapolis, which was six miles away, and continued another ten miles to Colosse after they left Laodicea. The water in Hierapolis came from a 95°F bubbling spring which had healing power. By the time the water reached Colosse it was cold and refreshing to drink. But as it passed through Laodicea it was not hot enough to heal and not cool enough to drink.

"Be earnest" (v 19) is literally means to be zealous or hot. The Greek word *zeleuo* means at boiling point. The inference is that they were once hot, but have cooled off, just as their water supply. Unless they rekindle the fire, they will continue to grow colder. They are warned in v 16 that at some point Christ will vomit them out. Clarke said, "They were too *good* to go to *hell*, too *bad* to go to *heaven*. . . . They rested in what they had already received, and seemed to think that *once in grace* must be *still in grace.*"[94]

Jesus warned the Ephesians that unless they repented he would remove their lampstand. He warned the church at Pergamos that unless they repented he would come and fight against them. He commanded the church at Thyatira to hold on to what they had. He warned in the letter to Sardis that it was possible to have ones name removed from the book of life. He told the church at Philadelphia to hold on to what they had so that no one would take their crown. Now he warns that he will spit out the backslider. Only those faithful to death receive the crown of eternal life.

But instead of repenting, some people are unmoved. Jesus asked, "To what can I compare this generation? They are like children sitting in the marketplaces and calling out to others: We have played the flute for you and you did not dance; we sang a dirge and you did not mourn" (Matt 11:16-17). They have heard it all before.

The second attitude which makes Christ sick is self-satisfaction. "I am rich; I have acquired wealth and do not need a thing" (v 17). This misguided opinion either means that they have equated material prosperity with God's blessings and therefore infer that they are prospering as a sign of God's favor or they feel that they are spiritually rich. While Smyrna was financially poor, they were spiritually rich (2:9). Apparently the condition at Laodicea was the exact opposite. The five adjectives used in v 17 described the condition of someone who is not a Christian.

Pride is the only disease that makes everyone sick except the person who has it! It is a sin to trust in yourself instead of in God. While they carry on in their smug self-confidence, they are actually destitute and did not realize it. In v 18 Jesus counsels them to obtain the very things they boasted in. If God actually gave the average congregation everything they testified to already possessing, a mighty revival would break out!

The thing we profess may be the very thing we lack. Laodicea was a famous banking center, but the church was wretched, pitiful,

---

[94]Clarke, *Commentary*, 6:985-986.

poor, blind, and naked. Christ counseled them to buy gold. This is an ironic statement. If they are truly wealthy, then they can buy gold from Christ. But since no one is self-sufficient, this "gold" must be accepted as a gift on the basis of faith.

"Come, all you who are thirsty, come to the waters; and you who have no money, come, buy and eat! Come, buy wine and milk without money and without cost" (Isa 55:1). In our humility we cry out to God and in his grace he "sells" us what we need at no cost.

Just as Jesus taught us to ask for our daily bread, he also taught us to ask for forgiveness from our debt. God gives us the gold that pays our debt of sin. This gold must be refined by fire (1 Pet 1:7), indicating the need to separate themselves from the idolatrous aspects of their culture.

Then Jesus counsels them to buy white garments to cover the shame of their nakedness. They exported black wool, but the symbolism is changed to white. *White* represents holiness and purity. We are to walk in white or live a holy life, undefiled by the world. Finally, Christ gives them a prescription for eye salve for their lack of spiritual discernment. We need spiritual vision (Eph 1:18). We need to see that which is invisible (Heb 11:27).

In v 20, Christ is standing at the door and knocking. The metaphor of a door in 3:8 symbolizes opportunity. In 3:30 it symbolizes salvation. In 4:1 it symbolizes revelation. While the other doors stand open, we must open the door to salvation. Binney observed that Christ knocks, but is not a house-breaker. No one is compelled by irresistible force.[95] While the sovereignty of Christ is implied in creation (v 14), and while the sufficiency of Christ is understood in the fact that only he can supply the riches, the robes, and the prescription, yet the condition is stated — *if anyone*.

The use of v 20 as an evangelistic text is sometimes criticized on the basis that Christ is speaking to the church. However, this church is no longer saved and v 20 extends the invitation to "anyone." The Lord seeks the individual in the midst of the crowd. He seeks a home

---

[95]Binney, *Commentary*, 678.

in the individual heart. But he also knocks at the door of the house where his church meets. This is a rebuke to the formalism and spiritual deadness of his people. The Lord is forever in the church knocking at the hearts of those who have not given him full admission so that he may complete what he has begun.

Supper was the main meal. The work day was over and it was more than meal time, it was a time to sit and talk and fellowship. Ever since God created the first man, he desired to come down and walk with him in the cool of the day. Christ used to come in and have fellowship with this congregation, as well. But here is a church which has gathered in the name of Christ, no doubt with an agenda, a program, an order of service, but they left out one thing — Christ is outside!

The overcomer is promised in v 21 that he will sit with Christ on his throne. Christ is the ruler and the overcomer, not the compromiser, will sit with Christ on his throne. Christ is already seated on the throne (Ps 110:1) and according to Ephesians 2:6 (see also Rom 5:17), we are now seated with him. However this promise, which is in the future, is connected with Revelation 22:5. We will reign with Christ forever.

The verb *overcome* (*nikao*) appears twenty-eight times in the New Testament; seventeen are here in Revelation. It occurs eight times in chapters 2-3 and nine times in the rest of the book. It is also significant that *nikeo* occurs in the present tense in this book some nine times — literally the one overcoming or conquering.

The promises in Revelation to the one overcoming through the blood of Jesus are *conditional*. According to 1 John 5:4-5 the overcomer has been born again and has a true, living faith. According to Rev 2:26 and 12:11 the overcomer is the one who keeps the works of Christ until the end.

Marshall wrote that the rewards for conquerors in Revelation 2-3 are elsewhere assigned to all Christians: 2:7 with 22:2; 2:11 with 20:6, 14; 2:17 with 22:4; 2:26 with 22:5; 3:5 with 22:14; 3:12 with 22:3; 3:21 with 22:5.

REVELATION 3:14-22

> The true Christian is the victorious Christian and he is promised salvation in the world to come. . . . The believer is required to show faithfulness unto death. . . . Being faithful entails keeping the commandments of God. . . . A further aspect of perseverance is . . . active endurance of trials. . . . All of this may be regarded as performing the works of God. The Christian life involves deeds, according to which men will be judged. . . . The possibility of failure to endure is mentioned. Christians who fail to persevere will come under judgment and their names will be blotted out of the book of life.[96]

---

[96]Marshall, *Kept by the Power of God*, 253, 174-175.

Chapters Two and Three Summary

II. Seven letters from Jesus Christ 2:1-3:22
- A. Ephesus 2:1-7
- B. Smyrna 2:8-11
- C. Pergamum 2:12-17
- D. Thyatira 2:18-29
- E. Sardis 3:1-6
- F. Philadelphia 3:7-13
- G. Laodicea 3:14-22

Ephesus and Laodicea have fallen into laxity. Smyrna and Philadelphia are both faithful. The three middle churches are a mixture of faithful and wicked. The first and last churches were in danger of apostasy and are exhorted to repent. Ephesus had become legalistic, while Laodicea had become lax. The second and sixth churches had persevered through persecution and receive no condemnation. The third through fifth churches had compromised through permissiveness, influence, and pride.

While each situation was different, Christ is adequate for every situation and has the answer to every problem. When a congregation is out of balance, Christ reveals himself as both transcendent and immanent. When people are threatened with persecution and even death, Christ declares to them that he has conquered death. A congregation with a mixture of truth and error is told that he will judge them with a sharp, double-edged sword. He is capable of separating truth from error. In an active congregation where authority has been usurped and the leadership encourages lawless living, the eyes of Christ blaze with omniscience and he stands in the fire with those who are oppressed. To a dead congregation Christ reveals himself as holding the Spirit of revival. He tells a congregation with little strength that he holds the key and can open and close doors of opportunity as he sees fit. To a compromising church, Christ is still faithful and true. They do not rule through their affluence; he rules.

These seven letters describe the state of the first century church. These letters were written to literal congregations, yet they contain some symbolism. The message of these letters can *apply* to the state of the church as a whole at any period of time, to the state of individual congregations at any period of time, or to the condition of members within a congregation at any period of time.

REVELATION 4

Interlude — Worship in heaven 4:1-5:14

After John received messages for seven churches, he saw the door opened to heaven and he was given the next vision. "Come up here and I will show you the things which are about to occur after these things." "These things" refer to the current situation described in chapters 2-3. Now the perspective has changed from earth to heaven.

N. T. Wright notes that Revelation 4-5 do not merely provide a vision of the future consummated kingdom. He argues that they also provide a picture of the present global church as "the heavenly dimension of our present life." The international multiethnic nature of the church is a prophetic sign of the kingdom of God in today's world.[97]

The phrase *after this* is found twice in 4:1. It does not introduce another period of time, but it introduces another message. After the vision of chapter 1 and the messages of chapters 2-3, John saw in a vision what he now describes. The command *come up here* was made only to John and cannot be stretched to include a rapture for the entire church. John is still on Patmos and in the first century.

While the word *church* does not appear again until 22:16 the church is represented in symbolic form throughout the book. This should be expected since the symbolic nature of the book has been established. Aune wrote that there were more than a hundred cognate expressions which express the church idea through the New Testament and many of these are to be found through the Apocalypse. The church of God is depicted as *the saints* or *holy ones, the called* and *the chosen, a kingdom* and *a priesthood,* and God's *people.* These terms all emphasize the divine initiative. From the perspective of human responsibility, the church is described as the *faithful ones,* God's *witnesses* and *servants.* The church is also seen as "the dwelling of God with man," a brotherhood, the woman clothed with the sun and her offspring, the Bride of Christ, the Lamb's wife, the two

---

[97]Wright, *Surprised by Hope*, 18-19.

witnesses, the seven lampstands, the twenty-four elders, the 144,000 witnesses, the innumerable multitude, and the New Jerusalem.[98] Thus, the church *is* an integral part of this whole book.

Before Moses constructed the tabernacle, he was shown a pattern (Exod 25:40). The tabernacle symbolized the heavenly reality (Heb 8:1-5). Everything described in Revelation 4 had a counterpart in the old tabernacle.

Tabernacle of Moses	The Heavenly Pattern
Mercy-Seat	Throne of God
Seven-Branched Lamp	Seven Lamps of Fire
Cherubim Four Living	Creatures
Sea of Glass	Bronze Laver/*Sea* (1 Kgs 7:23)
Twenty-four courses of priests	Twenty-four elders
Brazen Altar	Altar 6:9-11
Incense Altar	Incense altar 8:3-5
Ark of the Covenant	Ark of the Covenant 11:19

Today *we* are the tabernacle or temple of God. The church is supposed to reflect the realities of heaven, not be influenced by the values of this world. The church is to reflect the glory of God. A fuller description of the bride's adornment will be given in 21:19-21. God's will is to be done on earth as it is in heaven. We are to be a colony of heaven.

A. The glory of God 4:1-6

John immediately focused upon the most important aspect of heaven, the throne (v 2). Thus, this chapter connects back to 3:21 where Christ is depicted as already on the throne. The throne of God, depicting God's sovereignty, is mentioned seventeen times in chapters 4-5. The word *throne* is used forty-six times in this book, far

---

[98]Aune, "St. John's Portrait of the Church," 131-149.

more than in any other book of the Bible. It may seem like things are out of control on earth, but God is on the throne and that throne is the center of the universe. Thus meaning is brought to chaos when God is at the center of our worship.

And worship is spiritual warfare. Caird described John as a privileged press reporter who was granted access to the military war room at Supreme Headquarters. What happens on earth has been determined in heaven.[99]

God is described only as *someone* or *one* (v 2). John's reserve is a reflection of Jewish reluctance to use the name of God. He does not give a detailed description, but expresses his awe at the brilliance. There is no way to give an adequate description. It may be best not to assign individual meanings to each stone in v 3. Taken collectively, we see that God is light and in him is no darkness at all (1 John 1:5; 1 Tim 6:16).

God had the appearance of jasper, carnelian and a rainbow, resembling an emerald, encircled the throne. The jasper was translucent, like a diamond, while the carnelian or sardius was a fiery deep red stone. The most important element here is not the color, however, but the fact that the sardius was the first stone and jasper the last stone in the breastplate of the high priest (Exod 28:17-20). This was called the breastplate of judgment (Exod 28:15) and so John's description of God emphasizes his attribute of justice.

A rainbow has seven colors, but this rainbow was emerald. Either green was the dominant color or it was seven shades of green. The rainbow itself is a symbol of mercy (Gen 9:12-17). The emerald green color also seems to suggest mercy, the promise of Spring, growth, and paradise restored. Upon the high priest's breastplate, the emerald stone represented the tribe of Judah (Exod 28:18; 39:11). It was through this tribe that God sent Christ to bring us mercy.

God is light and this light was reflected upon the sea of glass and diffused down through the firmament to the earth (Exod 24:10). This sea of glass corresponded to the basin where the priests washed (Exod

---

[99]Caird, *Revelation,* 60-61.

30:18-21). In Solomon's temple this enormous bronze basin was called *the sea* (1 Kgs 7:23-26).

This sea of glass is the sky (Gen 1:7-8). In the Jewish mind there was a "sea" between heaven and earth. In Exodus 24:10 the elders saw under the feet of God something like a pavement made of sapphire, clear as the sky itself. This also compares to Ezekiel 1:22-26 where a throne of sapphire appeared in the expanse over the heads of the creatures. Commentators frequently note that *sea* carries connotations of evil (13:1; 20:13) and that in the new heaven there will not be any sea (21:1). However, this sea does not connote evil because it is in heaven and it is a sea *of glass*. Instead, it radiates the glory of God.

While it was transparent as John looked upon it, it is blue (or sapphire) when we look up to it. Thus, this *sea* symbolizes the transcendence of God. No matter what upheavals are occurring on earth, God sits above the strife and this *sea* is always calm. From the throne all history is crystal clear.

Before the throne was the sevenfold Spirit blazing like seven lamps (see 1:4; Ezek 1:13; Zech 4:2). It is the work of the Spirit to illuminate God. In spite of all the light we have in nature, we still need his revelation and this revelation should lead to worship. From the throne came flashes of lightning, rumblings and peals of thunder. This is an awesome display of God's power and here indicates that heaven is the source of the judgment which John describes in 8:5-7; 11:19; 16:18-21. Carpenter noted that the rainbow was a token of God's covenant with Noah to preserve life, the lamp of fire passed through Abraham's sacrifice when God made covenant with him (Gen 15:17), and the thunderings and lightnings were present at Mt Sinai with the giving of the Mosaic covenant. Thus, there is an emphasis upon the covenant-keeping character of God.

B. The worship of the natural world 4:6-9

Verses 6-9 describe four living creatures. These creatures are mentioned fourteen times in Revelation. However, they are not to be equated with the wild beast of chapter 13. A different Greek word is used of the beast in 13:1; they are living ones. *Zoon* is from *zoe*, the word for *life*. Our word *zoo* is derived from *zoe*. *Zoon* is used eleven times in chapters 4-5. Here the emphasis is on living beings. *Therion*, which is used sixteen times in chapter 13, denotes a wild beast.

These living ones form the innermost circle surrounding the throne of God. Ezekiel 1:10; 10:14 gives a similar description of creatures that are called *cherubim*. These cherubim participate in God's providential workings and this expresses figuratively by the "wheels within the wheels." They also incorporate the description of the *seraphim* in Isaiah 6.

These angelic creatures symbolize what is the noblest, strongest, wisest, and swiftest in creation. Four corresponds to the four corners of the earth. Thus, all God's creatures worship him. Not only do these four cherubim stand for God's world, but they remind us that angels are active within God's world. According to Psalm 148, God uses the forces of nature to accomplish his will.

In Numbers 2 the encampment of the Israelites in the wilderness is described. On the east the standard of Judah was a lion. On the south the standard of Reuben was the face of a man. On the west the standard of Ephraim was an ox and on the north, the standard of Dan was the eagle. This becomes all the more significant in light of the previous reference to the breastplate of the high priest in v 3. These references, plus the twelve "Old Testament" elders in v 4, make three symbolic references in this chapter to the twelve tribes of Israel.

Of all the birds, the eagle is considered the greatest. Of all animals, the lion is considered king. Of all domestic animals, the ox was the most important. Man is the crowning work of all God's living creatures. Therefore, these four creatures represent all of God's creation—all things wise and wonderful. "They seem to represent all the created powers and agencies by which God administers his providential government (15:7), which are all pervaded and directed by his omniscient Spirit."[100]

---

[100]Binney, *Commentary*, 678. Binney also ties this passage to Ezek 1:5-21.

Are then these creatures angelic creatures above us or animal life beneath us? They are angels who are over creation; angelic beings used by the Creator in executing his rule and divine will in all of his creation. Their description as having eyes everywhere indicates that they could see everything. The more clearly we see God's plan, the more we will worship him. Their wings suggest their swiftness to carry out the will of God. The most important aspect of God's creation is that it continually and instinctively glorifies him. Notice v 8 "day and night they never stopped" praising him. There is a beauty in every season; a majesty in every location; a wonder in every specie of animal. Eugene Peterson wrote, "Worship does not divide the spiritual from the natural, it coordinates them. Nature and supernature, creation and covenant, elders and animals are all gathered."[101]

"All Thy works shall praise Thy name in earth, and sky, and sea."[102] The whole earth is full of his glory. The glory of God is reflected in his creation. Even if we did not have the Bible, God has been made so plain that we are without excuse (Rom 1:19-20).

This is my Father's world,
And to my listening ears
All nature sings, and round me rings
The music of the spheres.[103]

In v 8 he is worshiped by nature for his attributes. He is almighty and eternal. But of all the attributes of God, it is his holiness that is emphasized (see also Isa 6:2-3). No other attribute is mentioned three times in succession. In this context it probably corresponds to the threefold nature of God — he who was, and is, and is to come.

Holiness means brilliance or radiance when it represents the unique nature and awesome presence of God. The glory of God is the

---

[101]Peterson, *Reversed Thunder*, 62.

[102]Reginald Heber, "Holy, Holy, Holy, Lord God Almighty" (1826).

[103]Maltbie D. Babcock, "This is My Father's World" (1901).

expression of his holiness (Lev 10:3; Isa 6:3). We have seen that depicted in the rainbow of light. Wesley said, "Holiness is covered glory, and glory is uncovered holiness."[104]

Holiness also means separation. God is distinct from and above his creation. He is transcendent; he is "wholly other."[105] Only God is inherently holy. Throughout the Bible there are holy places, holy things, holy days, and holy people, but they are holy only because they have been set apart for God's use. God alone is absolutely holy and altogether pure.

Holiness is absolute purity with no mixture of impurity. While he is repulsed by sin, he does not abandon us. Holiness is his essence; love is his expression of holiness. Oden wrote, "Wherever holiness is spoken of in Scripture, love in nearby; wherever God's love is manifested, it does not cease to be holy."[106] His love is holy, but his anger is also holy. Yet while wrath is his reaction to sin, this wrath is temporary. His love is eternal (Ps 103:8-11; Isa 54:8; Hos 14:4).

C. The worship of the church 4:10-11

In v 10 the twenty-four elders fell down before him. The twelve tribes of Israel plus the twelve apostles of the New Israel represent the universal church of all times. In 21:12-14 the church is depicted as a holy city with twelve gates. On these twelve gates were written the names of twelve tribes. The city also had twelve foundations and on them were written the names of twelve apostles.

Thus, the church under both covenants is portrayed at worship. This interpretation is further supported by the two songs in 15:3, the song of Moses and the song of the Lamb. The only other group of people who sit on thrones are the overcoming church in 20:4-6. These twenty-four elders "represent the entire company of God's faithful

---

[104]Wesley, *Notes,* 667.

[105]This phrase comes from Rudolf Otto, *The Idea of the Holy* (1923).

[106]Oden, *The Living God*, 124.

who are seated on thrones and reign with Christ."[107]

The ultimate priority of the church is the worship of Almighty God (2 Chr 16:9; Ps 92:2; 95:6; 96:9; John 4:23). Nature often does a better job at giving praise to God than does the church. Sometimes, though, we fail to hear the praise and instead hear the groan of nature (Rom 8:19-22). Here both nature and the church join together antiphonally in praise.

Verse 4 describes the majesty of God's church, dressed in white, washed from her sins in his own blood (1:5). We are a kingdom and are depicted as having crowns and as sitting on thrones surrounding the throne. We share in God's rule. In the beginning God told man to subdue the earth and rule over it. Mankind lost his dominion and fell into bondage to the devil. But Christ has redeemed us and has reinstated us as his agents. We have a double reason to give God praise. As part of nature we glorify God and especially as part of his church we worship him. We are to bring every aspect of this world under the lordship of Christ. Whether it be the state or the family, science, the economy, or the arts, education, law, medicine, technology — civilization in its entirety is to be brought under the authority of Christ. In v 11 the church ascribes worth to God. Our word *worship* is a contraction of the old Anglo-Saxon word "worth-ship." The word *axios* (worthy) refers to what is fitting and proper. Originally the word meant tipping the scales, counterbalancing something of like value. Thus, it carries the meaning of "weighty." Our worship of God should be weighty and not light.

From this chapter we learn that it should be "in the Spirit," that God and not man should be central, that we are to give God all glory, honor, and thanks, that we should fall down and worship him in humility, and that we should recognize that he alone is worthy of such worship. This word *proskuneo* (worship) occurs twenty-four times in Revelation and it originally meant to kiss an idol, to fall down, prostrate oneself, and adore on one's knees. Regardless of the position of the body, God desires that we worship him in spirit and in truth (John

---

[107]Mulholland, *Revelation*, 143-145.

4:23).

God is worshiped by the church for what he has done. He created all things. First he willed the creation, then he spoke it into being. The creation was created on account of God's will. The concept that God takes pleasure in creation is valid biblically and is to be preferred above the nonbiblical idea that God created out of loneliness.

Because of his will they have come into being and continue to exist (Col 1:16-17). This speaks both of the creation and the preservation of that creation. Therefore, the elders lay aside their crowns. Both the Greek words *diadema*, meaning a crown of authority, and *stephanos*, a victor's or overcomer's crown, are used in Revelation. In 4:4, 10 *stephanos* is used. It would seem that these overcomer crowns would rule out any identity of the elders other than representing humans. Furthermore, angels are never called *elders* (*presbyteros*). This term is reserved for men who have authority in the church and their description includes three elements promised to overcomers in the church: white garments (3:5), crowns (3:11), and thrones (3:21). This is a higher form of worship than instinct; it is deliberative.

REVELATION 5

D. The Lamb is Worthy 5:1-14

In chapter 4, the distinction between the One on the throne and the other beings is a distinction between God and creation. The significance of chapter 5 is that the Lamb never appears outside the confines of the throne. The Lamb does not participate in the worship, rather he receives worship.

Judaism drew the line between God and creature at the point of worship. God must be worshiped; no creature may be worshiped. Even angels refuse worship in 19:10; 22:8-9 and John is directed to "worship God." With this backdrop it is highly significant that John portrays the worship of Christ in heaven in Revelation 5. "There can be no doubt that in 5:8-12 John portrays explicit divine worship paid to Christ: the parallels between 4:9-11 and 5:8-12 make this clear.[108] Kiddle wrote, "Nowhere else in the New Testament is Christ adored on such absolutely equal terms with the Godhead."[109] Swete wrote, "This chapter is the most powerful statement of the divinity of Christ in the New Testament, and it receives its power from the praise of God the Creator which precedes it."[110]

1. The closed book 5:1-4

After Daniel was given an overview of the future, in Daniel 8:26 and 12:4 he was told to seal up the words of the scroll until a later time. The time of the unsealing was not the end of time but the time of the end (Dan 8:17, 19; 11:35, 40; 12:4, 9). These *last days* began with the coming of Christ. Daniel's prophecies were set in motion by the finished work of Christ. What Daniel sealed, John is about to see opened. The breaking of these seals symbolizes new revelation.

---

[108]Bauckham, *The Climax of Prophecy*, 137.

[109]Kiddle, *Revelation*, 105.

[110]Swete, *Apocalypse*, 127

Since the description of the heavenly scene found in this chapter is based upon Daniel 7:9-14, and since that passage describes the ascension of Christ, the unsealing of the scroll occurred when Christ was exalted to the right hand of the Father.

The position of the right hand of the throne was the chief place of honor, dignity, and power (1 Kgs 2:19; Ps 45:9; 80:17; 110:1). Matthew 26:64; Mark 14:62; 16:19; Romans 8:34; Colossians 3:1; Hebrews 1:3; 8:1; 1 Peter 3:22 all teach that this is the present position of Christ.

Wesley said, "The book and its seals represent all power both in heaven and earth given to Christ." Wesley recognized that Psalm 2:8, which refers to the inauguration and session of Christ, after his ascension, was here fulfilled "in the most glorious manner."[111] This interpretation is further confirmed by the fact that in 6:1-7 it is the Lamb who opens the scroll. Christ has begun to execute his sovereignty (see also Acts 2:32-36; 1 Cor 15:27; Eph 1:20-22; Heb 1:1-5). Notice the parallels to the installation of King Joash in 2 Kgs 11:12-17; 2 Chr 23:11-20.

Isaiah 29:11-12 also speaks about a sealed scroll. The hand of God also contained a rolled-up scroll which God unrolled for Ezekiel in 2:9-10. To many, the Scriptures are closed until Christ is revealed to them. In Acts 8:30-31 Philip met an Ethiopian eunuch. Philip asked him, "Do you understand what you are reading?" The eunuch answered, "How can I unless someone opens it to me and guides me." Christ is the subject of this revelation. Prophecy is the testimony of Jesus (19:11). Therefore, Christ alone is worthy to open this scroll.

Those in the first century knew a scroll with seven seals was a will or testament. "When a testator died the testament was brought forward, and, when possible, opened in the presence of the seven witnesses who sealed it; i.e., it was unsealed, read aloud and executed."[112] While the conclusion is often drawn than this scroll is a will

---

[111]Wesley, *Notes*, 668-669.

[112]Zahn, *Introduction to the New Testament*, 3:393-396.

which leaves us an inheritance, the Greek word *diatheke* is translated both as *testament* and *covenant*.

Hebrews 9-10 teaches that a will or testament or covenant is not in force until the one who made it dies. Jesus came to set aside the first and to establish the second. Through his death the new covenant was established. When he served his disciples in the upper room he took the cup and said, "This is my blood of the new covenant, which is poured out for many for the forgiveness of sins" (Matt 26:28). When he died the curtain separating the Most Holy Place was torn (Matt 27:51; Heb 10:20) and a new and living way opened for us.

It was God's plan to establish his kingdom upon earth by entering into covenant with his people. But the Jewish people broke their covenant with God and rejected their Messiah. Therefore, a new covenant was needed because the old one had been broken. This will or testament represents the new covenant and the destiny of the human race is wrapped up in it. John wept because no one was worthy to open it; no one had the authority to break those seals and execute the plan. Man is not competent to conquer the world's evil. We are impotent to determine our destiny.

Thus, John's tears are the culmination of several thousand years of human misery. John had been raised with the messianic hope that one day God would punish evil, establish his kingdom, deliver the oppressed, and end their persecution. Prophets and angels alike had searched and longed to understand day of salvation (1 Pet 1:10-12). Abraham had rejoiced to see this day (John 8:56), yet this hope appears to be out of reach.

The human race was under the curse of sin and death. We needed a substitute who has identified with the race as a human. However, this substitute could not atone for our sin if he himself had sin. We needed a sinless human. But sin entered the world through one man, and death came to all men because all sinned (Rom 5:12). Thus we need a human who did not have Adam for his father. But Adam was the father of the race. Therefore, we needed someone who was conceived by a virgin. Since this is humanly impossible, John wept much.

But one sinless human life could only substitute for one sinful human. How could one perfect, sinless human become a substitute for untold billions? He would have to be of infinite worth. What we really need is for God to become man and enter the human race while remaining God. We need a substitute who is fully God and fully man, yet not tainted with the sinful nature inherit within the human race. Did anyone in heaven or on earth or under the earth qualify to execute the plan of God? In other words, does mankind have any hope? Symbolically, the hope of the world is contained in this scroll and its execution and a human agent must break it open. Curtis explained that the scroll symbolizes the difficulties of redemption and illustrates that the Lamb of God alone has power to save.

2. The Lion and the Lamb 5:5-7

Until this point John was apparently a spectator. But for the first time, a participant takes notice of John, who is weeping. When the situation appeared hopeless, one of the elders, who represented the church, said, "Do not weep! Behold the Lion of the tribe of Judah, the Root of David, has triumphed once and for all."[113] Because Christ came and wept with us (John 11:35), and carried our sorrows (Isa 53:3-4), those who know him need not sorrow as those without hope (1 Thess 4:13). Someday he will wipe every tear from our eyes (7:17; 21:4).

In Genesis 49:9-10 Judah is told that he is like a lion's cub and that "the scepter will not depart from Judah, nor the ruler's staff from between his feet, until he comes to whom it belongs and the obedience of the nations is his." The scepter and the staff were symbols of authority. A line of kings would continue to descend from Judah until the King of Kings came and established his authority universally. David's throne was symbolized by a lion in 1 Kings 10:19-20. God was depicted as a warrior lion in Job 10:16; Isa 31:4; Jer 50:44; Hosea 5:14; Amos 3:8. Now Christ assumes this role as the lion king.

---

[113]Mounce, *NICNT*, 132. See John 16:33; Rev 3:21.

This demonstrates that Christ is Lord, not only of the church, but of the world.

Jesus Christ is also the Root of David (see 22:16). David was the great king of Israel and Jesse was his father. Isaiah 11:1 foretold that "a shoot will come up from the stump of Jesse; from his roots a Branch will bear fruit" (see also v 10; Jer 23:5; Zech 6:12). He will rule the world in righteousness and peace. "Righteousness will be his belt and faithfulness the sash around his waist" (v 5). "The earth will be full of the knowledge of the Lord as the waters cover the sea" (v 9).

Verse 5 emphasizes another truth — the Lion has prevailed. This is also the same word which has been used eight times in chapters 2-3 for the *overcomer*. Our victory is based upon his. We can overcome because he has overcome

Since there is no direct object, Christ conquered everything. John tells us that at a point in time Jesus Christ triumphed, overcame, conquered, prevailed once for all. *When* did Jesus overcome? At his death (v 9). "And having disarmed the powers and authorities, he made a public spectacle of them, triumphing over them by the cross" (Col 2:15). He *is* Lord! He has already won! In John 16:33 he declared, "I have overcome the world."[114] George Eldon Ladd explained,

> The Second Coming of Christ will mean nothing less than the disclosure to the world of the sovereignty and lordship which is already his. He is *now* the Lord; he is *now* reigning at the right hand of God. However, his present reign is seen only by the eye of faith. It is unseen and unrecognized by the world. His second advent will mean the unveiling — the revelation — the disclosure of the lordship which is already

[114]Arndt and Gingrich defined *world* as "the sum total of everything opposed to God" [*Lexicon,* 539].

his.[115]

But how did he prevail? The Jewish rabbis struggled to reconcile passages which spoke of their coming Messiah as a king and other passages which spoke of his suffering. Some of them concluded there must be two Messiahs, one to suffer and one to reign. However, the New Testament makes it clear that the Lion and the Lamb are one. The lion represents royalty, but the lamb symbolizes redemption. The lion is his deity; the lamb is his humanity. The lamb suffered death, but the lion overcame death.

In Isaiah 11:6 we are also told that in his kingdom, the lion will lay down with the lamb. Not only will nature be redeemed from the curse, but man himself will be transformed until humans can get along with each other. But we cannot be transformed from a lion into a lamb unless we have a Savior who is both a lion and a lamb.

The significance of the lamb is based on Exodus 12 where the passover lamb is sacrificed, then the people of God are delivered from 430 years of bondage. Isaiah said, "He was oppressed and afflicted, yet he did not open his mouth; he was led like a lamb to the slaughter, and as a sheep before her shearers is silent, so he did not open his mouth" (53:7; see also John 1:29, 36; Acts 8:32; 1 Pet 1:19). Christ is symbolized as a lamb twenty-eight times in this book.

In other words, the lion conquered by becoming a sacrificial lamb. Ewing called this "Lamb power." He explained, "Lamb power is the power of vulnerable but strong love to change the world."[116] We are called to choose between the way of the Lamb and the way of the Beast. This is the manifold [multifaceted] wisdom of God (Eph 3:10).

A. W. Tozer wrote,

> On earth, the lion is stronger than the lamb. But in the kingdom of God and before the throne of God, the Lamb is

---

[115]Ladd, "Historic Premillennialism," 32.

[116]Ewing, *The Power of the Lamb,* 198.

> stronger, and He is victor! . . . Unless we know Jesus Christ as both Lamb, our Redeemer, and Lion, our strength to live for Him day by day, we are not Christians in the right sense of the word. In the kingdoms of earth, the spirit of the lion dominates; in the kingdom of God, the Lamb rules.[117]

When Satan influenced wicked men to crucify the sinless, spotless lamb of God he thought he was gaining the upper hand, but he played into God's plan. Osborne wrote, "When Satan placed Christ on the cross, it was his greatest tactical error, for he took part in his own defeat."[118] The lamb that was slain arose three days later as the lion. Satan was so blinded by his pride and ambition that he never saw what was coming. John's message to the church is that, like Christ, while they are apparently defeated they are actually overcoming.

This lamb is portrayed as having seven horns and seven eyes. The horns symbolize his authority and the eyes symbolize his knowledge (see 1:4). In Daniel 7:7-8 the fourth beast, which is Rome, eventually had seven horns, although it began with ten. In Revelation 13 the beast which had ten horns, receives a fatal wound to his head and is superceded by another beast with only two horns. This beast is *like* a lamb. The message here to the early church is that the Lamb, not Rome, has authority. He had complete power and full knowledge. His suffering was not an indication of weakness or ignorance. He also had the fulness of the Spirit (see also 3:1). The one Holy Spirit is described in his completeness in Isaiah 11:2-3: the Spirit of the Lord, the Spirit of wisdom and of understanding, the Spirit of counsel and of power, the Spirit of knowledge and of the fear of the Lord.

If Satan could have blocked anyone from opening the sealed book, the human race would have been doomed. But the lion king established his kingdom in a world under the control of Satan by

---

[117]Tozer, *Jesus is Victor!*, 86.

[118]Osborne, *BECNT*, 253.

slipping in as a lamb. He humbled himself to the plan of God. Everyone who humbles himself will be exalted. And everyone who exalts himself, as did Satan, will be brought down. Jesus became the lion by first becoming the lamb.

Now it is time for the world's greatest drama to begin. The stage was set in chapter 4. However, Christ was conspicuous by his absence. Now the Lion is announced, "Behold the Lion," but instead (v 6) a wounded Lamb appears. The bleeding Lamb takes the scroll of the New Covenant from the hand of God and opens it. When he takes the scroll the angels and the church fall before the Lamb in worship. In chapter 4 they worshiped God the Creator. In chapter 5 they worship the Lamb. It is blasphemy to worship anyone other than God. Angels never accept worship. Therefore, the true church worships Christ, who is truly God. Thus, Christ, and not Caesar, receives universal worship and all bow and sing to Christ.

3. Worship of the Lamb 5:8-14

It is the church, not the four creatures, which worships with the harp and the bowl. The word *harp* appears in some form six times in Revelation. Music was not a human invention. The earliest reference is Job 38:7. If the angels sang at creation and mankind was not created until the sixth day, music is older than us. All primitive people believed that music was of divine origin. Music was born in the heart of God. God wants to hear us sing. When we are afflicted, in pain, discouraged, bewildered, when we don't know what to do — sing! It will confuse the devil and drive him away.

Heaven is full of music and praise. According to v 10 we are a kingdom of priests. The function of the Old Testament priest was to offer sacrifices. The Levitical priest offered sacrifices continually. There were sin offerings, trespass offerings, burnt offerings, peace offerings, meal-drink offerings, heave or wave offerings, the red heifer offering. All this was fulfilled in Christ, our once for all offering. But we are priests; "Let us continually offer to God a sacrifice of praise" (Heb 13:15).

REVELATION 5:8-14

We worship God through music. In v 9 we learn that they sang a new song. The Greek language utilized two different words for *new*. Here the emphasis is that this song is new in kind, not simply new in the sequence of time. The old song was the song of chapter 4, a song of praise to God our Creator. The new song is the song of re-creation in chapter 5 to Christ our Redeemer. In the language of John 14, chapter 4 says, "Believe in God," while in chapter 5 Christ says, "Believe also in me." Caird said that "the heavenly choir breaks out into a new song, new because it is a response to the new covenant, of which the Lamb has now become the mediator."[119]

Not only is the church pictured with a harp, but with a bowl or vial full of incense. Lest there be any mistake in the symbolism, John interprets it for us in v 8. According to Exodus 30:1-10 incense was burned every morning and every evening. Our prayers should rise continuously like the smoking incense from off the altar. Psalm 141:2, "May my prayer be set before you like incense; may the lifting up of my hands be like the evening sacrifice." Tennyson wrote, "More things are wrought by prayer that this world dreams of."[120]

These golden bowls are full of incense, which are the prayers of the saints. Revelation 8:3-5 describe our prayers ascending like the smoke of incense to the throne of God. Our prayers are collected in bowls and not lost or forgotten. In God's own timing he sends fire from heaven in answer to our prayers. Prayer is our priestly function (v 10). Prayer is spiritual warfare and we fight this battle through worship. Just as Gideon prevailed with trumpets and torches (Judg 7), so the church overcomes with harps and bowls. The seal, trumpet, and bowl judgments which follow are in response to these prayers.

A new day had dawned on the world. The Lamb had been slain. Atonement had been made. Through his blood the gates of heaven are open. The church is ablaze with the light of the gospel. The prayers of God's people ascend to the throne of God. The worship began with

---

[119]Caird, *Revelation*, 76.

[120]Tennyson, *Idylls of the King*, 111.

creation in 4:8. It was joined by the Old Testament church in 4:10. Now the New Testament church begins the worship, singing "You are worthy." They praise Christ for three reasons:

- He was slain. The verb *sphazo*, found in vv 6, 9, 12; 13:8, indicates a violent slaughter. While this verb is not used to describe the death of Christ elsewhere in the New Testament, it is drawn from Isaiah 53:7. The perfect tense of the verb in vv 6 and 12, and 13:8, emphasizes not only that Christ was slain at a point in time, but that "the efficacy of his sacrifice is still present in all its power." The fact that this lamb was standing indicates life, but the marks of death are still visible.

- He has redeemed us. They understand that through the blood of the Lamb we were purchased or redeemed. This is atonement language. *Redeem* (*agorazo*) means to buy. As a noun (*agora*) it means "marketplace." Our plight was slavery. We were on the auction block in the marketplace. According to 1 Corinthians 6:20, we were bought with a price. Our freedom was purchased with the price of his blood. The penalty of our sin was paid and we are no longer under the condemnation of the law. But salvation is not simply for the individual.

- He has made us a kingdom and priests. This is not just a local religion belonging to one nation or race of people. The church will be composed of men from every nation (Acts 17:26). Here John expands the extent of God's election from the nation (Israel) to the nations (incorporating non-Jews). However, *nation* does not refer to political divisions. *Nation* (*ethnos*) refers to the same culture. While *ethnos* comes last in this phrase of four divisions, it is the most general term and includes tribes, language and people. Thus, the Scripture gives three levels of evangelism:

- every political division. *People* (*laos*) refers to race or nationality.

- every linguistic division. *Tongue* (*glossa*) refers to the 6913 languages spoken.
- every cultural division. *Tribe* (*phule*) refers to the same lineage or descent.

Four times in the Gospels, Jesus emphasizes the necessity of penetrating this third level.[121] This phrase *tribe, tongue, people* occurs in some form seven times in Revelation and six times in Daniel.[122] We have an unfinished task. We are to take the gospel to every tribe and language and people, and as we do so the kingdom of God will spread over the world until the reign of Christ through his church will be extended over the whole earth (v 10). John Piper concluded that the goal of missions is the glory of God. God will be glorified when the nations worship him (Ps 67:4).[123] Fletcher argued against limited atonement by pointing to the great multitude which no man could number in 7:9.[124]

We reign because he now reigns. The phrase *on the earth* also indicates that the kingdom of Christ cannot be reduced to nothing more than a spiritual concept. The will of Christ shall be done on earth, as it is in heaven. Wesley anticipated a "*Christian world*."[125] Genesis 1:26 28 teaches man was created to rule this earth for God. Redeemed mankind will rule the world for God to complete God's purpose in history. "The earth shall be filled with the knowledge of

---

[121]Matt 24:14; 28:19; Mark 13:10; Luke 24:47. The foundation for this concept of unreached peoples goes back to Gen 12:3, 28:14.

[122]The passages in Daniel are 3:4, 7, 29; 5:19; 6:25, 7:14 (Nebuchadnezzar also uses the phrase in 4:1). The passages in Revelation are 5:9, 7:9, 10:11, 11:9, 13:7, 14:6, 17:15. The order is different each time in Revelation.

[123]Piper, *Let the Nations Be Glad*, 197-198.

[124]Fletcher, *Works*, 2:73-75.

[125]Wesley,"Scriptural Christianity," Sermon #4, 3.1.

the glory of the Lord, as the waters cover the sea" (Isa 11:9; Hab 2:14). His rule will extend to the ends of the earth (Zech 9:10; Ps 2:8; Matt 5:5; 6:10).

Then in v 11 angels beyond number join the chorus singing "worthy is the Lamb." Verse 11 uses a definite number and an indefinite number. The definite number is *chiliad*, which means thousand. But the Greek language had no word for any higher number. So John just repeated it by saying thousands of thousands. If he had the vocabulary, he could have said billions and billions. This interpretation is confirmed by his use of the indefinite number *myriad*, a numberless multitude.[126]

Their doxology is seven-fold. They ascribe to Christ power, riches, wisdom, strength, honor, glory, and blessing. These are divine attributes (compare to Dan 2:20-23; 37). However, it is the church in v 9, not the angelic host, which praises Christ for redemption.

Then in v 13 all nature, every creature in heaven and on earth and under the earth and on the sea, joins in, offering praise, honor, glory and power to Christ forever. The worship of God by nature is described in Psalm 148. According to Colossians 1:20 Christ has reconciled the whole universe to himself. Praise of God (4:9-11) and praise of the Lamb (5:9-12) are united in v 13. "Christ cannot be an alternative object of worship alongside God, but shares in the glory due to God."[127]

In v 14, all nature is represented by the four living creatures, who were first introduced in 4:6. The chapter closes with the church worshiping prostrate before God. Every living creature was singing and God was the audience. In worship God is the audience; with entertainment we become the audience. Kierkegaard wrote that God should be the audience, the pastor and choir the prompters, and the congregation the participants. We should seek God's applause.

---

[126]See Dan 7:10. In Rev 7:9 the church is also described as an innumerable host.

[127]Bauckham, *Climax of Prophecy*, 138-140.

REVELATION 5:8-14

Kierkegaard warned that when the spiritual is reduced to the worldly the speaker becomes an actor, the listeners become the critics, and God is no more present than he is in the theater.[128]

John's message was written to a discouraged church in the first century who did not understand God's great plan. They were under persecution from without and, as chapters 2-3 indicated, they also had problems within. Yet they are admonished to keep on praying and singing. They may have felt they were defeated, but if the seeming defeat of the lamb turned into the actual victory of the lion, then the seeming defeat of their persecution had to be understood as victory.

A persecuted church does not need a detailed forecast of future events, but a fresh vision of Jesus Christ to cheer the faint and encourage the weary. This chapter portrays the Lamb slain, the Lamb triumphant, and the Lamb worthy of our praise.

---

[128]Kierkegaard, *Purity of Heart*, 180-181.

Chapters Four and Five Summary

Interlude — Worship in heaven 4:1-5:14

- A. The glory of God 4:1-6
- B. The worship of the natural world 4:6-9
- C. The worship of the church 4:10-11
- D. The Lamb is worthy 5:1-14
    1. The closed book 5:1-4
    2. The lion and the lamb 5:5-7
    3. Worship of the Lamb 5:8-14

Things may appear one way on earth, but we see them in their true light when God reveals to us his perspective. While the church is undergoing persecution on earth, the church in heaven is worshiping.

To the extent that we are connected with heaven's agenda, we too will worship, even through tribulation. In fact, praise and worship are weapons which defeat Satan. No two chapters anywhere else in Scripture teach us more about worship than Revelation 4-5. This chapter contains the first two of sixteen hymns which are sung in heaven.

The door of revelation opened for John and remains open for us. Christ is that open door (John 10:9; Rev 3:8; 11:19; 15:5; 19:11). He gives this book of revelation and is the key to understanding it. As the door, Christ controls the destiny of human history and everything which happens must pass through this door. Through the open door John is allowed to see the triumphant church worship in heaven and to see the church pass through tribulation on earth from a heavenly perspective.

This vision was not meant to reveal God's future time table, but it does reveal heaven's priorities. Chapters 2-3 express the concern of Christ for problems within his church on earth, but now the focus shifts to the worshiping church in heaven. Unless we take frequent glimpses into glory, the imperfections of the church in this world will discourage us. However, the door is still open and we can still look in. *Open* is a perfect participle, meaning that is was opened and still stands open.

REVELATION 6

III. The Seven Seals 6:1-8:5

A. Six Seals 6:1-17

Before moving into the heart of John's vision we need an overview. Jesus will open the scroll with seven seals — one seal at a time. After the sixth seal there will be an interlude. At the seventh seal, seven trumpets are sounded one at a time. At the seventh trumpet, seven bowls are poured out one at a time. In each case between the sixth and seventh there are digressions. This pattern of six plus one set apart from the rest reflects the Sabbath (see another example in Prov 6:16). These seals, trumpets, and bowls comprise chapters 6-16.

Chapter 6 – the first six seals are opened
Chapter 7 – interlude
Chapter 8-9 – the first six trumpets
Chapter 10-11:13 – interlude
Chapter 11:14-19 – the seventh trumpet
Chapter 12-14 – interlude
Chapter 15-16 – the seven bowls

It is generally understood that the seals, trumpets, and bowls are parallel and cover the same period of time, There is a connection between the doubling of dreams (Gen 41:32) and the repetitive nature of Revelation. As the seals are opened, a new day dawns and judgment is released upon the old system. The trumpets repeat the judgment of the seals, but they are a call to repentance. With the trumpet warnings, judgment is intensified with the emphasis on the destruction of one-third. The bowls repeat the message but reveal God pouring out his judgment. Here the emphasis is upon total destruction of the old system.

The basis for seven judgments is found in Leviticus 26 where God warns Israel of a progressive sevenfold judgment if they disobey. It is important to understand there are seven, not twenty-one, judgments in Revelation. Actually, John is describing one great judgment, with a fourfold picture from earth and a twofold picture from heaven.

The fourfold judgment, according to Jesus in Matt 24:6-7; Luke 21:10-11, was accomplished through wars, famines, pestilences, earthquakes. From the heavenly perspective, the battle is waged with harps and bowls. It is not necessary, then, to find an exact fulfillment of each of these judgments in the past, present, or future.

This recapitulation, as opposed to linear, style is consistent with the way John writes. But there is a more profound meaning behind this repetition. It is based upon the three offices of Christ, as prophet, priest, and king. This was introduced in chapter 1:5, which describes him as all three. As our prophet, Christ opens the seven seals which usher in the new covenant. As our king, Christ is announced by the seven trumpets. As our priest, Christ pours out the seven bowls.

God's purpose for this world is the establishment of his kingdom. Now we see the great struggle between the kingdom of darkness and the kingdom of light. Before Israel was delivered from Egypt and established as a nation, God sent ten plagues. Now God establishes the new Israel by sending judgment upon their persecutors — Judaism (religiously) and Rome (politically). It is significant that on the Mount of Transfiguration, Moses and Elijah came to earth to meet with Jesus and to talk with him about his *exodus* (Luke 9:31). He was going to lead his people out of the captivity of sin. This is a spiritual struggle and the seals, trumpets, and bowls are not to be interpreted physically and literally. As this struggle unfolds, we see God work behind the scene and through secondary causes, such as war, calamity, famine, plague, and earthquake to accomplish his purpose. From man's perspective, this was the great tribulation. But, while everything seems out of control, the early church is assured that God is demolishing the old in order to make way for the new. Jesus taught that war, famine, pestilence, earthquake — the events of the seals, trumpets, and bowls — were not the end, but the beginning (Matt 24:6-8; Mark 13:19; Luke 21:9-10). He also taught clearly that the great tribulation would not occur at the end of time. He said, "For then there will be great distress (or tribulation), unequaled from the beginning of the world until now and never to be equaled again"

(Matt 24:21).

While these judgments are frightful, we must not lose our perspective. God is on the throne. The seven seals are opened in heaven, the seven trumpets are sounded in heaven, the seven bowls are poured out from heaven. These judgments all come from a righteous God. They are not poured out upon the church, but upon the enemies of the church. They are poured out in response to the prayers of the church (see 6:10; 5:8 and then chapter 16). This great tribulation was the day of God's vengeance (Luke 21:22). These judgments are depicted symbolically and were executed in the first century AD. God has not given his children the spirit of fear (Rom 8:15). The true Christian has nothing to fear from his Father in heaven.

FOUR HORSEMEN

Zech 1:7-11; 6:1-8

1. Red - war
2. Black - death
3.White - conquest
4. Dapple/grizzled

Zechariah 6 is another and fuller symbolism of the vision in chapter one. These horsemen are agents of divine judgment — the four winds [Jer 49:36; Ps 18:10; 104:4]. While there is something ambiguous about their specific function, in general they represent the means God uses to control history. Hag 2:6-7, 21-22 foretold that there would be a shaking or spiritual earthquake before the kingdom of God was established. But the horsemen report no activity; it would be another five hundred years.

OLIVET DISCOURSE

Matt 24:4-35; Mark 13:7-31; Luke 21:9-36

1. War
2. Conquest
3. Famine
4. Pestilence (Luke 21:11)
5. Earthquake
6. Persecution

If we combine the three gospel accounts, the big four judgments are: war, famine, pestilence, earthquake, but the complete list gives six. There is no mention of horses, because Jesus here is speaking literally.

SEVEN SEALS

Revelation 6

1. Conquest
2. War
3. Famine
4. Pestilence
5. Persecution
6. Earthquake

In Revelation 6, John sees four horses — the horses of Zechariah, and four judgments — the judgments from the Olivet Discourse. This, then is an expansion on Zechariah's original revelation. This does not depict four judgments, but a fourfold picture of one great judgment. Yet in this chapter six seals are broken. These six seal judgments are the four horsemen of Zechariah.

7. The seventh seal (8:1) opens to the seven trumpets.

TEN PLAGUES

Exodus 7:14-11:10

1. Water to Blood
2. Frogs
3. Gnats
4. Flies
5. Livestock
6. Boils
7. Hail
8. Locusts
9. Darkness
10. Firstborn die

Just as Israel cried out under Egyptian bondage until deliverance came, so the church cried out under Roman persecution until deliverance came. Our deliverance from the bondage of sin came after the death and resurrection of God's firstborn (Rev 1:5).

SEVEN TRUMPETS

Revelation 8-9

1. Hail/Fire/Blood. A third of the earth burned up
2. A third of the sea turned to blood; a third of marine life/ships destroyed
3. A third of the water poisoned
4. A third of sun/moon/stars darkened
5. Demonic locusts torment
6. Demons released from Euphrates River
7. Lightning, thunder, earthquake, hail (11:15-19). This seventh trumpet introduces the seven bowls.

#1 corresponds to 7th and 1st plagues
#2-3 corresponds to 1st plague
#4 corresponds to 9th plague
#5 corresponds to 8th plague
#7 corresponds to 7th plague

SEVEN BOWLS

Revelation 16

1. Sores on the land
2. Sea becomes blood
3. Rivers become blood
4. Sun scorches
5. Darkness
6. Invasion of frog-demons from Euphrates River
7. Earthquake; hail

These seven bowl judgments are introduced in Rev 15:1 as *plagues* and that those who overcame sang the song of Moses and the Lamb. In 11:8 Jerusalem is linked to Egypt.

#1, 4 correspond to the 6th plague
#2-3 correspond to the 1st plague
#5 corresponds to the 9th plague
#6 corresponds to the 2nd plague
#7 corresponds to the 7th plague

REVELATION 6:1-2

This section parallels the Olivet Discourse, in which Jesus answered the question concerning when the temple would be destroyed. This chapter is a composite of Leviticus 26:18-28, Ezekiel 14:21, and Zechariah 1:7-11; 6:1-8.

The Olivet Discourse of Matthew 24, Mark 13, Luke 21, describes war, international strife, famine, pestilence, earthquake, persecution. If we combine the three gospel accounts, the big four judgments are: war, famine, pestilence, earthquake, but the complete list contains six. Jesus makes no mention of horses, because he is speaking literally. But when we go to Revelation 6, John sees four horses — the horses of Zechariah, combined with four judgments — the judgments from the Olivet Discourse. This, then is an expansion on Zechariah's original revelation. This does not depict four judgments, but a fourfold picture of one great judgment. The horsemen ride together. Yet in this chapter six seals are broken. These six seal judgments are the four horsemen of Zechariah.

1. First seal — the white horse 6:1-2

John watched as each horseman was sent forth." It is the four living creatures, representing all of creation, who each call forth the four horsemen. Thus, both nature and the church are crying for deliverance (Rom 8:19-22; Rev 6:10).

The white horse represents the conquest of the gospel. And yet the white horse has a rider. Only the rider of the fourth horse is actually named, but the rider of the first horse is described sufficiently to identify him as Christ. Eugene Peterson wrote, "Christ is in history ruling and conquering. The only way to understand history is to begin, openly and firmly, with Christ. Christ is the first word. Whatever the subject, we begin with Christ. He is the Alpha in the alphabet of historical discourse."[129]

As the leader, the first rider can be seen as a summation of all that is to follow. The first rider introduces warfare, while the riders

---

[129] Peterson, *Reversed Thunder*, 75.

which follow delineate the conditions of war. While destruction follows in the wake of these horsemen, it should not be forgotten that the result of their destruction is the deliverance of the church.

In Zechariah 1:8-11 four horsemen patrol the earth and control human destiny. They report to the angel of the Lord (v 11). God's people at that time were suffering under Babylonian captivity and these horsemen are poised to respond to the cry of v 12, "How long will you withhold mercy from Jerusalem?" Zechariah gave this vision to comfort the people of God (v 13). The four horsemen rush to cover the earth in Zechariah 6 and as a consequence the temple of God is established. In Revelation 6 the people of God are under Roman persecution and they ask the same question "How long until you judge the inhabitants of the earth and avenge our blood?" (v 10). The same horsemen ride again under the command of Christ. They ride to avenge the church in answer to their prayers. As a result the people of God are sealed (chapter 7).

The rider of the white horse carries a bow. Habakkuk 3:8-15 and Psalm 45 depicts the Messiah as riding forth in victory with sharp arrows which bring down the nations. Habakkuk 3 describes the Lord riding in victory. "You uncovered your bow, you called for many arrows. . . . Sun and moon stood still in the heavens at the glint of your flying arrows, at the lightning of your flashing spear" (vv 9,11; see also Zech 9:13-14).

The rider of the white horse was given a crown. There are two Greek words for *crown* — *stephanos* is a crown of victory; *diadema* is a crown of authority. The devil is depicted as having a realm of authority, but never as having a crown of victory. Yet the rider of the white horse wears a *stephanos*.

The rider of the white horse rides as a conqueror. The Greek word for conquer or victory is *nikeo*. This word has already been used eight times by John and each time it describes Christ or his church. The last phrase of v 2 literally reads, "conquering that he might conquer." This implies his victorious nature, even *before* he proceeds to do battle. He even wears the crown of victory *before* the battle begins.

The rider of the white horse is again described in 19:11-16. The opening phrase of v 2, "And behold, a white horse and the one seated on it," is repeated verbatim in 19:11. There he is identified as the King of Kings and Lord of Lords. And, according to 19:11 he judges and makes war — exactly what he does in 6:1-2.

Make no mistake, it is Christ who controls human destiny. Yet he often works through secondary causes. The symbolism here suggests the opening of the Roman war against Jerusalem. Christ does not visibly appear to the church on earth until 20:9, but he has been working throughout human history implementing his will through war, calamity, famine, plague, and earthquake. He even said, "Do not suppose that I have come to bring peace to the earth. I did not come to bring peace, but a sword" (Matt 10:34).

2. Second seal — the red horse 6:3-4

The red horse of war brought upheaval to the *pax Romans*—the peace of Rome (Matt 24:6) and took peace from the land of Palestine. About three years after the death of Christ, war broke out between Herod and Aretas, king of Arabia Petraea. Then Caligula ordered his statue to be placed in the temple and there was so much civil unrest the Jews neglected even to farm their land. During this same period of time about 5000 Jews, who had moved from Babylon to Seleucia, were slaughtered. About five years later many Jews were killed over a dispute respecting the city of Mia. Four years later, 10,000 Jews were trodden to death in the streets of Jerusalem, over an incident within the precincts of the temple, instigated by a Roman soldier. Four years later the Jews fought and ravaged the Samaritans. Then, in another dispute, the Jews rose against the Syrians and were defeated. In Caesarea alone nearly 20,000 Jews were slain. This animosity prevailed throughout the region. In Damascus, 10,000 Jews were slain in one hour; 13,000 were slain one night in Scythopolis. In Alexandria 50,000 Jews were slain. Then in Jotapata, another 40,000 perished.[130]

---

[130]Holford, *The Destruction of Jerusalem,* 11-13.

During an eighteen-month period between AD 68-69 Rome changed emperors four times. Jerusalem, who had persecuted the prophets, fell under siege in AD 67 until it fell in AD 70. In his preface to *The Wars of the Jews*, Josephus wrote, "All the misfortunes of man from the beginning of the world are not as great as what happened here to the Jews."[131]

3. Third seal — the black horse 6:5-6

According to Matthew 24:7 famine would come. The black horse of famine rode bringing worldwide famine. According to Acts 11:28 a severe famine spread over the entire Roman world during the reign of Claudius.[132] Claudius was emperor from AD 41-54. Also, during the final days of the siege of Jerusalem there was terrible famine.[133] Titus, the Roman general ordered his troops to destroy "gardens" on the outskirts of Jerusalem, which would include olive trees and vineyards. At the end of the first century Domitian also issued an edict to destroy half the existing vineyards, because too much wine and not enough grain was being produced. This edict proved so unpopular that Domitian had to rescind it.[134]

Yet war tends not to affect the wealthy as much as it hurts the poor. Since a denarius[135] was a day's wages, according to Matthew 20:2, 9, the working class spent their entire wages for bread. Yet by vv 15-17 even the rich and powerful have not escaped the justice of

---

[131]Josephus, *The Wars of the Jews*, Preface ¶ 4.

[132]This famine was also recorded by Josephus, *Antiquities of the Jews*, 3.15.3; 20.2.5; Eusebius, *Ecclesiastical History*, 2.8.1.

[133]Josephus, *Wars of the Jews*, 5.10.2-5.

[134]Aune, *WBC*, 52B:398-400. There is a reference to the actions of Titus by Josephus in *Wars of the Jews*, 5.3.2.

[135]*Denarion* is translated *penny* in the KJV. However, since a penny is worth very little in our economy, this gives the wrong impression.

God.

4. Fourth seal — the pale horse 6:7-8

Death rode the pale[136] horse and hades, the place of death, followed close behind. Here death and hades are personified. While the word *pestilence* does not appear here, as it does in Matthew 24:7, the Greek word for death, *thanatos*, is translated *pestilence* over thirty times in the Septuagint, the Greek Old Testament. This was the aftermath of war, famine, pestilence and wild animals inhabiting the ruins (v 8) and these four plagues are a summary of the curses stated in Leviticus 26 and Ezekiel 14:21. Josephus described houses in Jerusalem that were full of the dying and the lanes of the city full of dead bodies.[137]

Grammatically, the phrase *they were given power* can, and probably does, refer to all four horsemen. These horsemen still ride wherever nations persist in opposing God's rule. War, famine, epidemics, death follow whenever men oppose the will of God. This is the wrath of the Lamb. Therefore, "Kiss the Son, lest he be angry and you be destroyed in your way, for his wrath can flare up in a moment. Blessed are all who take refuge in him" (Ps 2:12).

5. Fifth seal — souls under the altar 6:9-11

Now the scene shifts from earth to heaven as the fifth and sixth seals are opened. The term *souls* can carry the meaning of "lives or persons." According to Leviticus 17:11-14 life is in the blood. These souls represent the first Christian martyrs, from Antipas and the persecution of Nero.

This parallels with Matthew 24:9-10. Jesus predicted that upon

---

[136]*Chloros*, literally *green*. Our word *chlorine* comes from this Greek word.

[137]Josephus, *Wars of the Jews*, 5.12.3-4; 5.13.7. Holford wrote, "The ground could not be seen for the dead bodies, over which the Romans trampled in pursuit of the fugitives" [*Destruction of Jerusalem,* 37].

Jerusalem "will come all the righteous blood that has been shed on earth, from the blood of righteous Abel to the blood of Zechariah son of Berekiah, whom you murdered between the temple and the altar. . . . All this will come upon this generation" (Matt 23:35-36).

John saw only their souls, because their bodies had not yet been resurrected. Apparently they were dead and resting from their labors (14:13). They had overcome and received their white robe (3:5). Their lifeblood had been poured out as an offering to God (Phil 2:17; 2 Tim 4:6). Those under the altar are near to God. This is the place of safety and protection. They are spared the judgment of the sixth seal. It is significant that John indicated he was exiled to Patmos for the same reason (1:9). Like the blood of Abel (Gen 4:10), the blood of these martyrs cries for vengeance.

The earthly temple was considered to be modeled after the heavenly temple. Yet there were two altars in the earthly temple: the altar of burnt offering and the altar of incense. Their blood was poured out according to the instructions of Exodus 29:12 and Leviticus 4:7.

As God demonstrates his righteousness, justice, and holiness in his punishment of sin, the church shouts *hallelujah* (19:1-4). While we take no pleasure in the death of the wicked, this punishment of the wicked results in his glory (11:17-18; 14:7; 15:3-4; 19:1-2) and vindicates the church (18:4-7). The church cries out to the Lord. This is the only time in the book of Revelation that God is addressed as *despotes*. The emphasis of this word is absolute power. The Master and Ruler is asked, How much longer until you judge the inhabitants of the earth? This phrase, "the inhabitants of the earth," occurs nine times in this book. Without exception, they are always enemies of Christianity. Lenski described them as having no home but earth and wanting no other home.[138] While these deceased Christians had also lived on earth, yet whether living or dead their citizenship is in heaven (Phil 3:20). Yet more specifically, they are people of the *land*, probably a reference to the land of Palestine.

God must judge sin because he is holy and true. But if he is

---

[138]Lenski, *Revelation*, 236.

sovereign, why are the people of God also afflicted? As if in anticipation of this question, Jesus answers it in Luke 18:7-8, "And will not God avenge for his chosen ones, who cry out to him day and night? Will he keep putting them off? I tell you, he will avenge them quickly." Jesus taught that those days of tribulation would be shortened for the sake of the elect (Matt 24:22). The sixth seal is God's reply, "It is mine to avenge; I will repay" (Rom 12:19). Apparently the seven seals, seven trumpets, and seven bowls are all a divine response to these prayers.

Yet these saints must wait and rest *a little time*. If language has meaning, that phrase cannot be stretched to mean thousands of years. Vengeance would come before that generation ended (Matt 23:36; 24:34). The dead are to wait and rest while God completes the living — their fellow servants and brothers. The term *complete* (*pleroo*) means to perfect. Jesus had warned the church at Sardis, "I have not found your deeds complete" (3:2). The church would be perfected through suffering and tribulation (2 Thess 1:4-5; 2 Tim 2:12; 1 Pet 5:10).

6. Sixth seal — shaking of earth and heaven 6:12-17

The events described in vv 12-17 are described from the perspective of heaven. This divine visitation has three elements: an earthquake which moves every mountain and island, a solar eclipse which results in the moon appearing as the color of blood, the stars fall and the sky vanishes.

A – a great earthquake
    B – a solar eclipse
    B′ – moon appeared as blood
        C – the stars fell
        C′ – the sky disappeared
A′ – every mountain and island was moved

The description of vv 12-17 corresponds to the words of Christ in Matthew 24:7, 29; Luke 21:11; 23:30. If this literally described the end of the world, the people described in vv 15-17 would not still be hiding in caves. Gary DeMar has explained these heavenly signs as symbolically fulfilled in the first century.[139] The basis for this is found in Genesis 1:14-16. Examples of such symbolic use are found in Genesis 37:9; Isaiah 13:9-10; 34:4; Ezekiel 32:7-8; Amos 8:9. Carrington wrote, "If they are to be taken literally, there is no room for any more apocalypse, or any more history; the physical structure of the universe is at an end."[140]

Yet something was coming to an end, for as Jesus unrolled the scroll of destiny, the sky, like a scroll was being rolled up (v 14). The old world order is rolled up and the new order is unrolled. This is the end of the old covenant. The elaboration on the sixth seal provides us further confirmation that the time frame for this chapter coincides with Matthew 24 and the destruction of Jerusalem because the events described in both passages are the same.

With the sixth seal came an earthquake (v 12). At Mount Sinai, when the law was given, the earth shook (Exod 19:18). Pentecost was the commemoration of the giving of the law. The establishment of the kingdom of God at Pentecost deposed every king, prince, general, rich, and mighty man (v 15) and overthrew our enemies. Peter explained that the outpouring of the Holy Spirit constituted a spiritual shakeup. He said the prophecy of Joel was fulfilled at Pentecost. A. T. Robertson said, "Peter's interpretation of Joel should make us cautious about too literal an exegesis of these grand symbols."[141]

> And I will show wonders in the heaven above and signs on the earth below, blood and fire and billows of smoke. The sun will be turned to darkness and the moon become as blood before the coming of the great and glorious day of the

---

[139]DeMar, *Last Days Madness*, 129-153.

[140]Carrington, *The Meaning of the Revelation*, 135.

[141]Robertson, *Word Pictures*, 6:345.

> Lord. And everyone who calls on the name of the Lord will be saved (Acts 2:19-21).

Haggai 2:6-7, 21-22 foretold that there would be a spiritual earthquake before the kingdom of God was established. This shaking is also described in Hebrews 12:28. Hebrews 12:18-21 recalls the fright associated with Mt Sinai. For three days the children of Israel prepared to meet God. Anyone who touched the mountain would be put to death. On the third day a thick cloud was over the mountain, there was thunder and lightning. From the mountain came loud trumpet blasts. The Lord came down in the form of fire, smoke billowed up, and the ground shook (Exod 19:18). It was awesome. An earthquake, thunder and lightning, fire and smoke, an air-raid trumpet blast all at once.

But the writer of Hebrews said that we have not come to Mt Sinai, but to Mt Zion. Zion was first the hill upon which Jerusalem was built and where the throne of David was located; then it came to symbolize the city of God built upon the mountain of the Lord. Zion is God's throne and the people over whom he rules. Verses 22-24 describe the superiority of the new covenant, as the book of Hebrews has consistently done.

Just as the old covenant was instituted with earthquake, so God promised to shake this world once more. That was the indication that the four horsemen were originally seeking in Zechariah. This earthquake began at the resurrection of Christ. It rolled away the stone and in continues to bring down everything in the way. The resurrection of Christ was the beginning of an earthquake that was not confined to the area of Sinai. God shook the whole world. Matthew 24:7 associates an earthquake with the destruction of Jerusalem. In v 27 this shaking is described twice with a verb that is a present participle. The shaking continues. It has not stopped. God will continue to shake this world until every stronghold comes down, until every argument has been demolished, every high thing that exalts itself against the knowledge of God, and every thought is taken captive (2 Cor 10:5).

Every time man tries to establish a kingdom, God will eventually send an earthquake. Across the span of human history is the rubble of man's empires. Binney said of vv 12-17, "These are all common symbols of great civil and social commotions, the fall of governments, and the wreck of society."[142] But rising from beneath that rubble is a kingdom which cannot be shaken (Heb 12:28). The kingdom of Christ is unshakable. It is unstoppable. If death could not hold him, nothing can stop his advance.

The sun turned black, the moon became as blood, the stars fell. Joel, Peter, and John are all describing the day of Pentecost. These "stars" fell like a fig tree. According to Matthew 21:19; 24:32-34, the fig tree is Israel. Jerusalem was about to fall. But the kingdom also came with blood. When Jesus shed his blood on the cross, the sun did become dark. Jesus said in Matthew 24:29 that the sun and moon would be darkened. At the inauguration of the new covenant on the day of Pentecost Peter explained that the prophecy of Joel was fulfilled at Pentecost (Acts 2:19-21). John again quotes the symbolic language of Joel, which Peter said was fulfilled at Pentecost, the moon became as blood (v 12). The sun turned black, the moon became *as* blood, the stars fell (v 13).

Peter said the moon became *as* blood; here in v 12 it is symbolized as blood red in color. In Joel 2:10 the moon ceasing to shine and in vv 30-31 the moon turning to blood both describe the same event. The moon turned to a blood-like color at Pentecost; symbolic of a spiritual eclipse. These verses describes the temporal judgment of nations and are used to describe the spiritual overthrow of the empires of this world system. God shakes the earth, darkens the sun and moon, and his sword is drunk with blood (Jer 46:10).

The wrath of the Lamb is a paradoxical statement, since lambs are usually gentle. Only in Mark 3:5 and here is wrath attributed to Jesus. Yet in Exodus 12, the judgment of God fell on the Egyptians who had not put the blood of the Passover Lamb on their doorposts. Thus, the blood of the Lamb turns away the wrath of God and those who are sealed by God are protected from the wrath of the Lamb.

---

[142]Binney, *Commentary*, 681.

REVELATION 6:12-17

The *great day of his wrath* is based upon the words of Joel 2:11, 31; Zephaniah 1:14-15, 18; 2:3. It corresponds to the last half of Daniel's seventieth week and the great tribulation which Jesus described in Matthew 24:21. While God's wrath against sin is both a present reality (Rom 1:18-32), as well as a future judgment (Rom 2:5), here John uses the aorist indicative verb to announce that the great day of Christ's wrath *has come*. Therefore, this day cannot be projected into the future. On his way to the cross, Jesus warned in Luke 23:30 that the time was coming when "they would say to the mountains, 'Fall on us!' and to the hills, 'Cover us!'" Both Jesus and John borrow their words from Hosea 10:6-8. The act of hiding in caves is based upon Isaiah 2:10, 19, 21. Men have been hiding from God ever since Adam (Gen 3:8). The next verse, Luke 23:31, establishes the time frame when this would happen — if men are going to crucify a tree that is green, how much more severe will be the fate of guilty Jerusalem, which is a dry tree?

Josephus verified that during the siege of Jerusalem, people did seek refuge in caves and under rocks.[143] Here John lists seven groups of people, which made up the predominate social strata of the ancient world. The "kings of the earth" should probably be understood as rulers of Judea. They are united, however, in their fear. "All these terrors actually fell upon the sinners in Judea and Jerusalem in the day of their destruction, and they will all, in the utmost degree, fall upon impenitent sinners, at the general judgment of the last day."[144]

This chapter closes with the rhetorical question, "Who can stand?" This question comes from Nahum 1:6 and Malachi 3:2. The question summarizes this chapter. As Jesus Christ opens the seals, who can stand under his judgment? Chapter seven will answer the question. Those standing as the seals are broken are those whom he has sealed. According to 7:9 a great multitude that no one can count will ultimately stand before the throne.

---

[143]Josephus, *Wars of the Jews*, 3.2.3; 3.7.35-36; 5.3.1; 6.7.3; 6.9.4; 7.2.1.

[144]Tong, *Matthew Henry's Commentary*, 6:1146.

REVELATION 7

Interlude — First fruits and final harvest 7:1-17

1. The sealing of the first fruits 7:1-8

The six seals have just been opened and there is a Sabbath break or interlude between the sixth and the seventh seal. Yet there is a connection between chapters 6-7. In chapter 6 Christ broke the seals and judged the enemies of the church. In chapter 7 the church is sealed, protecting them from God's wrath, but not exempting them from tribulation.

> The first six seals represent the early stage of the Jewish war, wherein Vespasian fought his way through Galilee toward Jerusalem. But before he had an opportunity to besiege Jerusalem, the action pauses as these angels seal the 144,000 from the twelve tribes of Israel.[145]

The four angels in 7:1 hold back the four horsemen from their ride of judgment until the church, the servants of God, is sealed. Reference to the "four corners" of the earth does not imply that John believed in a flat earth, but simply referred to the four points of the compass.

The wind which was restrained was described in 6:13. In Scripture, wind is used in connection with the coming of God or his angels, either in blessing or in judgment (Gen 8:1; 41:27; Exod 10:13, 19; 14:21; 15:10; Num 11:31; Ps 18:10; 104:3-4; 135:7; 147:18; 148:8; Hos 13:15-16; John 3:8; Acts 2:2).

Clarke wrote that these four winds were held back until the church had time to prepare for its flight from Jerusalem to Pella, prior to the total destruction of Jerusalem by the Romans. He found it significant than not one Christian perished in the siege of Jerusa-

---

[145]Gentry, "A Preterist View of Revelation," 56.

lem.[146] William Tong wrote,

> If the destruction of Jerusalem was not yet over (and I think it is hard to prove that it was), it seems more proper to understand this of the remnant of that people which God had reserved according to the election of grace, only here we have a definite number for an indefinite.[147]

It may also be significant that Josephus recorded that four years before the siege of Jerusalem began, during the feast of tabernacles, a common farmer suddenly began to cry aloud in the temple, "A voice from the east, a voice from the west, a voice from the four winds, a voice against Jerusalem and the holy house, a voice against the bridegrooms and the brides, and a voice against this whole people."[148]

The cry of the angel in v 2 is connected to the cry of the martyrs in 6:10. According to Matthew 24:22, if these days were not cut short, no one would survive.

Verses 5-8 name the twelve tribes of Israel. If the church is the Israel of God, what is the point of specifying each tribe if spiritual Israel is meant? There is no need to determine whether this is a reference to Israel or the church. The first converts to Christianity were Jewish. The gospel went to the Jew first (Rom 1:16). The Jewish converts in Jerusalem were the first fruits of the ministry of Jesus.

---

[146]Clarke, *Commentary*, 4:330; 6:726-727; 996. See Josephus, *Wars of the Jews*, 4.9.2; 4.10.5, where the distraction of the advancing Roman generals, Vespasian and Titus, in AD 68 allowed time for the Jewish Christians to escape Jerusalem. See also Eusebius, *Ecclesiastical History*, 3.5.3. Eusebius then referenced the account of Josephus, citing three million as the number of Jews who would be in Jerusalem for Passover [*Antiquities*, 17.9.3]. Over a million died in the siege of Jerusalem.

[147]Tong, *Matthew Henry's Commentary,* 6:1147.

[148]Josephus, *Wars of the Jews*, 6.5.3.

They were the first fruits of those first chosen to receive the gospel. Yet even before the fall of Jerusalem, the church has been dispersed due to persecution (Acts 8:1) and so James began his letter by addressing it to the twelve tribes scattered among the nations (1:1; see also 1 Pet 1:1). Notice that in James 1:18 these twelve tribes are described as "a kind of firstfruits." As *firstborn*, they are the new Levites serving God in the new temple, the New Jerusalem.

While it is not necessary to take 144,000 as a literal exact number, since God has not decreed to save only an exact quota, it is probably a realistic estimate of the number of Jewish Christians in Jerusalem at this time (Acts 21:20). The symbolism is that God sealed 12,000 from each of twelve tribes.

These early Jewish Christians took seriously the warning of Jesus in Matthew 24:15-21 and escaped Jerusalem before it fell. In Exodus 12:13 those who had the mark of blood were spared when the death angel passed over. In Ezekiel 9:3-4 a man with a writer's inkhorn is commanded to set a mark upon the foreheads of all the righteous. God still knows his own. The beast also has marked his own. However, in these references a different Greek word is used. This mark provides no protection.

Twice in Ephesians Paul tells us that God marks those who believe with the seal of the Spirit (1:13; 4:30; see also 2 Cor 1:22; 2 Tim 2:19). This promise of the seal of protection recurs in 9:4, 14:1, 22:4.

The real significance of the 144,000 is that they were the first fruits (14:4). In their agricultural society, reproduction was very important. Their future depended upon it. They took a risk by planting seed in the ground. When the first ear of corn, head of wheat, or grape on the vine appeared, it was cause for great rejoicing because it was a sign that more was to follow. The firstfruits was allocated for the Levitical priests and thus considered to be holy (Deut 18:4).

- Jesus died on the cross and was buried. His resurrection made him the "firstfruits of those who have fallen asleep" (1 Cor 15:20, 23). We have the hope of bodily being resurrected because he was the first.

- The Jewish converts in Jerusalem were the firstfruits of the ministry of Jesus. Not all disciples of Jesus have been spared. Many were martyred for their faith, but these were sealed because they had a special significance as first fruits. James addressed the twelve tribes and explained that "they were a kind of firstfruits of all he created" (Jas 1:18). Then after the seven trumpets in Revelation John returns to the subject of the 144,000 and in 14:4 states that they are firstfruits to God and the Lamb.

The significance of firstfruits is that more is to follow. The other view treats them as "last fruits," but according to Romans 11:26 at the end *all Israel shall be saved*, not just 144,000. One of the Jewish feasts was the day of firstfruits (Exod 23:16; Num 28:26-31). It is significant that the day of firstfruits was also known as Pentecost.

It is also significant that the day of firstfruits was followed on the Jewish calendar by the week of ingathering or harvest. When all of the crop had been harvested they celebrated a week of ingathering (Exod 23:16b). We are involved in a harvest of souls. The Scriptures give us reason to hope for a great end of the age harvest.

2. The final harvest 7:9-17

After John had delivered messages to the seven churches, 4:1 begins with *after this I saw*, indicating another vision. Once more this same phrase is used after John saw the beginning of the church, he now describes another vision of its end. In both cases the scene moves from earth to heaven. This group is not sealed for protection because they no longer need it.

In vv 4-8 the number 144,000 is presented; in v 9 a great multitude that no one could count is described. In contrast, this final harvest is from every nation. This fulfills the promise made to Abraham that his descendants would be innumerable (Gen 13:16; 15:5; 16:10; 22:17-18; 26:4; 28:14; 32:12) and that he would be the father of many nations (Gen 17:4-6, 16; 28:14; 32:12; 35:11; 48:19). This multitude is described as wearing white robes and holding palm branches. Palm branches were part of the feast of tabernacles (Lev 23:40; Neh 8:15), which came after the feast of first fruits and was the celebration of the full ingathering of the harvest. Thus, 7:1-8 is based upon the Feast of Firstfruits or Pentecost and 7:9-17 is based upon the Feast of Tabernacles or Ingathering (see Exod 23:16; 34:22).

The only other mention in the New Testament of palm branches refers to the crowd at Jesus' triumphal entry into Jerusalem who also carried palm branches (John 12:13). Notice that God is their tabernacle (v 15) and the saints stand before the throne with palm branches in their hands (v 9). Tong said v 10 could be understood as either a *hosanna* or a *hallelujah*.[149]

The Old Testament prophets predicted an early and later rain of the Spirit. James held up the patient farmer, who waits for the early and latter rain, as an example to all Christians (5:7). Hosea promised, "As surely as the sun rises, he will appear; he will come to us like the winter [latter] rains, like the spring [former] rains that water the earth (6:3)." Joel's reference to these rains comes in the context of his great pentecostal prophecy (2:23). Zechariah encourages us to "ask for rain (10:1)."

The early rain was needed so that the planted seed would germinate. The latter rain was necessary for the plant to fill out and produce fruit. The purpose of the latter rain is to guarantee an abundant harvest. Just as Pentecost was the early rain which established the kingdom, the latter rain, which we are to pray for, will produce a great end of the age harvest of souls.

As a result of the atoning death of Christ and the drawing of the Holy Spirit, there will be people in heaven from every nation, language, ethnic group, and lineage. First used in 5:9, now this phrase reappears in 7:9. Christ is at the center (vv 9, 17) of the throne of God (v 15) and shares the throne (v 10).

These blood-washed serve God day and night. Under the old

---

[149]Tong, *Matthew Henry's Commentary*, 6:1148.

covenant this function was reserved for the Levitical priesthood. No Gentile could even enter the temple. Now the church, of all nations, tribes, and languages is a kingdom of priests (1:6; 5:10). Tong observed, "Heaven is a state of service, though not of suffering; it is a state of rest, but not of sloth."[150] The word *temple* does not refer to the Jewish temple, but would be better translated "sanctuary." God dwells with his church (see 21:3-4). God will provide for them, Christ will lead them, and every tear shall be wiped from their eyes (Isa 25:8).

There will be no hunger nor thirst nor burning heat (compare to Isa 49:9-10; Ezek 34:23-25; 37:24-28). We will be led by the Lamb. This image reverses the roles in Psalm 23, where the shepherd leads the sheep. In 14:4 we are described as following the Lamb. Our shepherd is the Lamb. At the end of Revelation 6, we are warned of the wrath of the Lamb; at the end of Revelation 7, we are promised the Lamb will feed and lead us. Swete observed that the purpose of chapter 7 is "to contrast the preparedness of the church for the coming end with the panic of the unprepared world."[151]

We shall be led unto living fountains of water. The emphasis in the Greek text is on *life*. The phrase *springs of water* serves as a symbol of that life. Ironically, it was at the Feast of Tabernacles where Jesus declared that whoever believes in him will experience rivers of living water (John 7:37-39).

Verse 12 contains a sevenfold doxology. It corresponds to the doxology of the Lamb in 5:12, but replaces *wealth* with *thanksgiving*. And unlike 5:12, this doxology begins and ends with *amen*. No other hymn in the Bible begins with *amen*. This opening *amen* is probably an antiphonal response to the hymn of v 10.

And so across history every saint of God has been cleansed by the blood and has come through great tribulation. All these may be said, more or less, to come *out of great tribulation*, of various kinds,

---

[150]Tong, *Matthew Henry's Commentary*, 6:1149.

[151]Swete, *Commentary*, 95.

wisely and graciously allotted by God to all his children." Whedon identified this tribulation as "the battle of probationary life under pressure of the world, the flesh, and the devil."[152] But across time, from the great tribulation to the end of the world, they keep coming through. Therefore, I do not interpret "the great tribulation" here as referring to a specific time period. This interpretation is confirmed by the fact that those who are coming out in v 14 are the same group described in v 9. Both groups are blood-washed.

Verse 9 says this group is innumerable and universal in representation, which indicates the redeemed through all the ages and is not restricted to martyrs. Peter said we were called to his eternal glory, but we must first suffer awhile (1 Pet 5:10). Yet while we are perfected through that suffering, we are sealed from God's judgment. An innumerable host will persevere, coming through every type of pressure and persecution. Their reward is threefold: they stand before the throne in worship, they will be delivered from every form of earthly deprivation, and the Lamb will lead them.

If the first group of Christian converts survived the attack of Satan and made it safely to heaven, so can those who follow. A universal atonement will ultimately result in an innumerable church. Therefore, the 144,000 are symbolic of the whole church and are the harbingers of a great end of the age revival. Tong quoted Isaiah 54:1 in his conclusion, "God will have a greater harvest of souls among the Gentiles than he had among the Jews."[153]

---

[152]Whedon, *Commentary*, 5:388.

[153]Tong, *Matthew Henry's Commentary*, 6:1148.

REVELATION 8

B. Seventh seal 8:1-5

Before daybreak the priests began their preparations, in the ritual of Old Testament worship. They carried out the ashes from the previous day and brought in the sacrificial lamb. Just at sunrise the trumpets sounded to summon the people to worship. At that moment the temple gates were opened and the lamb was slain. The lamb's blood was sprinkled and five candles were refit. After prayer and Scripture reading, a priest would fill his golden censer with incense. Slowly the priest would enter the Holy Place with incense and the crowd would wait outside praying silently. When the prayers had ended, the priest would reappear and give the benediction. The final two candles were lit. Then the meat offering was laid upon the altar and the drink offering poured out. This was the signal for the music to begin, with the priests blasting their silver trumpets. Cymbals were struck and the choir began singing. At the close the priests again gave three trumpet blasts and the morning service was over.[154]

John's revelation was influenced by this liturgy. This is the Lord's Day (1:10). The seven churches are candlesticks blazing the light of the gospel (Rev 2-3). The Lamb has been slain (Rev 5:6). Through his blood the gates of heaven are opened. The prayers of God's people ascend to the throne of God (6:10). This chapter opens with this description of prayer rising like incense. They have filled the golden bowl and have been brought before the altar. Edersheim noted that it took the priest a half hour to offer the daily incense.[155] In this chapter there is silence for half an hour as our High Priest intercedes for us. "The Lord is in his holy temple; let all the earth be silent

---

[154]Edersheim, *The Temple*, 152-173. See also Farrer, *Revelation*, 112.

[155]Edersheim, *The Temple*, 167-169. According to Luke 1:10, when Zechariah offered the incense, all the assembled worshipers prayed and waited outside. Whedon said half an hour was about the length of time this took [*Commentary*, 5:391].

before him" (Zeph 1:7; Hab 2:20; see also Zech 2:13). Thus, the silence of 8:1 is an indication that God has heard the prayers of his people. It is no accident that the heavenly altar is immediately before the throne (9:13). God cannot help but see the smoke. Then the trumpets sound and the bowls are poured out (8-9; 15-16). Heaven is filled with singing (19:1-8).

Peterson also noticed that the first seal is a revelation of Christ triumphant over evil, while the seventh seal is a revelation of the attentive silence in heaven in which the prayers of every believer are heard and answered. "All evil takes place between that beginning and ending. Evil is contained."[156]

Here God lets us see behind the scenes. "John sees the truly revolutionary dynamic of the prayers of the saints."[157] According to vv 3-5, here is what happens when we pray. While 5:8 referred to the prayers of the saints, and the prayers of the martyrs were recorded in 6:9-10, here John clarifies that he is describing the prayers of *all* the saints. Thus, the emphasis in Revelation is not upon literal martyrs, but upon all who overcome. Our prayers rise up before God (v 4). "May my prayer be set before you like incense" (Ps 141:2). In vv 3-4, the incense is not mingled *with* prayer; incense symbolizes prayer. The symbol is interpreted for us in 5:8.

Our prayers are assisted by angels (v 4). Yet angels do not have superior status, since they acknowledge to John they are "fellow servants" (19:10; 22:8). As priests (1:6; 5:10), the saints have direct access to the throne. Thus, angels present our prayers, but do not make them acceptable. Nor do angels or saints intercede or mediate for us (1 Tim 2:5). Although our prayers are imperfect, God assists us supernaturally as we pray. No prayer is ever lost; every prayer we pray is added to the bowl. "You put my tears into your bottle when I cry out to you" (Psalm 56:8). "Prayers prayed in accordance with the

---

[156]Peterson, *Reversed Thunder,* 85.

[157]Mulholland, *Revelation,* 188.

will of God are never lost."[158]

The censer was filled with much incense and the answer was poured out (compare to Exod 9:8-10). The judgments upon earth — the thunder, rumblings, lightning, and earthquake were in answer to prayer (compare to Exod 19:16-19; Ps 18:6-19; Ezek 10:2-7). Ezekiel 9:4-6 describes those who are marked for protection, while the following chapter then describes the scattering of fire from the temple. John follows the same sequence in Rev 7:3 and 8:3-5. The seventh seal becomes the seven trumpets. Then the seven trumpets sound their warning in chapters 8-9 and the seven bowls are poured out in chapter 16. Everything that unfolds is simply the effect; the cause is the prayer of the persecuted church. Swete wrote, "The prayers of the saints return to the earth in wrath."[159] Thus, worship and warfare are connected.

This imagery is also based upon the concept of holy war. Under the old covenant, a holy war was initiated at God's command against extreme cases of immorality and blasphemy. Such peoples were placed under a ban. Fire was taken from the temple altar and used to burn up cities conquered in a holy war (Num 21:1-3; Josh 6:15-19; Judg 1:17; 20:40). This fire had originally fallen from heaven (Lev 9:25) and was to be maintained. God did not accept "strange fire" (Lev 10:1-4). Under the new covenant, the principle of holy warfare is advanced through prayer.[160] Fire is taken from the heavenly altar and cast down. In this instance, it is Jerusalem herself which is under the ban. Nothing under this curse will survive.

However, under the new covenant, we are now God's temple and what is voluntarily dedicated to God is spared as a living sacrifice (Rom 12:1). The true fire first fell at Pentecost and the fire on the altar in the old temple had become "strange fire" (see Lev 10:1). And so the fire from heaven cleanses us (see Isa 6:6) and that fire of the

---

[158]Duewel, *Touch the World Through Prayer*, 223.

[159]Swete, *Apocalypse,* 109.

[160]Bright, *The Authority of the Old Testament*, 243-251.

Spirit is not to be quenched (1 Thess 5:19; 2 Tim 1:6). Thus, fire from heaven either destroys or sanctifies.

In 5:8 the church has both harps and bowls. In 15:2 we see the church which has come through tribulation. While they retained their harps, they no longer have their bowls. Their bowls had been poured out. God had answered their prayers.

The Seven Seals Summary – Revelation 6:1-8:5

III. Seven seals 6:1-8:5
  A. Six seals 6:1-17
    1. First seal — the white horse 6:1-2
    2. Second seal — the red horse 6:3-4
    3. Third seal — the black horse 6:5-6
    4. Fourth seal — the pale horse 6:7-8
    5. Fifth seal — souls under altar 6:9-11
    6. Sixth seal — shaking of earth and heaven 6:12-16
Interlude — First fruits and final harvest 7:1-17
    1. The sealing of the first fruits 7:1-8
    2. The final harvest 7:9-17
  B. Seventh seal 8:1-5

Jesus opened the scroll with seven seals one seal at a time. After the sixth seal there was an interlude. As our prophet, Christ opens the seven seals which usher in the new covenant. While everything seems out of control, the early church is assured that God is demolishing the old in order to make way for the new.

Christ controls human history. It is Christ who breaks open the book of destiny and who rides out in conquest, leading the angelic army against those who rebel against his rule. He has ushered in the new covenant and avenges his church by sending judgment upon their enemies. He holds the book of destiny and opens the seals. As the executor of our inheritance, he opens the seals. But he must also evict the powers of darkness who have refused to surrender and vacate a creation they had held hostage.

If the scroll with seven seals represents the new covenant, then the opening of the seals would take place when the new covenant came into force. It is important to understand that these judgments come from God. They are called forth from his throne and executed by his angels.

IV. Seven trumpets 8:6-11:19

Verse 2 is a parenthetical introduction of the seven trumpets, referring to the order of service. Chapters 8-9 cover six of the seven trumpets. Beale wrote, "The trumpets must be seen as judgments ultimately executed as an expression of Christ's assumption of kingship and consequent sovereignty over history, following from the resurrection."[161]

During the six days of creation God created the earth, sun, moon, stars, firmament, animals, and man. When God brings judgment upon a people, he sends destruction or de-creation to their world. This should not be misunderstood as the end of the world, but it is the end of order, government, and their world. We have already seen with the breaking open of the seven seals that symbolically the earth was destabilized by earthquake, the sun went black, the moon became like blood, the stars fell, their land was occupied through Roman conquest, and the people themselves destroyed through famine and war.

This parallels with the people of God held captive in Egypt. God told Moses at the burning bush, "I have indeed seen the misery of my people in Egypt. I have heard them crying out because of their slave drivers, and I am concerned about their suffering. So I have come down to rescue them from the hand of the Egyptians" (Exod 3:7-8). So God raised up Moses and sent ten plagues: blood, frogs, gnats, flies, livestock, boils, hail, locusts, darkness, death. They were delivered 430 years after they moved to Egypt. This deliverance was celebrated in Psalm 78:42-55. Revelation 15:2-3 connects the deliverance of Moses and the Lamb. The message to the first century church is that while their exodus is preceded by plagues, the plagues will be followed by their deliverance.

The ultimate purpose of the Egyptian plagues was to glorify God. They were also an attack on the false gods of Egypt. And they served as a warning, then as punishment for unrepentant idolaters and perse-

---

[161]Beale, *NIGNT*, 468.

cutors. Now the people of God have broken covenant with God by rejecting his Son as their Messiah. And so God is destroying his old creation. He is creating a new Israel who will follow Jesus Christ. Just as Ishmael tormented Isaac (Gal 4:29), so the old heir to covenant blessing persecute the new people of God. The persecuted have become the persecutor. And the true sons of God cry out, "How long, Sovereign Lord, until you judge and avenge?" These seven trumpets serve the same purpose as the ten plagues. In fact, these six trumpet judgments are called *plagues* in 9:20 and in 8:12 the verb *smitten* or *struck* is the verb form of *plague.*

Just as the first six days around Jericho were a warning, so the first six trumpets also sound a warning, with their partial judgments of a third. This is not prediction that a third of the world's population will be destroyed. In chapters 8-9 the word *ge* is used seven times and refers to the land of Israel.

Third occurs twelve times in vv 7-12 and is based upon Ezekiel 5:2. Mercy is mingled with wrath. This is the beginning of birth pains (Matt 24:8), not the end of the world. God serves notice that he has exalted his Son, but mankind does not repent (9:20-21). The last trumpet is the battle horn.

Trumpets were used in warfare and worship. They symbolize God's intervention in history. Osborne wrote that in Jewish life there were at least twenty-one trumpet blasts daily in the temple; on feast days there were as many as forty-eight.[162] Trumpets were used to sound an alarm, warning Israel of approaching judgment and to summon the army for battle. In Numbers 10, trumpets were used to convene worship (v 3), to begin pilgrimages (v 5), as a call to war (v 9; Num 31:6; Judg 7:8-22; 2 Chr 13:12; Jer 20:16; Ezek 33:3; Hos 5:8; Amos 3:6), and to celebrate sacred feasts (v 10; Lev 25:9; Num 29:1; Neh 12:41; Ps 81:3). The old covenant was inaugurated by the blast of a trumpet (Exod 19:13, 16, 19; 20:18; Heb 12:19). In the Old Testament, trumpets were sounded as a call to repentance (Jer 4:5; 6:1, 17; Isa 58:1; Hos 8:1; Joel 2:15), to sound a retreat (2 Sam 2:28;

---

[162]Osborne, *BECNT*, 342.

18:16: 20:22), or to announce news (1 Sam 13:3).

Trumpets were also used in worship (1 Chr 16:6, 42; 2 Chr 5:12-13; Ps 47:5; 98:6) and processions (1 Chr 15:24). The most memorable procession in Israel was when they marched in silence around the walls of Jericho for six days. The seventh day they marched seven times. Then the trumpets sounded and the walls came down. Once again, at the sounding of the trumpets, the walls of opposition to the church will come down. And just as Egypt hardened itself against the judgment of God under the ten plagues, so chapter 9 closes with the report that the rest of mankind did not repent. But God would once again lead his people out of bondage and persecution.

In Israel trumpets were also blown to proclaim a new king (1 Kgs 1:34, 39; 2 Kgs 9:13). When the seventh trumpet sounds in 11:15, the kingdom of Christ is also announced.

Trumpets were also sounded to bring in the new year. The feast of trumpets marked Rosh Hashanah or beginning of the religious year. Here they mark the dawn of the day of the Lord. The prophets said trumpets would announce the day of the Lord (Isa 27:13; Joel 2:1; Zeph 1:14-16; Zech 9:14; Matt 24:31) and the return of Christ (1 Cor 15:52; 1 Thess 4:16).

These seven trumpets, while significant, are not to be interpreted literally. The first trumpet and first bowl both effect the land. The second trumpet and bowl both effect the sea. The third trumpet and bowl both effect the rivers and fountains. The fourth trumpet and bowl both effect the sun, the fifth trumpet and bowl both deal with darkness from beneath. The sixth trumpet and bowl both dry up the Euphrates River and the seventh both clear the air for the kingdom of God. Yet the seven bowl judgments are more intense and not divided into two sets of four and three.

This progressive judgment is consistent with the warning God gave in Deuteronomy 28 where Israel was told if they kept covenant with God that he would bless them. But they were also warned that they would come under a curse if they broke covenant. Disease, plague, drought, boils, darkness or blindness, foreign siege, and conquest would come until things would get so bad they would eat their own offspring, and finally uprooted from their land and scattered. This would be the "last days" for Israel as the people of God. They would be cut off as Paul warned in Romans 11:17-21.

It is significant that this warning in Deuteronomy came on the heels of the plagues of Egypt. Just as God gave Pharaoh ample opportunity to repent, so these warnings were progressive and would not all come at once. But once they began, they would intensify and the backslider would know from the judgment which had already come exactly what was going to come if he persisted in rebellion. God would continue to tighten the screws. At the end of the seals (6:16) and near the end of the trumpets (9:6) both speak of those who sought death and could not find it. Josephus said that during the siege of Jerusalem that those who survived "called them that were dead happy."[163]

Deuteronomy 28 and the judgments described in symbolic language in Revelation reveals that everything John described in Revelation was included in the warning of Moses. And if we study the history of the siege of Jerusalem from AD 67-70 we would see that it all happened at that time. While there have been other times of crisis in the history of the world, the importance of the siege of Jerusalem is that old Israel had rejected the Messiah and was persecuting the church. They had broken covenant with God and brought his wrath upon themselves. Carpenter concluded, "Perhaps no period in the world's history has ever been so marked by these convulsions as that which intervenes between the Crucifixion and the destruction of Jerusalem."[164]

It is generally understood that the seals, trumpets, and bowls are parallel and cover the same period of time. Yet their sequence varies. The trumpets repeat the revelation of the seals but are a call to repentance. The bowls repeat the message but reveal God pouring out his judgment. Whedon saw the function of the seals as revelation, the

---

[163]Josephus, *Wars of the Jews*, 4.6.3 (see also 5.10.5; 5.13.6).

[164]Carpenter, *Ellicott's Commentary*, 6:146. See also Josephus, *Wars*, 4.4.5.

trumpets as proclamation.

God's message back to his people throughout this book is that he will act soon. He will act through his Son whom he has appointed to be the judge. As our prophet, Christ opened the seven seals which usher in the new covenant. As our king, Christ is announced by the seven trumpets. As our priest, Christ will pour out the seven bowls. The judgments which are described in terms of seals broken, trumpets sounded, and bowls poured out correspond to the plagues of Egypt. Yet they are not exact repetitions. Six of the ten plagues are duplicated, sometimes more than once, in the judgments of Revelation.[165]

While the judgment described by the trumpets is worse than the seals, and the judgment of the bowls is worse than the trumpets, they all seem to be describing the same events from three perspectives. It is significant that as the seals are broken a fourth of the earth is killed (6:8). In five of the seven trumpets we are told that a third of whatever is destroyed. In the bowl judgments, which are God's final judgment on apostate Israel, the destruction is total.

A. Six trumpets 8:6-9:21

Revelation 8 covers the first four trumpet warnings. The first four trumpets are grouped together, just as the four horsemen were a unit. These four judgments describe a disruption of nature (Rom 8:20-22). Fire and blood were cast down to the earth. The sun, moon, and stars fell (see Luke 21:25). The first three trumpets all involve the fire of divine wrath from the censer (v 5): vegetation is burned up, a burning mountain is cast into the sea, a blazing star falls. However, the fourth trumpet describes a fire which has burned out and turned to darkness.

These four judgments could be summarized by the words of Joel,

---

[165]Four trumpet judgments correspond to Egyptian plagues and five bowl judgments correspond to the plagues of Egypt. When these two lists are combined, at total of six Egyptian plagues are symbolized in the trumpet and bowl judgments. This analysis also confirms the overlap of the trumpets and bowls.

quoted by Peter, "And I will show wonders in the heaven above and signs of the earth below, blood and fire and billows of smoke. The sun will be turned to darkness and the moon become as blood" (Acts 2:19-20). Peter said this was fulfilled at Pentecost (see the seventh trumpet in 11:19).

1. First trumpet 8:7

With the first trumpet comes hail and fire. This is the result of the fire which was cast down from heaven in v 5. This storm is based on Exodus 9:23-26, which records hail and lightning as part of the seventh plague. grass and trees are destroyed. Josephus recorded that the invading Roman army scorched the vegetation through their methods of warfare.[166] However, this fire is mixed with blood, which also incorporates the first Egyptian plague (Isa 9:5; Ezek 21:32; 38:22). Luke 13:1 speaks of the blood of some Galileans who were put to death by Pilate as they offered their sacrifice. Thus, their blood was mixed with sacrifice. In this instance the blood is that of the early martyrs, while the fire is God's judgment on their persecutors. Joel 2:30 also speaks of blood and fire, which Peter said was fulfilled at Pentecost (Acts 2:19).[167]

2. Second Trumpet 8:8-9

The second trumpet turned water into blood, just as the Nile was turned to blood in the first plague on Egypt. Again, Josephus described a battle in which the Romans pursued many Galileans to the sea of Galilee and slaughtered them there, so that the sea over a wide

---

[166]Josephus, *Wars of the Jews*, 6.1.1. He also recorded trees cut down for warfare [*Wars*, 3.7.8; 5.6.2; 5.12.4].

[167]Wesley's comments on Acts 2:19 elaborate on the events which preceded the destruction of Jerusalem [*Notes,* 278-279]. See also the comment of Josephus that Galilee was all over filled with fire and blood [*Wars*, 3.4.1].

area was full of blood and dead bodies.[168] Here John describes something *like* a great burning mountain. The particle *hos* serves as a reminder that this is not literal.[169] Jeremiah 51:25 also speaks of a destroying mountain. Jeremiah was describing the kingdom of Babylon, which would sink to rise no more (vv 63-64). In Revelation 18:21, John compares Babylon with a large millstone thrown into the sea.

This fall of Babylon destroys the sea commerce which had captured the souls of men (18:11-19). As surely as Egypt and Babylon were destroyed, so will God destroy the covenant-breaking nation of Israel. In a context in which Jesus spoke of the destruction of the fig tree, symbolizing Israel, he also said that faith would move mountains (Matt 21:21). Thus, the mountains of opposition which threatened to destroy the church would be overcome by their faith.

3. Third trumpet 8:10-11

The third trumpet repeats the warning of the second trumpet by heralding a falling star, instead of a burning mountain, which poisoned the rest of their water supply. This symbol of bitter water was a reversal of the miracle recorded in Exodus 15:23-25. This star was named *Wormwood*, a reference to Deuteronomy 29:18, Proverbs 5:4, Jeremiah 9:15; 23:15, Lamentations 3:15, 19, and Amos 5:7. Isaiah 14:12-15 also describes a fallen star, the king of Babylon.

Hebrews 12:15 describes a bitter root which defiles many. Steve Gregg wrote that the bitter herbs at the Paschal meal still remind the Jews of the bitterness of Egyptian bondage. Their rescue from Egypt

---

[168]Josephus, *Wars of the Jews*, 3.9.3. Holford said 4200 dead bodies were strewn along the coast [*Destruction of Jerusalem*, 26]. See Josephus, *Wars,* 3.10.9; 4.7.6, for similar accounts.

[169]*Hos* occurs again in v 10; 9:2, 3, 5, 7-10, 17, 19. This particle occurs a total of 65 times in Revelation.

is described as a "healing" in Hosea 11:1-3.[170] The bitter water here symbolizes the Jewish apostasy from the fountain prophesied in Zechariah 13:1 (see also Jer 8:14; 9:15; 23:15). But the gospel will ultimately heal the nations (22:2).

4. Fourth trumpet 8:12

The fourth trumpet corresponds to the sixth seal in 6:12-13. This judgment brought darkness. The ninth plague of Egypt was thick darkness (see Amos 8:8-9). Now the lights go out for Jerusalem. If we conceive of the Roman leaders as great lights, during this same time many were committing suicide or were assassinated. Farrar wrote that

> Ruler after ruler, chieftain after chieftain of the Roman Empire and the Jewish nation was assassinated and ruined. Gaius, Claudius, Nero, Galba, Otho, Vitellius, all died by murder or suicide; Herod the Great, Herod Antipas, Herod Agrippa, and most of the Herodian Princes, together with not a few of the leading High Priests of Jerusalem, perished in disgrace, or in exile, or by violent hands. All these were quenched suns and darkened stars.[171]

Generally it was becoming a time of spiritual darkness and deception. The Jewish people were divided into two factions and they fought each other, when they were not fighting the Romans. The insanity, warned against in Deuteronomy 28:28-34, called madness, blindness, and confusion, prevailed. Women did eat their own offspring. Jesus had warned that such a time would come (Luke 21:25-26), but while that was happening on earth, in heaven he was being seated at the right hand of the Father (Luke 21:27-28; Dan 7:13-14).

---

[170]Gregg, *Revelation: Four Views,* 216.

[171]Farrar, *The Early Days of Christianity,* 519.

a. First woe 8:13-9:11

The phrase *then I looked and heard* begins a new section, which divides the last three trumpets from the first four. Thus, v 13 should begin chapter 9. This chapter ends with a warning of woe to the inhabitants of the earth (see 3:10; 6:10), because there are three more trumpets to be sounded. The word *woe*, which announces calamity, is never repeated three times anywhere except here. It is repeated three times to announce the three trumpets yet to come. The second woe will come in 9:12-21 and the third woe in 11:14-19.

The best Greek manuscripts have the word *eagle*. Perhaps the angel appeared in the form of an eagle. Notice that Hosea 8:1 ties together the symbolism of a trumpet warning and an eagle about to descend upon Israel. While the Greek word *aetos* can mean either "vulture" or "eagle," in Exodus 19:4, after the Jewish exodus from Egypt, God compares himself to an eagle. Yet God can work through ungodly nations to punish Israel. Clarke observed that the eagle was the symbol of the Romans.[172] Israel was warned in Deuteronomy 28:49 that if they broke covenant, an eagle would swoop down upon them. Note also in Matthew 24:28 there is a reference by Jesus to the gathering of eagles, which Clarke interpreted again as the Roman armies. Those vultures gathered at the carcass of Israel. And yet this eagle, flying high, is a reminder to the church that these plagues are birth pains of a new day. In 12:14 this eagle brings deliverance to those who keep covenant.

---

[172]Clarke, *Commentary*, 6:1000.

REVELATION 9

5. Fifth Trumpet 9:1-11

Chapter 9 was introduced in 8:13 with the designation that the last three trumpets were called *woes*. Again notice that the trumpets, as the seals, are divided into four and two, then the last trumpet. The trumpets warn of the total destruction of the Jewish nation which will follow in the bowl judgments. The last three trumpets are warnings of *woe*. Clarke commented,

> These woes are supposed by many learned men to refer to the destruction of Jerusalem. *The first woe* — the seditions among the Jews themselves. *The second woe* — the besieging of the city by the Romans. *The third woe* — the taking and the sacking of the city, and burning of the Temple. This was the greatest of all the woes, as in it the city and temple were destroyed, and nearly a million of men lost their lives.[173]

This chapter opens with the description of a fallen angel (see 8:10). John did not see this *star* fall; he described a star which had fallen. This star or fallen angel is identified in v 11 as a king named Abaddon in Hebrew or Apollyon in Greek, both of which mean *destroyer*. In chapter 12 he is called "that ancient serpent, the devil or Satan" (v 9). He fell because he rejected truth and became the father of lies (John 8:44). He also came under judgment because of his pride (1 Tim 3:6).

He influenced a minority of the angels, which 12:4 designates as *a third*. 2 Peter 2:4 tells us that there were angels who sinned. Jude 6 tells us that these angels did not keep their positions of authority but

---

[173]Clarke, *Commentary*, 6:1006. To the first woe, which comprised the rebellion of the Jewish zealots, I would also add the actions of Gessius Florus, governor of Caesarea, who incited much of that rebellion. Farrar described this uprising in *The Early Days of Christianity,* 478-482.

abandoned their own home. They lost their place in heaven. Jesus said, "I saw Satan fall like lightning from heaven" (Luke 10:18). Apparently this fall occurred prior to Genesis 3.

John saw this star (Satan) which had fallen from heaven to earth (9:1). John begins here with a reference to an event which had already occurred. Satan then releases demonic spirits, symbolized as locusts. Literal locusts did come in the eighth plague upon Egypt (Exod 10:12-15). And Deuteronomy 28:38, 42 warned that if Israel broke covenant with God that he would send the plagues of Egypt upon them (vv 27, 60), which included locusts (see also Amos 4:9). Jeremiah 46:23; 51:14; Nahum 3:15-17 all incorporate the image of a locust invasion to describe a military invasion sent by God. However, these *locusts* cannot be literal because they were commanded not to harm grass, plants, or trees — precisely what locusts always destroy. Thus, the famine resulting from locusts, which Joel prophesied, has been spiritualized.

In response to the prayers of the saints which rose like incense, God allowed the abyss to be opened and demons rose from beneath like smoke to punish those who had persecuted the church. This smoke obscures the sun and sky creating darkness (v 2; see 8:12; Joel 2:10, 30-31). These *locusts* were demons who were allowed to torment those who were not sealed (7:3). Their torment, compared to the agony of a scorpion sting, was so severe that their victims sought death.

Compare this description of locusts to Joel's description (Joel 2:3-10). It is a frequent observation that the head of a locust resembles a horse head (see Joel 2:4). Yet these *locusts* have long hair, scorpion tails, and human faces. On their heads appeared to be crowns (*stephanos*). The text does not say they actually had crowns. While this is the only instance in Revelation where *stephanos* is used to describe anyone other than Christ and the saints, even in this instance this appearance which resembled a crown was not real nor did it symbolize a permanent victory.

Teeth like lion's teeth is a reference to Joel 1:6, and describes an insatiable appetite. The thorax is covered by a breastplate of iron.

Without attempting to assign significance to each part, the overall description is a combination of man and beast, resulting in an unnatural and demonic figure. Verse 9 describes their roaring sound as the thundering of horses and chariots. Again, this is drawn from Joel 2:5.

In his description of the siege of Jerusalem, Josephus wrote of the Jewish paramilitary zealots, led by Simon of Gerasa, who moved through the countryside of Edom, saying that "as one may see all the woods behind despoiled of their leaves by locusts, after they have been there, so was there nothing left behind Simon's army but a desert."[174] Josephus also told of gangs of Jewish zealots who terrorized the citizens of Jerusalem. They dressed like women, complete with long hair and makeup, but would suddenly draw their swords and become fighting men.[175] Certainly they were demon possessed, just as the militant homosexual movement of today. Whenever society rejects the Word of God, all the latent evil forces come to the surface. This is the opening of the abyss.

However, the demons were subject to God's control. Satan was given a key (v 1), but Christ holds the keys (1:18). In contrast, an angel from heaven has the key to the abyss in 20:1. This good angel came down from heaven in 10:1 and 18:1, while the angel in 9:1 had fallen from heaven.

The demons which were released were under God's restraint and permissive will (v 5). God is sovereign and can use the devil to advance his own plan. "The fact that the demons are enchained does not mean that they are completely devoid of power and utterly without influence in the world," wrote Bahnsen.

> They have been committed to chains from the time of their fall into sin, and yet the Gospel records show them to have

---

[174]Josephus, *The Wars of the Jews,* 4.9.7.

[175]Josephus, *The Wars of the Jews*, 4.9.10. *Satyr* was a Hebrew word for demon used in the Old Testament in Lev 17:7; 2 Chron 11:15; Isa 13:21; 34:14, which meant "hairy goat" or "hairy demon."

> been extensively active, just as Revelation 9 teaches that God makes them serve His purposes in history. Thus, being enchained does not imply being destroyed or immobilized; it simply signifies that the demons are strictly under God's control and restrained in their activities. Their operations never set them free from the ultimate end to which God's chains have assigned them.[176]

What was the significance of a five-month period (vv 5, 10)? Biologically, locusts have a five-month life span. In May, 66 Gessius Florus, appointed the governor of Caesarea by Nero, began to terrorize the Jews killing 3600 peaceful citizens over a five-month period. Florus did this in an attempt to incite the Jews to rebel, although Satan was actually behind it. He also raided the temple treasury, claiming the money was owed Rome. Josephus dates the beginning of the Jewish War from this occasion.[177] But those who were sealed by God would only witness a short period of upheaval, then would flee Jerusalem to Pella. Just as the plagues of Egypt did not harm the Israelites (Exod 8:22-24; 9:4-7, 26; 10:21-23), the evil one cannot harm them (1 John 5:18) through these plagues (v 20). Just as the church at Smyrna was prepared for ten days of persecution (2:10), so the church in Jerusalem is here prepared for five months of instability. Yet these brief periods of tribulation, when evil appears to be in control, will be followed by a "thousand years" of peace.

b. Second woe 9:12-21

Verse 12 serves as a division between the first and second woe, as well as a transition between the fifth and sixth trumpets. The "locust plague" of Gessius Florus beginning in May 66 incited a Jewish rebellion, which provoked Cestius Gallus to invade Palestine

---

[176]Bahnsen, "Person, Work, and Present Status of Satan," 17-18.

[177]Josephus, *The Wars of the Jews,* 2.14.3-2.22.2.

in the fall with large numbers of mounted troops from the region of the Euphrates. This constituted the second woe. After ravaging the countryside, his forces arrived at the gates of Jerusalem in November 66 but were unable to make any progress for five days.

Then, when it appeared that victory was attainable, Cestius unexplainably withdrew his forces. It was during this lull that the Christians inside Jerusalem escaped to Pella, following the command of Jesus in Matthew 24:15-21.[178] Not one Christian perished because they had been sealed. This lull, from November 66 to Spring 67, was given by God to allow time for Jerusalem to repent. Instead, it emboldened the zealots to believe they could defeat Rome. They became over confident from their resistance of Florus and Cestius and miscalculated their success. They believed the temple was invincible and that the entire city was under divine protection. They also believed that Nero was approaching his end and that the Roman empire would end with him.[179]

Nero replaced Cestius with Vespasian and his son, Titus in Spring 67. It was the final siege of Jerusalem under Titus that constitutes the third and final woe.[180] At the very time that the seventh trumpet is sounded in chapter 11, we are told that the gentiles would trample on Jerusalem for 42 months (11:2). This is 3½ years, the duration of the siege on Jerusalem in AD 67-70.

6. Sixth trumpet 9:13-21

The sixth trumpet was sounded in 9:13-21. This is an intensification of the fifth trumpet, with the added woe of death (v 18). In response to the Jewish uprising, described under the fifth trumpet, the Romans invaded Palestine. Yet behind the scene, this action is both

---

[178]McClintock and Strong, *Cyclopedia*, 3:728.

[179]Renan, *Antichrist*, 138-139; 254-255.

[180]Josephus, *The Wars of the Jews*, Book 2-Book 6; Farrar, *The Early Days of Christianity*, 473-474.

in response to the prayers of the Christians which have ascended to the golden altar of incense (v 13; 6:9-10; 8:3) and in response to God's predestination (v 15). God has determined the exact moment — the year, month, day, and hour when the four angels would be released. John does not explicitly state this time, but only assures the people of God that God is in control and that things happen on his time table.

The voice in v 13 came from the altar with horns, or corner projections, the altar of incense (see Exod 30:2, 10). This voice represents a personification of the altar. Again in 16:7 the altar speaks. The Greek text indicates that it was a single or solitary voice. Mounce understood this to signify "the universal desire of the church."[181] Thus, the church speaks with one voice.

Since these four angels were bound, they should be understood as demonic spirits. Notice in 7:1 four angels held back the four winds. The four winds of 7:1 are these four evil spirits. However, this time they are at the Euphrates River and not at the four corners of the earth.

The Euphrates River ran through Babylon. The Euphrates River, which will come up again in 16:12, refers to the region where sin first entered this world. It marked the northern boundary between Israel and their pagan neighbors (Gen 15:18; Josh 1:4). This had been the traditional location of Israel's enemies. The Assyrians, Babylonians, and Persians had all invaded Israel from the north. Thus, the boundary which had protected the city of God from the city of man has now been removed. Even though John is describing an invasion of Romans from the west, at that time the dominion of Rome extended to the Euphrates and Titus drew troops from Syria and the Euphrates region.[182]

This Roman invasion was demoniacally inspired, yet it was also orchestrated by God. God uses the devil to advance his own agenda.

---

[181]Mounce, *NICNT,* 193.

[182]Josephus, *Wars*, 5.1.6.

As Samuel Rutherford said, "The devil is but God's master fencer, to teach us to handle our weapons."[183]

There is no basis for insisting that the number of the troops was literally 200 million. In Greek it literally reads a double myriad of myriads or an indefinite number. *Chiliad* was the highest word for a number in Greek; it meant a thousand. *Myriad* is an indefinite number (see 5:11). Twice 10,000 x 10,000 does equal 200,000,000 but we must remember John is counting demon spirits (vv 7-11; 17-19). Apparently it is the horses, not the riders, which bring judgment. The *horses* in v 17 are the *locusts* of v 7. There are four similarities: both focus on men, both have power in their tails, both appear as horses, and both have breastplates.

John reminds the reader that this is a vision (v 17) and therefore symbolic. The comparative particle (*hos*), which means *like* or *as* is used ten times in this chapter, the adjective (*homoios*), which also means *like* occurs four times, and (*homoioma*), a noun from *homoios*, which indicates resemblance in used in v 7.

The description of these "horses and riders" links them to the fire and smoke and brimstone associated with the destruction of Sodom and Gomorrah (Gen 19:24, 28). Only in this account of Sodom and Gomorrah are the words fire, smoke, and brimstone used together in the Old Testament. Red is associated with fire, blue with smoke, and yellow with the sulfur or brimstone. These colors symbolize the source of their power and the sulfur, in particular, connects them with the lake of fire (14:10-11; 19:20; 20:10; 21:8).

Verse 18 describes the destructive results of the three plagues of fire, smoke, and sulfur. These demons employ the same strategy which was used by the devil in the garden. The smoke and darkness depicted in this chapter symbolize obscurity and deception. According to v 19, their power is in their mouth. Verse 19 adds another symbol of evil; their tails were like snakes (12:9; 20:2).

Thus, these *horses* are evil from head to tail (Joel 2:3). When this

---

[183]Rutherford, *Letters*, 290. See Judg 2:21-3:2 for a scriptural example of this principle.

aspect of judgment is retold in 16:12-14 John will see three unclean, frog-like, spirits emerge from the mouths of the dragon, the beast, and the false prophet. Satan's ability to steal, kill, and destroy (John 10:10), lies primarily in his ability to deceive. During the siege of Jerusalem this deception was demonstrated in the factions which divided the Jewish population, the fanatical zealots, the false Messiahs which arose almost daily, and the Jewish refusal to accept the offers of peace made by Titus.

Chilton summarized the final stages of the siege, as depicted by Josephus:

> The loss of all ability to reason, the frenzied mobs attacking one another, the deluded multitudes following after the most transparently false prophets, the crazed and desperate chase after food, the mass murderers, executions, and suicides, the fathers slaughtering their own families and the mothers eating their own children. Satan and the host of hell simply swarmed throughout the land of Israel and consumed the apostates.[184]

In spite of the torment, those who survived did not repent. Nor did Pharaoh repent when he witnessed the ten plagues of Egypt. Instead, he hardened his heart. Yet in spite of God's message of warning, many choose not to hear it.

Vespasian and Titus marched toward Judea in the spring of AD 67, and for fifteen months they devastated all the strong areas in Galilee and western Judea, killing at least 150,000. They proceeded only as far as Jericho, however, before receiving word that Nero died on June 9, 68. Therefore, they awaited new orders. The lapse between the appointment of Vespasian in Spring 67 and the final assault on Jerusalem in June 69 constituted a second opportunity for repentance. Holford wrote, "Thus the Almighty gave the Jews a second respite, which continued nearly two years; but they repented not of their

---

[184]Chilton, *Days of Vengeance*, 246.

crimes, neither were they in the least degree reclaimed, but rather proceeded to acts of still greater enormity."[185]

Mulholland suggested that the rest of mankind in v 20 represents a third group of humanity. While one group is sealed by God and a second group has been judged by God, there is always a third group — those who still have a choice between life and death.[186] Yet they continued to worship demons and idols. Demonic power is behind all idolatry. The *and* in v 20 is probably epexegetical, or an additional explanation, meaning the unrepentant worshiped demons, *which were* idols. Deuteronomy 32:16-17; Psalm 96:5; 106:37 make the same point. MacArthur explained, "When people worship idols, gods that do not exist, demons who do exist will impersonate those gods and hold those idolaters captive to their demonic power and deception."[187]

These idols are impotent; they cannot see, hear, or walk. Here John alludes to Psalm 115:4-7. Idolatry not only included the emperor worship of the Romans, but Stuart argued that many Jews were heathen in their practices. He pointed out that Judea was rife with all the crimes of v 21, during the time Palestine was invaded.[188]

There is a connection between what is worshiped and how people live. There is a link between idolatry and immorality. Murder, including abortion, sorcery, immorality, and theft are all interconnected. Here John appeals to the fifth, sixth, and seventh commandments, as a further indictment that the unrepentant had also broken the second commandment. Ladd observed that apocalyptic literature always envisioned the people of God under attack through foreign invasion, but here John sees this invasion as a divine judgment upon a corrupt

---

[185]Holford, *Destruction of Jerusalem*, 27.

[186]Mulholland, *Revelation,* 199.

[187]MacArthur, *Revelation 1-11*, 273.

[188]Stuart, *Apocalypse*, 2:201-203. Stuart cited Josephus, *Wars*, 4.9.10; 5.9.4; 6.2.1-2; 7.3.3 as examples of the wickedness of the Jews prior to the destruction of Jerusalem.

people.[189]

There will be another digression in chapter 10 and through the first half of chapter 11. Then the seventh trumpet will sound in the last half of chapter 11and the walls of Jerusalem will come down! This follows the same pattern as the seal judgments. The first four seals were opened as a group. Then two more came, followed by a digression in chapter 7. We returned to the last seal in chapter 8.

---

[189] Ladd, *Commentary*, 135.

REVELATION 10

Interlude – The little scroll and the two witnesses 10:1-11:13

After six seals were opened, there was an interlude before the final seal. Once again six trumpets have sounded and we move into another interlude before the final trumpet sounds. Between the three visions of judgment — the seals, the trumpets, and the bowls — the interludes provide perspective. The interlude within the seals focused on the protection of God's people. This interlude focuses on the proclamation of the gospel.

A. The sweet and sour book 10:1-11

Angels have been mentioned twenty-one times in the first nine chapters. This chapter opens with the introduction of another angel which is clothed with God's power, mercy, and glory. Tozer wrote, "Something of the splendor and glory of God at His throne clung to the angel as he moved from the heavenly scene to command the judgments of God on the earth."[190] While some angels apparently have more power and authority than others, the question is whether this angel is mighty or almighty. It is best to view the angel as a servant of Christ (22:16) and not Christ, since the incarnation is permanent.

Christ may have been the "angel of the Lord" before his incarnation, but Hebrews 1:4-14 is clear that Christ is superior to angels. While the book of Revelation may portray Christ symbolically as a lamb or a lion, it does not describe Christ as an angel. However, the voice in vv 4, 8, 11 may be the voice of Christ.

Three times in this chapter the mighty angel is portrayed as having one foot on land and the other foot on the sea (vv 2, 5, 8). "By having one foot on the land and the other on the sea, John was stressing the dominion of the angel over the whole world and the signifi-

---

[190]Tozer, *Jesus is Victor!*, 150.

cance of the message in the scroll for the whole world."[191] This angel came from heaven to stand on sea and land and that he swore by him who created heaven, earth, and sea. In so doing he not only emphasized God's sovereignty over all three realms, he was taking possession on behalf of Christ the King.[192] The act of swearing an oath is the basis for a covenant. Thus, the angel who swears is the same angel with the open book — an indication of the covenantal nature of the book. The rainbow above his head is also a sign of the covenant (Gen 9:12-17).

The little scroll is also significant. Chapter 5 described a book (*biblion*) sealed with seven seals. At this point six trumpets have sounded and again there is an interlude. The focus returns to the same book depicted in chapter 5 and another angel like the one who spoke in 5:2. However, the book is now described as an open book because the seals have all been broken off. It is also described three times in this chapter as a little book (*biblaridion*) because at this point it is open and contains only what remains to be fulfilled from chapter 5. Yet in v 8 John also calls it by the usual name, *biblion*. Tong explained that the little book was "probably the same that was before sealed, but was not opened, and gradually fulfilled by him."[193] With only one more trumpet to sound, the purpose of God will soon be accomplished (vv 6-7).

When the seventh angel sounds his trumpet, the old Jerusalem will fall and the new Jerusalem will be established. According to v 7 the mystery has been accomplished. God's mystery had been previously concealed, but now is revealed. Binney explained that God's scheme of redemption will be more and more clearly revealed, as the gospel develops itself to its fullest consummation at the end of the

---

[191]Osborne, *BECNT*, 396.

[192]In Josh 10:24 the victors place their foot on the neck of the defeated kings as a statement of sovereignty. So here the angel places his feet on land and sea, claiming the whole cosmos for Christ.

[193]Tong, *Matthew Henry's Commentary*, 6:1154.

world.[194] The church will no longer be centered in Judaism, but will be open to gentiles (Eph 3:3-6; Col 1:26-7).

In answer to the question "How long?" (6:10), the answer is that this will happen without delay (v 6). "Rev. 10:6 does not mean that time itself comes to an end. All that is meant is that the judgment of God will be delayed no longer."[195] In 6:11 the church was told that they must wait a little time. Now we are told that their wait is over. Tozer explained that the "time-out" has ended.[196] God had delayed his judgment forty years from the time of the crucifixion. Judgment would be delayed no longer. The execution of the will and establishment of the covenant, we are told, will not be delayed into the distant future.

The contents of this book were unfolded in the first century and accomplished at the time the seventh trumpet was sounded. In 11:15-19 the kingdom of the world became Christ's. Christ began to reign. The temple was opened, and judgment was poured out.

God not only revealed to the prophets *when* but *how* this mystery will be accomplished. Daniel explained that the kingdom of evil would be defeated as it broke the power of the holy people (12:7). "That is, the prophecy of God's defeat of the evil kingdom is being ironically fulfilled by this evil kingdom's apparent physical victory over the saints. God's people are already beginning to win spiritually in the midst of their physical defeat. Their enemies are already beginning to lose spiritually in the midst of their apparent physical victory."[197] This is an extension of the paradox of the cross. Caird wrote, "The persecution of the church is thus the secret weapon by which God intends to win his victory over the church's persecu-

---

[194]Binney, *Commentary*, 685. Binney also associated this mystery of redemption with Rev 14:6 and Matt 24:14.

[195]Delling, "χρόνος," *TDNT*, 9:592.

[196]Tozer, *Jesus is Victor!* 145-146.

[197]Beale, *NIGNT*, 544.

tors."[198]

In a general sense the book may be thought of as the Bible. Walvoord wrote, "The book itself seems to be a symbol of the Word of God as it is delivered to men, that is, divine revelation already given."[199] Specifically, the contents of the book declare the last days of the old covenant, God's divorce lawsuit against unfaithful Israel,[200] and the establishment of the new covenant, which is the content of Revelation. In chapter 5 only Christ was worthy to open the book and institute this covenant. Now five chapters have passed, in which the dissolution of the old covenant has been nearly finalized and the new covenant has been established. Now the emphasis is on trumpets, not seals. God has preached his mystery to the prophets. The verb in v 7 is *euangelizo*, the basis for our word "evangelize." As God reveals the gospel to us, we then become his messengers (*angelos*) and our message is contained in the book, the *biblos*, which we call the Bible. It is significant that the mighty angel is depicted as coming down from heaven with an open book. This symbolizes the supernatural origin of scripture. The Word of God is also portrayed as a sword coming out of the mouth of Christ (1:16; 2:16; 19:15, 21). Thus, the authority of the Word stems from its source.

We have been given sufficient revelation, but not exhaustive revelation. In v 4 John was told not to record the words spoken in a voice like seven thunders (compare to 2 Cor 12:4). Psalm 29 describes the voice of God as thunder and uses the word *voice* seven times. The voice of the Lord is powerful, full of majesty, breaks the cedars, divides the flames of fire, shakes the wilderness, makes the deer give birth, and strips the forest bare.

Just as seven is often used in Revelation to refer to something complete, so the sevenfold voice of God is a description of his com-

---

[198]Caird, *Revelation*, 128.

[199]Walvoord, *Revelation*, 173.

[200]The certificate of divorce is also called a *biblion* in Matt 19:7; Mark 10:4.

plete or full glory. We have yet to see the fullness of God's glory; the complete glory of God is still sealed. Daniel apparently knew more than he was allowed to tell. He was told to "close up and seal the worlds of the scroll until the time of the end" (Dan 12:4). Then about six hundred years later, in the time of the end of the old covenant, the seals were broken (Rev 5-6). Once more John is told to seal up some things because they pertain to the future and not to the first century church.

There is a parallel between Revelation 10 and Daniel 12. In Daniel 12:6 the question is raised, "How long will it be before these astonishing things are fulfilled?" (compare to Rev 6:10). Then an angel, clothed in linen, swore by him who is eternal (compare to Rev 10:6), that it would be for 3½ years. This same span of time will be referenced in Revelation 11:2-3. Basically, John is giving encouragement to the early church that by the end of the trumpet judgments, the great tribulation will be over and there will be no delay in the execution of God's plan. Israel's time is up and her temple is about to be removed (Rev 11).

According to v 8, God's Word is to be actively received. John is told to take the book for himself. God's revelation must be actively appropriated rather than passively received. Too many scholars stand in judgment over it, but John was told to receive it and assimilate it. John was literally told to *eat down* the little book. For the first time John does not merely watch, but he participates in the vision.

This same command was given to Ezekiel before he went out as God's spokesman (Ezek 2:8-3:3). Jeremiah also ate God's words (Jer 15:16). Amos 8:11 describes a famine, "not a famine of food or a thirst for water, but a famine of hearing the words of the Lord." "Man does not live on bread alone, but on every word that comes from the mouth of God" (Matt 4:4). How else can we take God's Word into the whole world except that we be full of it ourselves? God's Word is to be kept open. The New Testament was written in the common street language of the people, Koine Greek. One of the great results of the Reformation was that it once again put an open Bible back into the hands of the common people. The perfect participle used in vv 2 and 8 conveys the idea that the book, having been opened, is to remain open. "The little book should ever be kept open, and its contents unfolded to the people."[201]

God's Word must be preached. The only way we can continue to obey God's call is to keep preaching and the only way we can keep on preaching is to keep feeding upon the Word. In v 8 John is told to take the book and in v 11 John was told he must prophecy again. This was not a new commission for John, but another step in his original calling. John was exiled on a lonely island and may have thought his ministry was finished, but God was not finished with him. John would preach again before many people. And his prophecy is still being read today.

John was told, and discovered, that to have God's Word in one's mouth was as sweet as honey. Ezekiel had the same experience (Ezek 3:3) and so have all of God's true messengers. David wrote, "How sweet are your words to my taste, sweeter than honey to my mouth!" (Ps 119:103; 19:10).

Yet Christ is especially addressing the first century situation. The early church was preaching the gospel throughout the whole of the known world, yet they were being persecuted for doing so. Christ assures the church that they will be victorious. The kingdoms of this world will become the kingdoms of Christ, but it will come through persecutions, apostasies, and judgments. There was a bitterness in seeing the old Jewish religion pass away, but a joy in watching the kingdom of Christ spread. The scroll is sweet because there is no longer a delay in its accomplishment — the triumph of the church.

But John was also told and discovered that God's Word turned his stomach sour. The Old Testament prophets knew what this meant. While Ezekiel made no mention of the bitterness of the scroll, yet it was also opened and its message was words of "lament, mourning, and woe" (Ezek 2:9-10). There was still persecution ahead for the early church. John was on the isle of Patmos because he had faithfully preached God's Word (1:9), but the bitterness turned to sweetness as

---

[201]Clemance, *Pulpit Commentary*, 22:280.

Jesus Christ was revealed to him. "The way of victory is the way of the Cross."[202]

There may be bitterness, but we neutralize the sourness of our stomach by filling our mouth again with sweetness. When we quit preaching faith, love, and hope, we are overcome by bitterness. It caused Jeremiah pain and grief to announce judgment to his people. At times he wanted to quit the ministry, but the Word was in him and it burned like fire shut up in his bones (20:9).

The church must carry the gospel to many peoples, nations, languages, and kings. God's Word is to cover the earth. This phrase *peoples, nations, languages, kings* was previously used in 5:9 and 7:9. Yet only in this third of seven repetitions, *kings* is substituted for *tribes*.

Jesus told us to go into all the world and make disciples. John reminds us that this is our mission and we will finish the task. The Word of God will be preached everywhere before the end comes. This gospel will cover land and sea (Ps 2:8) and there will be no further delay. It will convert people within every race, nation, language, and culture. We must proclaim God's Word to a hungry world! We must place an open Bible in their hands!

---

[202]Caird, *Revelation*, 130.

REVELATION 11

In order to interpret this chapter, we must take into account three time indicators which place its fulfillment within the first century of the church:

- The temple is still standing. John says that for forty-two months the Gentiles will trample Jerusalem. This will result in the destruction of the temple. Clarke called this fact "another presumptive evidence that it was yet standing."[203] Thus, John was writing this prior to AD 70.

- But could not this temple merely symbolize the church? Although the church is portrayed symbolically in this chapter as the two witnesses, which are two olive trees and two lampstands, and the twenty-four elders, there is a mixture of literal and figurative language regarding the temple. "This mixture of literal and figurative language should not alarm us," according to Gentry, who pointed out that the earthly and heavenly temples are contrasted in Hebrews 8:5 and 9:24. In Galatians 4:22-26 Jerusalem below is contrasted with Jerusalem above and in Hebrews 12 historical Sinai is contrasted with spiritual Zion.[204]

Here John contrasts an earthly temple with a heavenly one, in order to teach us that the church is no longer centered in Jerusalem. This cannot be interpreted as the heavenly temple, as is the temple in v 19, because the outer court will be taken over by the Gentiles. If both Jew and Gentile are united in one church (Eph 2:11), why are the Gentiles segregated in this temple?

Therefore, to interpret the measuring of the temple merely as God's protection of the church is to miss the big point of this chapter. The *new* temple is the church. Old Israel is passed over, and the old

---

[203]Clarke, *Commentary*, 6:1005.

[204]Gentry, "A Preterist View of Revelation," 67.

temple destroyed, as God transfers his kingdom to the new and living way. But since the temple in heaven (v 19) is contrasted with the earthly temple (v 1), the earthly temple cannot merely be a figure of speech. And since it was a literal temple, it could not be measured after its destruction.

- Verse 8 implies that if bodies are lying in the street of Jerusalem, that Jerusalem was still standing. According to v 13 Jerusalem is still in existence. According to v 13 the events of vv 3-12 happened at the same time as the earthquake of vv 13, 19. Josephus recorded that before Titus, the Roman general, ever laid siege to Jerusalem,

> There broke out a prodigious storm in the night, with the utmost violence, and very strong winds with the largest showers of rain, with continued lightnings, terrible thunderings, and amazing concussions and bellowings of the earth, that was an earthquake. These things were a manifest indication that some destruction was coming upon men, when the system of the world was put into this disorder, and anyone would guess that these wonders foreshewed some great calamities that were coming.[205]

This historic earthquake is indicative of the spiritual earthquake which also occurred in the first century. Hebrews 12:18-29 speak of the establishment of the new covenant and the heavenly Jerusalem. What can be shaken — the old system — will be leveled. Christians are part of a kingdom that cannot be shaken.

- According to v 14, this is the time of the second and third woes.

---

[205]Josephus, *War of the Jews*, 4.4.5. This earthquake was also described in 6:12 and will be described again by John in 16:18-19. This earthquake made way for a kingdom that cannot be shaken (Heb 12:27).

Clarke said these woes refer to the destruction of Jerusalem.[206] In Matthew 23, just before Jesus describes the destruction of the temple and fall of Jerusalem, he pronounced seven *woes*.

Beale noted that "if the events described in 11:1-13 occurred chronologically after the 'no delay' in 10:6-7, then there would be a contradiction." Although the angel has sworn that there will be no delay, there would, in fact, be a delay before the seventh trumpet sounded. Therefore, 11:1-13 is not a chronological delay, but a parenthetical delay which is a literary device like the one John used in chapter 7.[207] If the trumpets were sounding a warning of judgment coming upon first century Jerusalem, then this chapter is dealing with the same time period. And if the trumpets recapitulate the seals, we are not dealing with the span of church history. Nor can all these events be projected into the future, if the scene of the opening of the seals is linked to the time of the ascension of Christ.

B. Measuring the temple 11:1-2

Jeremiah described the measuring line being stretched as Jerusalem was rebuilt (31:39). Ezekiel saw a man with a measuring rod and chapters 40-48 are given over to a description of the new temple. Ezekiel foresaw God dwelling with man and expressed it in the language of the Old Testament. Ezekiel described this temple as being filled with the glory of God. Then he saw water flowing from under the threshold of the temple until it flooded the whole earth. Jesus interpreted this in John 7:38-39. We are the temple of the Holy Spirit and rivers of living water flow from us. Therefore, this description from Ezekiel should not be interpreted as a literal temple to be built in the future. The covenant community forms the spiritual temple in which God's presence dwells and is the fulfillment of what

---

[206]Clarke, *Commentary*, 6:1006.

[207]Beale, *NIGNT*, 521.

Ezekiel saw. Thus, the book of Revelation redefines the vision of Ezekiel, stating both that there would be no temple (21:22) and that "now the dwelling of God is with men, and he will live with them (21:3).

Amos described the Lord measuring Israel with a plumb line (7:7-8). Zechariah saw a man with a measuring line measuring Jerusalem (2:1-2). Now John is given a measuring rod and told to measure the temple. Between the sixth and seventh seals, God's people were sealed. Between the sixth and seventh trumpets, God's temple was measured. In 21:15 John will see an angel measuring the new Jerusalem. However, the new Jerusalem has no temple.

The Jewish temple was about to be destroyed. It would literally be torn down block by block because the cornerstone, Jesus Christ had been rejected. The holy city would be trampled on for forty-two months (v 2; see also Dan 8:13-14; Zech 12:3; Luke 21:24). John is building on five layers of biblical tradition.

- In v 6 he refers to Elijah who shut off the rain for 3½ years (James 5:17). So Jerusalem will be judged the same length of time.

- Daniel had predicted that from the rebuilding of this temple until its destruction would be a period of 490 years (9:24-27). He specified that from the time the decree is issued to rebuild the temple until the Messiah came, 483 years would elapse — leaving seven. The public ministry of Jesus was 3½ years. Daniel also specified that in the middle of the last week Christ would confirm the new covenant which put an end to sacrifice and offering. We are now left with 3½ years to account for. John is telling us the same thing Daniel predicted — that the city will be invaded and the temple destroyed.

- The abomination of the temple under Antiochus Epiphanes, the Greek king, was from 167-164 BC. His persecution was foretold in Daniel 8:9-14; 11:21-39.

- Matthew opens with the genealogy from Abraham to Messiah which was forty-two generations. Now that the Messiah has come, in forty-two months the temple will be destroyed.

- The public ministry of Jesus Christ was 3½ years. It ended with his death and descent into hades for three days (compare to vv 8-9), followed by his resurrection and the establishment of his kingdom.

What John measures here is time. If Revelation 11:2 represents Gentiles, then the temple measurements are symbolic — perhaps they are a time line. Notice the chiasm that John uses in his measurement of time:

A 11:2 – 42 months
  B 11:3 – 1260 days
    C 11:9 – 3½ days
      D 12:14 time, times, and half a time [from Dan 7:25; 12:7]
    C′ 11:11– 3½ days
  B′ 12:6 – 1260 days
A′ 13:5 – 42 months

Destruction must take place. It is the judgment of God upon those who have rejected his Son. But the bigger picture of God's plan must not be overlooked. Actually the old temple was being leveled to make way for the new temple. There must be destruction before there can be construction. There is only one reason to measure, set stakes, and stretch plumb lines and that is *construction.* Metzger wrote, "Measuring is done in order to build and repair, and John is given a measuring rod so that he can restore and revive the church."[208]

Yet it is the inner court, not the entire temple area which is measured. It is significant that the Greek language has two words for *temple*: *naos* refers to the inner sanctuary, while *hieron* refers to the

---

[208]Metzger, *Breaking the Code,* 69.

entire temple area. *Hieron* is never used in a figurative sense in the New Testament and is never used by John in the book of Revelation. Nor is the temple in Jerusalem ever used in early Christian literature to symbolize Christians or the church.

In contrast, *naos* is used sixteen times in Revelation and is used in the New Testament symbolically for the church as indwelt by God (1 Cor 3:16-17; 6:19; 2 Cor 6:16; Eph 2:21-22; 1 Pet 2:5). *Naos* is used in vv 1-2 in reference to the Jewish temple and in v 19 in reference to the heavenly temple. Thus, the outward form of Judaism was destroyed, but the temple in heaven is opened and true spiritual worship was preserved (v 19; Heb 9:8; 10:19-20). Even though the temple would be destroyed, all that was essential — the "holy of holies" where the Shekinah glory of God dwelt — would not be destroyed. Since every believer may come boldly to the throne of grace, entering into the most holy place through the name of Christ, there is no longer any need for anything more of the physical temple.

Both the people of God and their enemies would be tested forty-two months. However, the church would rise above its opposition, while the apostate Jews would be leveled under their opposition. The destruction of the old temple prepared the way for the construction of the new temple of God, the church.

God's purpose is to dwell with man. God is building a building, but it is not a temple in Jerusalem. It is the holy temple described in Ephesians 2:19-22. According to 1 Corinthians 3:9, we are God's building. The old covenant was the scaffold and was taken down after the foundation was laid, the cornerstone set, and the building was constructed. As the temple of God is constructed of people from every nation, language, culture, and tribe, God is not going to put up the old scaffold again. The emphasis of 21:22 is "no temple," not a rebuilt temple.

Therefore, a rebuilt temple in Jerusalem would have no spiritual significance, if we are the temple of God and the new Jerusalem (Heb12:22-23). The book of Hebrews is clear that the new covenant is better. A rebuilt temple in Jerusalem would be a regression and the re-institution of animal sacrifices would be an insult to the finished work of Christ (Heb 10:1-12). Jesus Christ is our high priest forever (Heb 7-8) and the church constitutes a kingdom of priests.

While Zechariah 14 anticipated the expansion of Christ's kingdom, v 21 refers to sacrifices. How are sacrifices and a return to Old Testament ritual consistent with the new covenant? The answer lies in the concept of accommodated language. God reveals truth to us in terms we can understand. While Ezekiel spoke of the "house of God" in terms of a temple — even giving its dimensions, and while Abraham was promised land, when we get into the New Testament the emphasis on land disappears (see Heb 11:10 where the emphasis is on the city of God). We become the temple of Ezekiel as we are indwelt by the Spirit (1 Cor 6:19). The sacrifices we offer are the sacrifices of praise (1 Pet 2:5). But Zechariah could not describe to a Jewish audience how God's kingdom would function except to use language with which they were familiar. Sacrifice denotes worship and there will come a time when God will be worshiped universally, though not under Old Testament ritual.

John was also instructed to measure the altar of sacrifice within the temple. Hebrews 13:10-16 also spiritualizes this altar, teaching that Christ is our altar.

Finally, John was commanded to measure the worshipers of the temple. Specifically, John is to measure the true worshipers of the inner sanctuary. These true worshipers are witnesses of Jesus Christ.

C. Two witnesses 11:3-13

The two witnesses (v 3) have the spirit of Moses and Elijah. While John did not name Moses and Elijah, they symbolize the ministry of the early church. Moses and Elijah came back to earth and met with Jesus on the Mount of Transfiguration (Matt 17:3) and Jesus spoke with them about his departure. Moses stands for the law, while Elijah stands for the prophets. "The law and the prophets" or "Moses and the prophets" were commonly used phrases referring to God's Word (Luke 16:29; Acts 13:15).

Therefore, the symbolism is that the true temple of God is

marked by the faithful proclamation of God's Word. This is in contrast to the apostate Jewish religion which honored the law and the prophets with their lips, but rejected the central figure of the law and the prophets — Jesus Christ.

The church is also symbolized by the two candlesticks and the two olive trees. The witnesses are called lampstands because their message is to burn like a lamp (see John 5:35). We dare not cover the light (Matt 5:14-16) or Christ will remove our lampstand (Rev 2:5). We are to proclaim Christ to the nations. And the lampstand is supplied by the olive tree (Zech 4:3, 12). Without the continuous flow of oil, which symbolizes the Holy Spirit (Zech 4:6), the light soon goes out. The church of Jesus Christ is the light of the world.

This corporate interpretation of the two witnesses is justified because in Revelation 1 it is seven congregations which are described as lampstands. The beast makes war against the entire church (v 7; Dan 7:21; Rev 12:17; 13:7), not simply two individuals. The two witnesses in 11:7 are the saints in 13:7. In 6:9, 12:11, 17; 19:10 and 20:4 the church is described collectively as those who testify. While the verb *nikao* is used seventeen times in this book to describe either the triumph of Christ or the church, here at 11:7 and 13:7 are the only two references where it is used of the triumph of evil. In both instances the victory of the beast is temporary.

Zechariah 4 describes one lampstand, while this passage mentions two. Here the two lampstands represent the word of God in the twofold sense of Old Testament prophecy and New Testament confirmation. In Zechariah the two trees refer to Joshua the priest and Zerubbabel the prince. John speaks of two trees, two lampstands, and two witnesses — all a reference to the church as a kingdom of priests and a reflection of the character of Christ. Just as Joshua and Zerubbabel were employed in building up and establishing the ancient temple and church, so, under the new testament, "faithful leaders and teachers are employed in building up the new and spiritual commonwealth of Christianity."[209]

---

[209]Stuart, *Apocalypse*, 2:229.

Moses was also used of God to turn the waters into blood — one of the plagues on Egypt. The connection here is that just as Egypt was judged and God's people were delivered, so now Jerusalem is being judged and God's new people will be delivered. Notice that v 8 calls Jerusalem spiritual Sodom and Egypt. John is speaking figuratively, and while the whole book is figurative, he reminds us again here so that we will not miss his message. The holy city was apostate and thus linked to the rebellion of Sodom and the bondage of Egypt, as well as the adultery of Babylon and the idolatry of Rome. Therefore, Jerusalem was under God's judgment. Just as Elijah shut off the rain for 3½ years (James 5:17), so Jerusalem's judgment would last the same length of time. Unbelieving Israel has been excluded to the outer court of the temple and are no longer counted. The remnant who believe in Christ are in the inner temple. Their worship alone counts. Stuart observed that John measured the *inner* temple for preservation, while all the rest of it is devoted to ruin. "The *essence* of the ancient religion is to be preserved, and is incorporated with Christianity, while all that was merely exterior and ritual is abolished."[210]

Zerubbabel and Joshua represented prince and priest; Moses and Elijah represented prince and prophet. All three offices are combined in Christ. The first pair rebuilt the temple, while the second pair talked with Christ on the mountain of transfiguration (Matt 17:2). Christ is our temple (John 2:19) and the glory of that temple.

Thus, the early church was prepared by John's revelation. John had a message that was both bitter and sweet. The good news was that the church would be protected from Jewish persecution. The original Jewish converts were sealed (7:1-8). They would be protected (v 5) so that they could witness to the truth. Thus, the early church is portrayed as the 144,000 which are sealed, as well as the two witnesses which are martyred.

In the early chapters of Acts, the opposition was restricted so that the message could become established. The gospel was preached over the known world, attested by signs and wonders. In those early days,

---

[210]Stuart, *Apocalypse*, 2:139.

when an apostle was locked up in prison, God let him out. Just as God had made his words a fire in the mouth of Jeremiah (Jer 5:14), so God has made the words of the two witnesses a fire. Just as Elijah had called down fire upon his enemies, so the early church was under the protection of God (v 5).

But divine sanction did not prevent persecution from coming. The bad news is that they would not be protected from Roman persecution. They would bear witness against the Jews, but be put to death by the Romans. According to v 7, they will be persecuted from another enemy — the beast. This is the second great enemy of the people of God. The beast will be the focus of chapter 13 and this is his first mention. John makes this reference without an introduction since it is a familiar concept from Daniel 7. Revelation 13 will identify the beast as the Roman Empire. In 13:5-7 we are told that the beast makes war with the saints and to conquer them, and that he was given forty-two months. Therefore, their preaching to the Jews and their persecution by the Romans occur during the same forty-two-month span.

Why did Christ allow his body, the church, to be persecuted? Because the servant is not above the Master (Matt 10:22-24) and because the world still hates truth (John 3:19). Jesus himself, is also the temple of God (John 2:19-22). The Lord God and the Lamb are the temple of the new Jerusalem (21:22). Beale wrote, "There is no reason to limit this identification to the new, future Jerusalem, since the identification began to be made when Christ was resurrected, and the resurrected Christ is the central feature of the heavenly temple scene in Rev 1:12-20."[211] His public ministry was 3½ years. Notice that Christ is called the "faithful witness" in 1:5 and 3:14. Then the Romans, with Jewish cooperation, crucified this temple and *three* days later God raised it up again. Jesus gave the sign of the prophet Jonah that he would be three days and three nights in the heart of the earth (Matt 12:40). Then he arose and ascended to his throne (vv 15-19).

---

[211]Beale, *NIGNT*, 562.

The message to the early church was that as the body of Christ they would be persecuted by Rome, with Jewish cooperation. They witnessed for Christ during the 1260 days, or 42 months, or 3½ years of Roman persecution — the same length of time as the ministry of Jesus. Then for 3½ days they lay dead in the street. This corresponds to the prophecy of Jesus in Matthew 24:9-13 and Luke 13:9-13; 21:12-16.

There is interplay between years and days. John is comparing the witness of the church to the testimony of Christ. John is comparing the death of the church to the death of Christ. In both instances, when it looked like they were finished, God raised them up.

The symbolic message to the church was that her witness would be measured in years, while her persecution would be measured in days. John made this same point in 2:10, where he told the church at Smyrna that they would have ten days of persecution. On the other hand, the devil knows his time is short (12:12). Because his time is running out, he intensifies his efforts. Yet to a persecuted church, that short time seems long. While Satan is bound for a thousand years, he is loosed for a "short time" (20:3). John gave these comparisons in order to provide perspective to a persecuted church.

But why would God allow his church to be temporarily defeated? This is simply an extension of the paradox of the cross, discussed in the previous chapter. The church cannot fail and Satan cannot succeed, but we must accept this truth by faith because our perception is often the opposite.

When the Christians in Jerusalem saw the events predicted by Jesus in Matthew 24 shaping up, they fled to the mountainous region of Pella before the actual siege of Jerusalem began (see Matt 24:16-22). But this chapter depicts the church not only as escaping tribulation, but as triumphing over it. While the Christian community escaped, Stuart felt that these must have been faithful and zealous evangelists, endowed with miraculous powers, who chose to remain and preach repentance and faith to their besieged countrymen. "These

I regard as being symbolized by the *two witnesses* in 11:3."[212] Like Antipas (2:13), we know little about these faithful witnesses.

Josephus also recorded that before the final campaign of Titus in AD 68, various factions of zealots actually barricaded themselves inside the temple. One faction allowed a group of Idumeans to enter the temple. These Idumean zealots were from Edom and thus would be Gentiles. This act was opposed by two high priests Ananus and Joshua (or Jesus), who were regarded as just and honorable men. Joshua actually made a speech declaring, "And this place, which is adored by the habitable world, and honored by such as only know it by report, as far as the ends of the earth, is trampled upon by these wild beasts born among themselves."[213] This is similar to the language of Jesus Christ in Luke 21:24.

These Gentile zealots were responsible for slaying Ananus and Joshua, actually standing upon their dead bodies, making a speech of ridicule, and then cast away their bodies without burial. Josephus expressed great horror at this event, marking it as the beginning of the destruction of Jerusalem. "I cannot but imagine that virtue itself groaned at these men's case, and lamented that she was here so terribly conquered by wickedness."[214]

In many respects this incident fits the revelation of John in this chapter, which in turn was based on Psalm 79:1-3. My conclusion is that John prophesied this event, using it as a basis for his symbolism of the church as two persecuted witnesses which God revives. If these old covenant witnesses were hated, *how much more* would the Christian church be hated.

It is significant that these witnesses were described as having the authority to strike the earth with plagues. While these "plagues" may be interpreted symbolically, yet John is connecting the power of the church with the deliverance of Israel from Egypt. Beale wrote that the

---

[212]Stuart, *Apocalypse*, 2:227.

[213]Josephus, *Wars*, 4.4.3.

[214]Josephus, *War*, 4.5.2.

plagues (v 6) and torment (v 10) ascribed to the "two witnesses" correspond to the trumpet judgments.[215]

Fire falls to earth at the sounding of the first three trumpets and fire comes from the mouths of the two witnesses. A third of the sea is turned to blood with the second trumpet and the two witnesses have the authority to turn the waters into blood. Michaels wrote, "The implication is that all the plagues described in connection with the first four trumpets are now under the control of the two witnesses! . . . The people of God themselves become the executors of divine judgments."[216] In other words, the phenomenon of vv 5-6 are a summary of chapters 8-9. Just as God used the prayers of the saints to pour out the seal judgments, so God is using the preaching of the church to execute the trumpet judgments. These trumpet judgments are meant not simply to punish the earth dwellers, but to protect the church. Yet this protection was not *from* persecution, but *through* persecution.

After the two witnesses were martyred, their bodies lay in the streets of Jerusalem (v 9). In fact, the slaughter in Jerusalem became so great that the ground could not be seen for dead bodies. The Romans trampled not only on the holy city, but upon the dead bodies as they pursued fugitives.[217] Just as there had been God-fearing Jews from all over the world in Jerusalem at Pentecost (Acts 2:5-11), so there were those representing all peoples, tribes, languages, and nations in Jerusalem to witness this holocaust. Jesus confirmed the tradition that it was impossible for a prophet to die outside Jerusalem (Luke 13:33). The earth dwellers thus rejoiced in the downfall of Christianity because of the spiritual and supernatural power demonstrated by the church (vv 5-6). Their gift giving is reminiscent of Esther 9:19.

---

[215]Beale, *NIGNT*, 585-587.

[216]Michaels, *IVPNTC*, 139-140.

[217]Holford, *The Destruction of Jerusalem,* 37. Josephus wrote that the lanes were obstructed with dead bodies [*Wars*, 6.8.5].

If Moses is dead, then they do not have to be reminded of the purpose of creation. If Elijah is dead, they do not have to be reminded of the destiny awaiting them. "We are free to exploit the earth, oppress our enemies, manipulate our friends, indulge our emotions, pamper our bodies. But," Peterson, concluded, "their party is always interrupted before it is well underway. . . . The work of witness cannot be stopped."[218]

At the end of this siege, in which the Christian witness should have been silenced, God breathed new life into his church. After 3½ days of death, they received a new breath of life, like the resurrection of dead men which Ezekiel saw rise up like a mighty army (Ezek 37:10). Like Elijah, who was taken to heaven in a whirlwind (2 Kgs 2:11), they go up into heaven. According to Ephesians the church is seated with Christ in the heavenlies. Thus, this chapter not only describes the proclamation of the church and its persecution, but its position.

While Judaism was a lying corpse, the true church is standing on its feet as a mighty army. Everyone who wants to live a godly life in Christ Jesus will be persecuted (2 Tim 3:12). However, the people of God will always triumph (2 Cor 2:14). Just when it seems the church is about to die, God will give us a new breath of life (v 11) and we revive and sit with Christ in the heavenlies (Eph 2:6). Christ's protection of his people and judgment on those who rejected him comes because he is seated on his throne and his reign has begun (11:15-19).

In v 15 the reference to both God and Christ together is followed by a singular pronoun. In 6:17, 20:6, and 22:3-4 singular pronouns are also used. In so doing, John places Christ on the side of deity in distinction to creation, but does not want to infer there are two Gods. Apparently John broke grammatical rules, with a singular pronoun replacing a plural subject, for the sake of theology.

Although at 11:13 we are not at the point of final destruction in John's revelation, John wrote this vision in chapter 11 to encourage the church to remain standing through all that would come. Even

---

[218]Peterson, *Reversed Thunder*, 115.

those who died as martyrs were not defeated. While their bodies were desecrated and refused a decent burial, their spirits are caught up to heaven — just as Elijah ascended bodily into heaven (2 Kgs 2:11). But the deliverance of vv 11-12 is not to be considered a literal rapture nor a literal resurrection.

Their witness was not in vain. The church was redeemed from all nations in order to witness to all nations. Verse 13 indicates that many who survived the initial judgment of Jerusalem repented and were converted. According to Acts 2:43; 5:5, 11; 19:17 the church evoked great fear. The word for *fear* is an intensive form which emphasizes the inward effect. It is used of Felix in Acts 24:25. It is the beginning of wisdom (Ps 111:10), which can lead to salvation.

The second term "gave glory to God," can refer to conversion. It is used by Joshua in calling Achan to repentance (Josh 7:19) and to describe Nebuchadnezzar's conversion in Daniel 4:34. A similar phrase is used in Acts 13:48. In Revelation 14:6-7 the angel with the eternal gospel calls on the earth dwellers to fear God and give him glory. The church issues a similar call in 15:4. In 16:9 the people blasphemed the name of God, refusing to repent and give him glory. The inference is that if they had repented, they would have given glory to God.

Ultimately the entire city fell, but Cestius Gallus, the Roman governor of Syria, led the first siege in November 66. Even before Titus arrived in June 69, and the final woe is announced in v 14, God took a tithe (tenth) as a warning that it was all his (v 13). While over a million Jews were finally killed,[219] figuratively speaking, seven

---

[219]Josephus, *Wars of the Jews*, 6.9.3. However, not all of this number were killed inside Jerusalem. The population of Jerusalem in the first century is estimated from 30,000-150,000 [see Aune's evaluation, *WBC*, 52B:628]. However, Josephus recorded that the population swelled to three million at Passover [*Wars*, 2.14.3].

thousand were killed initially.[220] This figure is considered significant because in Elijah's day there were seven thousand faithful (1 Kgs 19:18). Now because of Israel's unfaithfulness, seven thousand are initially destroyed. Ultimately all who destroyed the land were destroyed (v 18; Matt 21:33-46). When it was over Jerusalem and the temple were in ruin.

c. Third woe 11:14-19

The word *woe* was commonly used by the Old Testament prophets. In Revelation 8:13 the word *woe* is pronounced three times. The first "woe" is identified in 9:12 as demonic spirits unleashed upon the land of Palestine. The second *woe* is the first wave of civil unrest and the invasion under Cestius (11:14) and the third *woe* was to follow quickly. The third *woe* was never specifically identified, but should probably be understood as the actual fall of Jerusalem since the first *woe* corresponded to the fifth trumpet, the second *woe* to the sixth trumpet, and the third *woe* would correspond to the seventh trumpet (11:15). Just as the seventh seal had no specific content, but opened to the seven trumpets, so the seventh trumpet has no specific content but opens to the seven bowls.

B. The Seventh trumpet 11:15-19

Now the vision shifts from earth to heaven. When the seventh seal was opened we were kept in suspense for a half hour of silence. Now as the seventh trumpet is about to sound, the silence is reversed

---

[220]We do not have an actual count of how many Jews were slain by Gallus, in the account by Josephus [*War*, 2.19.4-9]. Yet we do have record that before the actual siege by Titus, 20,000 Idumeans from Edom were called by the Zealots to help defend Jerusalem. Instead, both parties gave themselves to rape and murder until the outer temple overflowed with blood. Josephus reported that when the sun came up there were 8,500 dead bodies in the temple [*Wars*, 4.5.1].

and there are loud voices in heaven. These voices announce the session of Christ. The seventh trumpet does not mark the end of time, but the accomplishment of the mystery of God (10:7). Thus, the seventh trumpet does not correspond to the last trumpet of 1 Corinthians 15:52.

At the ascension of Christ, he was seated on his throne, and his kingdom began. In the first hymn, sung by angels, *became* is aorist participle (v 15; see same usage in Luke 19:9). Again in the second hymn, sung by the church, Christ has taken power (v 17; perfect tense - emphasizing permanence) and has begun to reign (aorist). In 1:8 and 4:8 the formula includes past, present, and future. Here John omits *is to come* and reverses the past and present. Thus, John is emphasizing the present, not merely future, reign of Christ.

The sounding of the trumpets marked the coronation of Jesus Christ and the beginning of a new year or age. He will continue to reign forever and ever. George Frederick Handel used v 15 as part of the text for his famous "Hallelujah Chorus." Yet the *Messiah* is most often sung at Christmas, in commemoration of Christ's *first* advent.

Yet Stuart explained that it is not necessary to suppose that as soon as the seventh trumpet sounded, that all the world has been at once converted. "A confident *anticipation* here, that the Gospel will now have free course and be glorified is sufficient for the purposes of the writer."[221] But before God can bless the world, he must remove the obstacle which blocks the flow of his Spirit. He must first judge those who have refused his Son and destroy their temple. Verse 18 is not a panoramic sweep of the major events to happen over a thousand-year period. Instead, it explains why the Jewish temple was destroyed in AD 70. The nations were angry and conspired against Christ. Psalm 2 is quoted in Acts 4:25-27 where it is connected both with the conspiracy of Herod and Pontius Pilate against Christ and the first wave of persecution against the church. God responded in wrath and judgment at their rejection of his Son (Ps 2:1-12). This is the vindication and reward of the righteous dead in 6:9-11, not the final

---

[221]Stuart, *Apocalypse*, 2:421.

judgment at the last day.

The time has come for destroying those who destroy the earth or the land, since *ge* with the definite article can refer to the land of Palestine. Just as God drove the first couple out of the garden for breaking the covenant, so part of God's covenant with Israel was to care for the land. They went into captivity because they did not allow the land to have its Sabbath. According to Leviticus 18:24-30 sin and violence defiles the land. The reference in Revelation is to the Jewish people who broke the covenant, defiled the land with their sin, and were driven out.

Then God's temple in heaven was opened (v 19). "The way into the Most Holy Place had not yet been disclosed as long as the first tabernacle was still standing" (Heb 9:8). The heavenly temple opened during the same generation that the earthly temple ceased. The ark is now visible because the curtain of the temple was torn in two from top to bottom (Matt 27:51).

The ark is now in heaven (v 19). The ark of the covenant held the two tables of the law. Presumably, this ark was lost when the first temple was destroyed by Babylon in 586 BC. There was no ark in the second temple.[222]

The temple on earth has lost what status it had. It never did contain the ark, which was lost when Nebuchadrezzar destroyed Solomon's Temple. It was a confident hope of some apocalyptic writers that in the Great day it would be restored; but St. John holds out no hope of any such restoration. God's covenanted presence is no longer the City of David; it is a universal covenant now "in Heaven," visible to all mankind, and available for all. The earthly, local, temple is to be destroyed.

Sutcliffe wrote that v 19 demonstrates "that the church above and the church below is one church. A flood of glory and righteousness is poured down from above, grace, grace, upon Zion." Flashes of glory sparkle from the altar. Voices create echoes of thunder. "And

---

[222]Josephus, *Wars*, 5.5.5. See also McClintock and Strong, *Cyclopedia*, 1:403.

the earth shall be shaken with the power of our God and of his Christ."[223]

The blessing comes from heaven. When God opens the windows of heaven, the church, which is his temple on earth, is the funnel through which he pours his blessing. God is building his church and the gates of hell cannot prevail against it. While we only seem to see destruction, the major lesson of this chapter is that God is not only bringing down the old; he is raising up the new. There is also construction going on! The new temple of God rises from the rubble of the old temple. Verse 19 does not describe the end of the world. Instead, it introduces the next vision which begins in chapter 12.

---

[223]Sutcliffe, *Commentary*, 2C:1080.

The Seven Trumpets Summary – 8:6-11:19

IV. Seven trumpets 8:6-11:19
- A. Six trumpets 8:6-9:21
  - 1. First trumpet — judgment on earth 8:7
  - 2. Second trumpet — judgment on sea 8:8–9
  - 3. Third trumpet — judgment on rivers 8:10-11
  - 4. Fourth trumpet — judgment of sun 8:12
    - a. First woe 8:13-9:11
  - 5. Fifth trumpet — judgment of locusts 9:1-11
    - b. Second woe 9:12-21
  - 6. Sixth trumpet — judgment of war 9:13-21

Interlude — The little scroll and the two witnesses 10:1-11:14
- A. The sweet and sour book 10:1-11
- B. Measuring the temple 11:1-2
- C. Two witnesses 11:3-13
  - c. Third woe 11:14-19
- B. Seventh Trumpet 11:15-19

These seven trumpets, while significant, are not to be interpreted literally. The trumpets repeat the judgment of the seals, but are a call to repentance. With the trumpet warnings, judgment is intensified with the emphasis on the destruction of one-third. The sounding of the trumpets marked the coronation of Jesus Christ and the beginning of a new year or age. He will continue to reign forever and ever. As our king, Christ is announced by the seven trumpets.

REVELATION 12

Interlude — War against the dragon and the beast 12:1-14:20

With the seventh trumpet having sounded and the temple opened in heaven, John begins describing a new vision. This chapter is a great dramatic depiction or epic poem of the conflict between the church and Satan. The Greek word *megas* is used six times in the chapter to express the significance of this vision. Our prefix *mega*, meaning large, great, weighty, or decisive, comes from this Greek word.

Except for the brief references to Satan or the devil in 2:9-10, 13, 24; 3:9, he has not been mentioned until now. This second half of the book takes us over the same conflict, but at a deeper level. The first half of Revelation emphasizes the victory of Christ, while the second half depicts the victory of the church. Three bindings of Satan are intertwined in this chapter.

Revelation 12:10 is an expansion of the seventh trumpet in 11:15-18. Just as the period of persecution is exactly the same in 11:3 and 12:2, the expression to "make war" is identical in 11:7 and 13:7, and the declaration of victory in 11:15 and 12:10 both use the same verb — *has occurred*. Thus, this chapter 12-14 interlude is a further elaboration on the seventh trumpet. The next chapter will focus on the satanic influence behind the Roman opposition and chapter 14 will focus on the triumphant nature of the church. But chapter 12 goes clear back to the beginning of time, and then describes the incarnation, in order to give a sweeping view of this great conflict — all in one continuous vision. The verb *ballo*[224] is used in v 4 of the first demotion, twice in v 9, v 10, and v 13, describing the second demotion, and in 20:10 of the third and final defeat. Since two of these defeats are past, the book of Revelation cannot be interpreted as continuously historical or as completely future.

---

[224]Peterson's translation of *ballo* is "bounced — unceremoniously tossed out" [*Reversed Thunder*, 120].

A. The holy war 12:1-17

John told us in 1:1 that his revelation was symbolic. Now he uses the this same word twice in this chapter to introduce the sign of the woman (v 1) and the sign of the dragon (v 3). A third and final sign will be introduced at 15:1. Those holding a literal interpretation of Revelation, tend to interpret these statements as implications that most of Revelation is to be taken literally. But John has already told us the whole book is symbolic. The emphasis here is that these are *great* signs in the sky, central to the interpretation of the whole book.

The woman is clothed with the sun, the moon under her feet, a crown of twelve stars. This description is based upon Joseph's dream in Genesis 37. Joseph saw his father as the sun, his mother as the moon, and the twelve sons as twelve stars. This was the beginning of the nation Israel. The moon was created to rule the night and it is God's purpose for his church to conquer darkness. Yet she is clothed with the sun. Christ is the sun of righteousness (Mal 4:2), and he is the light and glory of the church. The moon under her feet indicates that the sun has risen and the night is ended (Matt 4:16). The twelve stars represent the twelve tribes of Israel.

This woman is depicted as being with child and almost ready to deliver. Metzger wrote that this was a personification of the ideal community of God's people, "first in its Jewish form, in which Mary gave birth to Jesus the Messiah, and then in its Christian form, in which it was persecuted by a political power as evil as the dragon."[225]

It is obvious from v 5 that this son is Jesus Christ. This description is based on Isaiah 7:14 and Psalm 2:9 which was quoted in Revelation 2:27 and 19:15.

The church existed prior to the coming of Christ (Acts 7:38), but had become apostate. Only a remnant, such as Simeon and Anna, were eagerly awaiting the birth of Christ. But with the institution of the new covenant many were brought into the church (see Isa 66:7-8;

---

[225]Metzger, *Breaking the Code*, 74.

Mic 5:3; Gal 4:16). She is the new Eve and her Son will crush the serpent. This woman is the antithesis of Babylon, the great prostitute, who will be introduced in 17:3.

Just as v 5 truncates the nativity and ascension of Christ, from mother to father, so vv 7-13 conflate the battle in heaven and on earth. Verse 6 is resumed in v 14. Satan is symbolized as a great red dragon with seven heads, ten horns, and seven crowns. This description is based on the vision in Daniel 7. Daniel described the world empires which were under satanic authority. A composite picture of these four kingdoms, Babylon, Medo-Persia, Greece, and Rome, would result in seven heads — the first three beasts plus the four heads of the fourth beast (Dan 7:6) — each with a crown. The last mutation of this beast was the Roman Empire, which Daniel described as having ten horns (Dan 7:7). John gives the same description in 13:1 of a beast with ten horns and seven heads (but ten crowns). Yet by 17:9 the seven heads refer to seven Roman *kings* or caesars. However, his emphasis in chapter 12 is on the dragon behind the beast. That dragon is clearly identified in 12:9, and in 20:2, as:

- the ancient serpent who lied to Eve in the beginning (Gen 3:1-15; 2Cor 11:3)
- the devil (*diabolos*) in Greek meaning slanderer
- Satan (*satan*) in Hebrew means adversary or accuser

This great cosmic battle began before the creation of the world. Satan fell because he rejected truth and became the father of lies (John 8:44). Pride brought the devil under judgment (1 Tim 3:6). Apparently this fall occurred prior to Genesis 3 because at that time the serpent deceived Eve. According to 9:1 this fall had already occurred and the result was that Satan fell to earth. Satan had lost his position in heaven, yet apparently still had access to heaven (v 10). In Job we find Satan presenting himself before the Lord to accuse Job (1:6; 2:1; see also 1 Kgs 22:21-22; 1 Chr 21:1; Zech 3:1).

According to v 4 a third of the stars of heaven were swept by Satan's influence and cast to the earth. This refers to the original war in heaven. After the dragon threw a third of the stars to earth, he continued to pursue the people of God. It has already been established that John uses stars to symbolize angels, whether human messengers or supernatural beings (1:20; 9:1), but the emphasis in Daniel 8:10, Revelation 9:1 and 12:4 is upon *fallen* stars. While we do not know the total number of angels, apparently the majority did not fall. God did not spare the angels who sinned (2 Pet 2:4). These angels which did not keep their original position of authority are bound until the day of judgment (Jude 6).[226]

Adam and Eve had been given dominion on earth (Gen 1:26-8), and so Satan attempted to gain control of the earth by holding the human race hostage. When Adam sinned, a curse came upon the world. But God announced the war when he told Satan that he would put enmity between the woman's seed and his seed. The woman's seed was the coming Christ who would crush Satan's head, while Satan would only strike his heel (Gen 3:15). From that day forward Satan watched for the child to be born. "The dragon stood in front of the woman who was about to give birth, so that he might devour her child the moment it was born" (12:4b).

Cain, the first offspring, killed his brother Abel. Seth replaced Abel and Satan attempted to corrupt his lineage. By the tenth generation only Noah was righteous. Back and forth throughout the Old Testament the battle of the ages was waged. Abraham did not have an heir until he was a hundred. Two nations struggled in Rebekah's womb. All the male children except Moses were aborted in Egypt. Five hundred years later a demon-possessed King Saul tried to kill David through whom the Messiah had to come. Later the royal line was completely destroyed except for Joash. Haman tried to annihilate the entire Jewish race. But all satanic attempts fail to stop the Messiah from coming. The woman gave birth to a son, a male child, who was about to become world ruler (v 5). The Greek verb for rule combines

---

[226]It is common to also include Isa 14:12-15 and Ezek 28:12-19 in the discussion of Satan's original fall, but it is debatable whether or not these are descriptions of Satan.

the ideas of ruling and feeding as a shepherd.

Satan, the deceiver, then tried to mislead Joseph into divorcing Mary. Herod slaughtered all the infants in Bethlehem, and Mary, Joseph, and baby Jesus had to escape to Egypt (Matt 2:16).

As Jesus began his public ministry, he confronted Satan in the wilderness for forty days of intense battle (Matt 4:1-11). Jesus encountered demonic opposition during his entire public ministry. Yet Jesus explained that his ability to cast out demons was proof that the kingdom of God had finally come (Matt 12:28).

Finally Satan entered Judas and one of the inner circle betrayed Jesus. As Jesus was condemned to die and was led to the place of execution, all of the losers in hell must have thought the battle had finally turned in their favor. But Satan did not understand that he had played right into God's hand.

The battle turned at the cross. When Jesus was lifted up from the earth on the cross, he began drawing all men to himself (John 12:32). He disarmed the powers and authorities. He made a public spectacle of them, triumphing over them by the cross (Col 2:15). Jesus died, but it was impossible for death to keep its hold on him (Acts 2:24). He preached to the spirits in prison (2 Pet 3:19) and when he ascended on high, he led captives in his train (Eph 4:8).

Again there was war in heaven (vv 7-9). Satan, who had already lost his position in heaven was now cast out of heaven. Satan fell at the beginning of the first creation and falls again at the start of the new creation.

Jesus said, "Now is the time for judgment on this world; now the prince of this world will be driven out" (John 12:31; 16:11; 1 John 3:8; Heb 2:14). "I saw Satan fall like lightning from heaven" (Luke 10:18). Now the accuser, who accused night and day is cast down (v 10). *Now* is *arti*, a temporal adverb. Along with the aorist verb, "became," John clearly records that salvation has been provided and the kingdom has been established at the time of his vision.

Mounce said that the war in heaven between Michael and the dragon "is the heavenly counterpart to the [earthly] victory of Christ in his death and resurrection."[227] The resurrection of Christ unleashed the victory of Michael. The defeat of Satan by Michael began the great tribulation.

Michael and the good angels prevailed. The dragon with his angels lost their place in heaven and were cast to the earth. Satan was cast out of heaven at the same time salvation was provided (v 10), when the blood of the Lamb was shed (v 11), at the same time the kingdom of God was established (v 10), and at the time of the persecution of the early church (v 13). This also corresponds to Michael's victory in Daniel 12:1.

At his ascension, Christ was caught up to God and to his throne (v 5b). As the result of his death, resurrection, and ascension, salvation and the power and the kingdom of our God and the authority of his Christ have been established (v 10). Now that Jesus has taken his throne, there is no room for Satan in heaven. Aune suggested that *victory* is a particularly apt translation of the word usually translated *salvation* (v 10).[228] Beale concluded, "Therefore, v 10 does not merely anticipate the future kingdom, but celebrates the fact that the kingdom has begun immediately following Christ's death and resurrection."[229]

But the early church was under intense persecution. They must have asked, "If Christ is reigning, why are we suffering?" But the invasion of Christ's kingdom brought war in heaven and tribulation on earth. Caird explained that Satan did not accept defeat without a struggle. Satan was full of fury because he has been cast down to earth. Satan was full of fury, literally a boiling rage, because Christ bruised his head at the cross. Christ was caught up and Satan was cast down. Satan was running out of time. Since the triumph of the cross, according to v 12, Satan's remaining time is short. The Greek word *oligos* means *few*.

Paul wrote the Romans in AD 57 that "the God of peace will

---

[227]Mounce, *NICNT*, 235.

[228]Aune, *WBC*, 52B:700.

[229]Beale, *NIGNT,* 658.

soon crush Satan under your feet" (Rom 16:20). The kingdom of God was replacing the kingdoms of this world. The heavenly saints would have to wait a little time (6:11) and then Satan would be bound, as the church began to enforce the legal verdict on earth which Michael enforced in heaven.

Satan cannot reach God. He will never again do combat with the ascended Christ. So Satan turned on the people of God (v 13). Swete wrote, "The historical moment in the Seer's mind is doubtless the dark day in A.D. 64 when Nero began the policy of persecution."[230] But the Bible teaches that the church is the apple of God's eye (Deut 32:10; Ps 17:8; Zech 2:8). Satan attempted to attack God by attacking his people. But Christ has given us authority over him.

In chapter 9 John saw fallen spirits released from the Abyss. Jerusalem experienced the invasion of a demonic army and the siege of a Roman army. But although Satan tried to annihilate the infant church, the true church escaped to Pella during that terrible siege of 3½ years (v 6).[231] Pella is about 20 miles south of the Sea of Galilee. Bahnsen wrote, "Satan thought that by sending the Roman army against Jerusalem he would destroy the people of God, but instead Satan was simply the tool of God's sovereign plan; his wrath was used by God for historical judgment and retribution upon the city which has rejected the Messiah and put Him to death."[232]

Again in v 14 the church was placed out of the serpent's reach and nourished for 3½ years. Here is a specific application of the words, "You prepare a table before me in the presence of my enemies" (Ps 23:5; 78:19-20).

Then Satan tried to flood the church by casting water from his mouth (vv 15-16). Beale argued that this was a symbol of decep-

---

[230]Swete, *Apocalypse*, 157.

[231]Matt 24:15-24; Eusebius, *Ecclesiastical History*, 3.5; Stuart, *Apocalypse*, 2:250, 261; Renan, *Antichrist*, 203-204. Swete said v 6 was doubtless a reference to Pella [*Apocalypse*, 152].

[232]Bahnsen, "The Person, Work, and Present Status of Satan," 36.

tion, since the three references to *mouth* in chapter 13 is associated with deception.[233] Deceit is his primary weapon. The counterpart to this river of lies (Matt 24:24; 2 Thess 2:9-11; Rev 2:9; 3:9; 13:14), is the river of life in 22:1.

Just as the Old Testament church was led out of Egypt into the desert, and Pharaoh was called a dragon in Ezekiel 29:3; 32:2, so the New Testament church fled the dragon out of Jerusalem, called spiritual Egypt in 11:8, into the desert. Just as the ark rose above the worldwide flood and the Old Testament church was delivered through the Red Sea, so when the enemy comes in like a flood, the Spirit of the Lord will put him to flight (Isa 59:19; see also Ps 18:4; 124:2-4; Isa 43:2). The earth "swallowed" the Egyptians who pursued Israel through the Red Sea (Exod 15:12). "God never lacks the means to frustrate the devices of Satan, often making the very wrath of men and of devils to praise him (Ps 76:10)."[234] The gates of hell cannot prevail against the church (Matt 16:18).

This chapter closes by tracing the conflict down through the ages to the present day. Satan now makes war against the rest of the woman's seed, who are also called Abraham's seed (Rom 4:16; Gal 3:16, 29). The true church is characterized as keeping (present tense) God's commandments and holding to the testimony of Jesus (see also 14:12; Matt 5:17-20; 19:17; 1 Cor 7:19; 1 John 2:4-5). When the devil could not touch Christ, he redirected his attack from the Son to the woman. While the early church was initially protected, the devil again redirected his anger to the following generations, first through Roman persecution and then through other antichrists. Satan is defeated, both through the seed of the woman (singular), and the seed

---

[233]Beale, *NIGNT*, 513, 673.

[234]Binney, *Commentary,* 689. Some writers think John may have been alluding to an incident in March of AD 68, when the Jews of Gadara were preventing from escaping the Romans because the Jordan River had flooded. Fifteen thousand were slain, while many more were forced to leap into the river [Josephus, *War of the Jews*, 4.7.5]. In contrast to this tragedy, God will provide the church a way of escape (1 Cor 10:13).

of the woman (collective).

In Genesis 3:15 *seed* is singular and refers to Christ. But while the decisive victory of Christ (v 11) corresponds to D-Day in World War 2, the battle is not over. Now the war is between the collective seed, the church, and the dragon. And Satan would soon be crushed under the feet of the church (Rom 16:20).[235]

Chapter divisions in the Bible are arbitrary. Some commentators feel the first part of 13:1 belongs with chapter 12. Thus, chapter 12 would end with the words, "And the dragon stood on the shore of the sea." This would indicate that the heavenly war continues on earth (see also v 12). While this dragon tries to control through fear, in the sixteenth century Thomas More wrote, "The devil, the proud spirit, cannot endure to be mocked."[236]

The theme of this chapter is that Satan has been defeated twice and will be defeated once more. John does not yet describe the final battle when Christ returns and the devil will be cast into the lake of fire and brimstone to be tormented day and night forever and ever (20:10). Yet Satan continues to lose ground and before Christ returns every enemy will be defeated (1 Cor 15:24). The early church was able to face the future, even if it meant a martyr's death, by looking back to the victory of the cross and the blood of the Lamb. They overcame because they preached this message. Verse 11 begins with the connective particle καί (*kai*) which could be translated *for* and thus gives an additional connection between the defeat of Satan and the death of the martyrs.

We overcome Satan because of the blood of Christ. "It is the blood of Christ that is the basis of every victory achieved by the people of God." This was the price of our redemption. Beale explained that the emphasis on Satan's role as our accuser in v 10

---

[235]Oscar Cullman first used the analogy of D-Day and V-Day from World War 2. However, this two-stage victory should not be used to imply defeat until Christ returns. V-Day was the triumph of the cross, but that victory is not fully realized. Thus, we speak of "already, but not yet."

[236]C. S. Lewis cited More at the beginning of *The Screwtape Letters.*

reveals that "the angelic battle of vv 7-9 was figurative for a court-room battle between two opposing lawyers, with one losing the argument and being disbarred for employing illegal tactics."[237] Wall wrote that Satan's case was thrown out of court because of two kinds of evidences: the blood of the Lamb and the testimony of the martyrs.[238] Christ is our advocate (Rom 8:34; Heb 7:25; 9:24; 1 John 2:1) and Satan is our accuser.

This legal battle is also described in Daniel 7:13-27. However, in Dan 7:21 the saints are defeated by the beast, while in Rev 12:11 the dragon has been conquered on behalf of the saints.[239] This reversal is due to the victory of the cross.

Bahnsen wrote, "The one who opposes and slanders God's people has lost his *power*; his accusations no longer have force after the substitutionary atonement of Christ."[240] This world belongs to God through creation and redemption. Satan is a squatter with no legal rights. He will attempt to develop a foothold and strongholds of bondage wherever he is not challenged (Eph 4:27), but when we plead the efficacy of the blood he must back down (Jas 4:7).

We also overcome through our witness. The testimony of Jesus (1:2, 9) becomes the basis for the testimony of the saints. Christ is the faithful and true witness (3:14) and we are called to be faithful witnesses of him through our obedience to his covenant stipulations — which is repeatedly called "the law and the testimony" in Psalm 119. Just as Jesus faithfully bore witness to the Word of God, so the church is Christ's witness. We overcome by the hope we gain from the testimony of those who have overcome. Bloesch wrote that Satan is dethroned not only by the crucified and risen Christ but by the

---

[237]Beale, *NIGNT*, 661.

[238]Wall, *NIBC*, 18:164.

[239]Osborne, *BECNT*, 471.

[240]Bahnsen, "The Person, Work, and Present Status of Satan," 35-36.

preaching of the gospel by the church under the cross.[241]

The hymn of vv 10-12 appeals to those who are not martyrs to confirm their testimony to Christ, even if that means death. While not all will be martyrs, all are called to take up their cross (Mark 8:34-35). Our sufferings link us to the cross. "This seems to suggest that in some mysterious sense the sufferings of the people of God are linked to the sufferings of Jesus in his triumph over Satan and evil."[242] The blood of Christ is not only the basis for Michael's triumph in heaven, but for the saints' earthly victory.

According to Revelation 2:26 and 12:11 the overcomer is the one who keeps the works of Christ until the end. Thus, the overcomer includes all who persevere. "They did not love their lives so much as to shrink from death" is a negative way of saying that they persevered in the faith to the end, despite persecution. "If they maintain their faith, they maintain their identification with and share in Christ's overcoming through death and resurrection."[243]

According to 14:12 those who persevere are those who keep the commandments and keep the faith. Marshall asked if sealing preserves the people of God from his judgments upon the world, does it preserve them from persecution and from falling away under persecution? He concluded that it does not necessarily follow that all who have been sealed will certainly persevere. The victory is not dependent upon the sealing of God's people, but on their endurance. "The Book of Revelation is, therefore, an appeal to Christians to be conquerors by holding out to the end against the onslaught of the demonic powers arrayed against them. It passes judgement upon Christians who fail to overcome and threatens them with loss of salvation, so that a pure and strong Church may be fitted to face the fury of the

---

[241]Bloesch, *Last Things*, 110.

[242]Johnson, *XBC*, 12:518.

[243]Beale, *NIGNT*, 665.

devil and antichrist."[244]

The church positionally dwells in heaven (Eph 2:6), but is the object of the devil's attack on earth. Yet we are to rejoice (v 12) because Christ's kingdom has been established, the devil has lost his position, and the saints have the grace to overcome. But the world does not know of the victory of Christ unless we tell them. Unfortunately, parts of the church have been convinced they are defeated and do not preach an overcoming gospel. But the full message of the cross will ultimately win the world.

---

[244]Marshall, *Kept by the Power of God,* 176-177.

REVELATION 13

B. The two beasts 13:1-18

While chapter 12 gives the heavenly perspective, chapter 13 provides the earthly perspective. After the dragon was thwarted in his attempt to abort the Messiah, he then empowered Rome to pursue the church of Christ. If apostate Judaism was the first enemy of the church, the Roman beast became the second enemy. The Roman Empire was across the Mediterranean Sea from the land of Palestine. Here the sea corresponds to the Abyss and the beast is the same as the one in 11:7 and 17:8. Rising above the sea of humanity is a political beast which had gone through several mutations (see Dan 7:3). When the Roman emperors frequently visited Ephesus, their ships on the horizon appeared to be rising out of the sea.[245]

This vision must be interpreted in light of Daniel 7. Daniel looked forward in time and saw four beasts come up out of the sea: like a lion, like a bear, like a leopard, and a monster. When each world empire was defeated, its spiritual life continued in the kingdom which followed. Now John looks back across history and mentions them in reverse order: a beast, like a leopard, like a bear, like a lion.

The *lion* represented the Babylonian empire (605-539 BC). A winged lion was the national symbol of ancient Babylon. Babylon is called a lion by Jeremiah in 4:5-7; 49:19; 50:17.

The *bear* represented the Medo-Persian empire (539-331 BC). This kingdom immediately follows the fall of Babylon (see Dan 2:39; 5:28).

The *leopard* represented Greece (331-146 BC). Alexander the Great conquered the world with the speed of a leopard. Daniel 8:20-21 made it clear that Greece would defeat the Medes and Persians. Daniel 8:22 describes the breakup of the Greek kingdom after Alexander's death and v 23 describes Antiochus Epiphanes, ruler of Syria between 175-164 BC.

The nondescript *beast* represented Rome (146 BC - AD 476). It is

[245]Ramsay, *Letters to the Seven Churches of Asia*, 74.

hard to put an exact termination date on the fall of the Roman empire because it was not conquered by another earthly empire. It had disintegrated by the time 10% of its citizens had converted to Christianity. In the days of the Roman empire the kingdom of God entered this world like a rock cut out of a mountain which smashed the idolatry and filled the whole earth (Dan 2:35). Again the symbolism is the same in Daniel 7, Daniel described the ascension of Jesus Christ and the establishment of his everlasting kingdom. While Daniel 2 portrays the attractiveness of these humanistic kingdoms, Daniel 7 reveals their beastliness.

In contrast with the Greek word for *living creatures* used eleven times in chapters 4-5, *therion* is used sixteen times in this chapter and denotes a wild beast. The beasts of Revelation 13 are counterparts to the two witnesses of chapter 11. They must also be understood in connection with Job's reference to Leviathan, the sea monster, and Behemoth, the land monster. These creatures, along with the dragon, all represent evil. They cannot stand up against God (Job 41:10-11). The extinction of these dinosaurs foreshadows the ultimate destruction of Satan himself.

Bahnsen wrote that government, as God originated it, was to reflect the image of God (Gen 9:5-6). But a beast which requires men to worship its own image (13:1, 14) is civil government degraded and deified. As such it represents the work of Satan (12:9; 13:4). According to Deuteronomy 6:8 the law of God was to guide the thoughts and actions of men. They are to keep the commandments of God (14:12). However, the totalitarian state demands that its own law be supreme and is thus symbolically represented as the mark of the beast upon the hand and forehead (v 16).

Therefore, the book of Revelation condemns any human government, such as imperial Rome, which replaces the law of God with the law of the state.[246] Mulholland concluded that when the church adopts the values and methods of "naturalistic humanism" it has been compromised and subverted by the beast. When the church baptizes the

---

[246]Bahnsen, *Theonomy*, 393-395.

destructive values of the world and adopts them as its own, it has been subverted by the dragon.[247]

1. The beast from the sea 13:1-10

This beast had seven heads. The description is based on the vision in Daniel 7. Daniel describes the world empires which were under satanic authority. A composite picture of these four kingdoms would result in seven heads — each with a crown. The Greek empire had four heads (Dan 7:6), plus Babylon, Medo-Persia, and Rome. The last mutation of this beast was the Roman Empire which Daniel described as having ten horns (7:7). According to Daniel 7:24 these ten horns were ten kings. These ten horns are explained in Revelation 17:12-14 as Roman provinces.

John illustrates the fact that, while this beast went through four mutations, in each form it was controlled by the same dragon. John explained to the people of God that Christ conquered at the cross and brought in a new world order. The first century church was living during a time of intense spiritual struggle. The Roman government demanded worship (v 4). Christians were required to pledge allegiance saying "Caesar is Lord." We noticed that some of the churches in Revelation 2-3 were already experiencing intense opposition and persecution. Apostate Israel, however, rejected Christ saying, "We have no king but Caesar" (John 19:15). In the ultimate sense they were worshiping the dragon and became the synagogues of Satan (Rev 2:9; 3:9).

While Christ wears the *diadem* in 19:12, the dragon and the beast have a *diadem* in 12:3; 13:1, representing usurped authority. On the seven heads of the beast are also names of blasphemy (see also 17:3). When directed toward the righteous, this word is translated *slander* (2:9). When directed at God, it is *blasphemy*. Both Daniel 7:8 and Revelation 13:5 refer to a mouth speaking great things. According to Daniel 7:25 the fourth beast would "speak against the Most High."

---

[247]Mulholland, *Revelation*, 230.

These words of blasphemy are the beast's claims to sovereignty. The Roman emperors referred to themselves as "God," "son of God," and "our Lord and our God." Nero called himself 'The Savior of the World." The Roman Senate officially declared them divine at their death.

The beast also spoke blasphemous words in vv 5-6. This flood of words was described as a river coming from the mouth of the dragon in 12:16. Both the name of God and the people of God are attacked in v 6. The Greek text does not have a final conjunction in v 6. Thus, the blasphemy is directed against two objects: the name of God and the tabernacle of God—which is those who are dwelling or tabernacling with God in heaven.

The temple of God was not only a place, but the worshipers of God are included in that temple (11:1). While the people of God constitute the true temple of God, it may be that this blaspheming of the tabernacle of God also includes the symbolic desecration of the temple in Jerusalem by the beast of Rome. According to Matthew 24:15 it was such a desecration of the holy place which was the signal that the people of God should flee Jerusalem. Antiochus Epiphanes had set up an altar to Zeus in the temple in 167 BC. The Roman emperor Gaius (Caligula) had threatened to erect a statue of himself in the temple around AD 30. Now the temple would be ultimately desecrated through its destruction (see Dan 9:27; Luke 21:20-21).

Rome was temporarily allowed to overcome the saints by destroying their lives and blaspheming their God (see also Dan 7:12, 21-27). The temporary defeat of the saints is the greatest blasphemy against God. This is allowed for a period of 42 months (v 5). Yet God decrees times and seasons and he imposed this time limit upon the devil. This period of 42 months corresponds to 11:2-3 when the holy city is trampled on for 42 months and during which time the two witnesses prophecy, as well as to 12:14 where the church is sheltered for 42 months. John now tells us that these events were all in response to the activity of the beast. According to 15:2 the saints ultimately overcome the beast.

While Jesus Christ had dealt Satan a death blow at the cross, crushing his head, it seemed that the beast had recovered (vv 3, 12, 14). Although Julius Caesar, the founder of the Roman Empire was assassinated in 44 BC, the beast had not died. Nero was the 6th emperor (see 17:10). Thus, he is the sixth king, whose name is 666. During the end of Nero's reign, the Roman empire was plunged into a period of civil war. After Nero's death, Galba, Otho, and Vitellius were each emperor of Rome for a matter of months. Josephus wrote that Rome was near "ruin."[248]Then the empire revived under Vespasian. Vespasian left his son, Titus, to continue the siege of Jerusalem and returned to Rome to restore order.

According to v 3 this Roman beast was healed of what appeared to be a fatal wound. This fact is again emphasized in vv 12 and 14. Yet in the first reference it is one of the beast's heads that is wounded, in the second reference it is described as a fatal wound to the beast, and in the third reference this wound was inflicted by the sword. It is typical for John to refer back to the same subject several times, each time supplying more information. These are not separate incidents; John refers to the head and to the beast interchangeably. Thus, the two beasts cannot be separated by hundreds of years.

This fatal wound and claim to healing was Satan's attempt to discredit the victory of Christ, first predicted in Genesis 3:15, that Christ would crush the head of Satan. Satan's wound was inflicted by the death and resurrection of Christ. Satan's death was real. The word *slain* is almost identical to the verb used in 5:6 of Christ's death. While both are also said to live again (2:8; 13:14), the resurrection of the beast is only an illusion; "the beast's continued existence is not a reversal of his actual defeat." He no longer has authority over the

---

[248]Josephus, *Wars of the Jews*, 4.11.5; 7.4.2. Tacitus wrote that "the year [AD 69] that was to be for Galba his last and the state almost the end" [*Histories*, 1.425; see also 3.48-49,71-73,83 for descriptions of chaotic conditions during this time]. But while the Roman Empire staggered, it survived. The mortal wound was healed [Carrington, *The Meaning of the Revelation*, 230]. Josephus said the government of Vespasian delivered the Romans from ruin [*Wars of the Jews*, 4.11.5].

saints nor any control over what God gives them. The dragon and the beasts, however, deceptively cover up the fact that their authority has been removed.[249] Walvoord wrote, "Expositors usually hold that the extraordinary powers given by Satan to the false prophet do not extend to giving life to that which does not possess life, because this is a prerogative of God alone."[250]

While it is common for writers to refer to the legend that Nero would return to life, it is better to understand that John is portraying this Roman beast as a parody of Jesus Christ in his death and resurrection. While the government of the world was laid upon Christ's shoulders (Isa 9:6), yet humanistic government has always attempted to usurp his sovereignty. Just as the Israelites exclaimed, "Who among the gods is like you, O Lord?" (Exod 15:11; Ps 35:10; Mic 7:18), so the whole world asked, "Who is like the beast?" (v 4). Elijah had declared that the God who answers by fire was the true God (1 Kgs 18:24), but this false prophet caused fire to fall from heaven (v 13). Yet notice that while he looked like a *lamb*, an obvious reference back to Christ in v 8, he spoke like a dragon (see Matt 7:15). In 5:6 Christ appeared as a lamb having been slain. Here the beast appears as having been healed of a fatal wound.

Rome's rule had been advanced through the use of occult powers (v 13). Fire from heaven refers first to the answer to Elijah's prayer (1 Kgs 18:38), then to the fire of the Holy Spirit at Pentecost (Acts 2:3). False fire goes back to the priests Nadab and Abihu in Leviticus 10:1-2. This fire is a parody on the fire which fell when Elijah prayed. Stuart was emphatic that John was not stating as fact that these false prophets actually wrought miracles, but only that they pretended to do so. The pretended miracles created the deception (v 14).

Everyone who was not in the kingdom of God, whose names were not written in the book of life, went along with the program of the beast. The names of the elect were recorded in the book of life

---

[249]Beale, *NIGNT*, 689.

[250]Walvoord, *Revelation*, 208.

before the foundation of the world. While the foreknowledge that mankind would need a Savior was the basis on which God predestined Christ to be that Savior, v 8 cannot be used to prove that God predestines the individual salvation of those whom he elected unconditionally. Nor does the statement that the Lamb slain before creation lead to a theology that God decreed the fall because he had already predestined his Son to die on the cross. God foreknew the fall, but did not predestinate it.

The beast frightens with his power and deceives with his illusions. The people of God wondered if the plan of God was working. They were tempted to doubt and disobedience. John confirmed that some would go into captivity or be martyred (v 10). If, in the providence of God, he allows persecution, then the Christian must accept this reality (Jer 15:2; 43:11). Peterson observed that fears lose half their potency when named. John was preparing the early church to endure under persecution and to keep faith by telling them what to expect, so they will at least not be surprised.[251]

But the second couplet is retribution. God has ordained that those who live by the sword will also die by the sword (Matt 26:52; Gen 9:6). Paul was decapitated by the sword of Nero[252] and Nero committed suicide by means of his own sword. Stuart saw this prediction in v 10 as an inference that Nero was alive at the time John wrote it.[253]

According to 17:14 the Lamb will progressively overcome [future tense]. This Lamb was slain from the foundation of the world (v 9). Therefore, the church is challenged to hear the promise of God. In each of the seven letters these words "If anyone has an ear, let him hear," accompany the promise to the overcomer.

John assured the early church, that regardless of their circumstances, God knows the future. The same God who planned salvation before the fall, knows their future. The success of the beast was only

---

[251]Peterson, *Reversed Thunder*, 125.

[252]Eusebius, *Ecclesiastical History*, 2.25.5.

[253]Stuart, *Apocalypse*, 2:451. This inference is confirmed in 17:10.

temporary. The kingdom of darkness may blaspheme and even challenge God, but he is still sovereign whether or not he chooses to respond. The people of God may be battered and resisted, but the meek will inherit the earth. They may be conquered, just as their Lord was crucified, but, like him, they too will overcome. On the other hand, the beast, who appears to be healed of his death blow, has actually been defeated. Some form of the phrase "tribe, people, language, and nation" occurs seven times in Revelation and there will be representation in heaven from every category. But here it is used to describe Satan's temporary authority (v 7).

How were the saints to react under tribulation? Verse 10 calls for patient endurance and faithfulness (see also 14:12). This word *endurance* (*hupomene*) was considered a manly virtue. It means to stand your ground. It was used to describe the ability of a plant to live under hard and unfavorable circumstances. We must also be faithful. We must be faithful even unto death (2:10).

2. The beast from the earth 13:11-18

Verses 11-18 describe the third part of a satanic trinity. We have already identified the dragon as Satan and the beast, in its present form as Rome. Now we have another beast of the same kind. He was a wolf in sheep's clothing. While the first beast came out of the sea, he came out of the earth. In 16:13, 19:20, and 20:10 he is called "the false prophet." He spoke through the beast and behind the beast was Satan, the dragon. Some commentators have conjectured that this "false prophet" must have a religious, rather than a political, identity. However, the concept of a state religion mixes religious and political authority. The head of state was then worshiped as God and salvation was through government programs.

Although Satan lost his legal right to accuse (12:7-12), he still has authority within his own realm and he delegates that authority to his evil earthly agents. In 12:3 that the dragon is described with seven heads and ten horns, just as the beast is described in 13:1 (see also 17:3). John's point is that the beast is really just a puppet used by

Satan.

Four times in vv 5-7, and again in v 15, we find the passive verb *was given*. This usage emphasizes that the beast has no power of its own. The beast was not in control, but was allowed by God to operate unrestrained.

It seems clear from v 12 that this second beast is the leader of the Roman empire; the one who exercises the Roman authority. The second beast was contemporary with the first beast. Nations and even churches are identified by their leaders. Since Nero was the embodiment of the Roman Empire, the two subjects were treated interchangeably at times. Notice that the seven heads are both identified as the seven hills of Rome *and* the seven rulers of Rome (17:9-10). F. F. Bruce wrote that "there is some oscillation in the imagery and its interpretation between the empire and the individual emperors who from time to time embodied the imperial power."[254]

Actually the symbolism of the beast is fluid. Daniel saw four beasts, as four world empires in Daniel 7. Then John saw the last of Daniel's beasts with seven heads. The seven-headed beast can refer collectively to the Roman Empire or the seven heads can refer chronologically to the succession of Roman emperors. This chapter ends with a reference to the beast as one individual emperor.

According to Revelation 13 there was a brief time span when God allowed the early church to be overcome. There was an intensc struggle at the time God's kingdom entered the world, but the Bible is abundantly clear that once the kingdom of God is established it is here to stay. We will experience tribulation and will fight all the way to heaven, but never again will Satan regain control.

Revelation 2:9 refers to economic pressure directed against Christians. The Roman coins had the head of the emperor with references to his divinity and worship. In their confrontation with Jesus, the Pharisees conceded that Caesar's portrait and inscription appeared on their coins (Matt 19:22). Nero's coins declared him to be the *Savior of the World*. Thus, no one could buy or sell without using

[254]Bruce, *New Testament History,* 411; *Revelation*, 1621.

coins which bore Nero's head. Everyone, regardless of social status, was confronted with this pressure to conform to emperor worship and participate in guild ceremonies in order to avoid economic repercussions. The warning in 14:9-11 refers to the apostate Jews who sold out to Rome, choosing salvation through the pagan state rather than accepting their Messiah. Anyone who is willing to violate God's commandments in order to transact business has been marked as belonging to Satan's realm. No one who worships this beast has their name written in the book of life.

This mark of the beast is referred to in 13:16-17; 14:9, 11; 16:2; 19:20, and 20:4. In Revelation 3:12; 7:2-4; 14:1 that the people of God are also marked. The mark of the beast parodies the sealing of the saints in chapter 7. Both groups are stamped with the image and character of their leader. The High Priest in the Old Testament had "Holiness Unto the Lord" on his forehead (Exod 28:36). In Ezekiel 9:4-6 God's remnant was marked. Paul tells us that Christians are sealed by the Spirit as a mark of ownership (Eph 1:13; 4:30).

Israel was instructed to write Deuteronomy 6:4-5, roll the parchment into small phylacteries or capsules, and fasten them to their foreheads and hands. Thus, their thoughts and actions were to be governed by the command to love God with the whole person. Peterson wrote that when the creed of the beast replaces these words, "religion becomes consumption — people become gross parodies of the gospel, buying all they can to show they are blessed by God, bowing down before every display of success. The buying and selling of religion is the mark of the beast."

The number 666 carries fear and superstition. Some approach this number as a complex riddle or secret code. But we should seek a *relevant* interpretation. The early Christians had not heard of any of the historical leaders or contemporary names often suggested. The solution needs to be someone who was contemporary in the first century, since John said that the events of Revelation were to occur soon. Aune wrote that the beast "is not a *future* but rather a *present* figure whose identity was probably well known to the readers of the book."

According to v 18 it is the number of a man. Some languages do not have separate numerals. Normally we use Arabic numerals, but sometimes we use Roman numerals which are also letters. However, the English language did not begin to develop until about AD 450. The solution, therefore, cannot be worked out in English. The extant languages in the first century were Greek, Hebrew, and Latin (John 19:20). None of these languages have separate numerals. Their letters all have numeric value. The solution would have to incorporate the languages in existence and the numeric value of the letters cannot be arbitrary.

The Roman emperor at the time Revelation was written was Nero. He was the sixth Roman emperor. His name in Latin:

N = 50
E = 6
R = 500
O = 60
N = 50

The Greek name *Nero Caesar* in Hebrew (with no vowels):

נ = 50
ר = 200
ו = 6
נ = 50

ק = 100
ס = 60
ר = 200

Thus, Nero becomes the only first century figure whose name adds up to 666, or the variant 616, in two of the major languages in use at that time. Nero became emperor in AD 54 and the first years of his rule were uneventful. Thus, he began as a lamb (v 11). Renan described him as evil, hypocritical, flippant, vain, egotistic, jealous, and intelligent, but mentally unbalanced. He liked literature, loved theatrics, perceived himself of something of an artist and musician, and ruled the world.

In 59 he caused his mother to be murdered. In 64 a terrible fire broke out in Rome and burned out of control for six days, then after it was thought to be put out it broke out again for two more days. Although Nero was out of town at the time, he blamed the Christians for this fire. Apparently he had been poisoned against Christians through his Jewish contacts. This began the first Roman persecution of Christians in November, 64. Nero was a homosexual and he found sexual excitement through torture. He was regarded as a demon in human form and depicted in art as a monster. Christians were sewn in the skins of wild animals and thrown into the arena to be torn by dogs. Others were crucified. Some had their clothing dipped in oil or pitch, they were attached to a stake, and set on fire to illuminate Nero's magnificent gardens at night. Every conceivable torture was inflicted on them. Nero also dressed in the skin of a wild animal and physically assaulted young men and women who were bound, naked, in the arena. Thus, to these Christian virgins he literally became *the beast*.[255]

Marcus Aurelius called Nero a *beast*. Apollonius of Tyana arrived in Rome during the reign of Nero and spoke of the emperor as a *beast*. The Sibylline Oracle referred to Nero as "the great beast" and a serpent.[256]

---

[255]Renan, *Antichrist*, 74-89; 134-135; 153-154.

[256]*Sibylline Oracle*, 8.157;5.29; 12.79, 81. Cited by Bauckham, *The Climax of Prophecy*, 409-410.

REVELATION 14

C. The church militant and triumphant 14:1-20

This chapter stands as part of a parenthetical set of three visions of John. In fact, the chapter 12-14 interlude is a sweeping overview which carries us beyond the first century. This chapter opens with a depiction of the final victory of the church (vv 1-5), which brings a conclusion to the theme of the 144,000 from chapter 7.

The next vision centers around what is happening above the earth, describing the church as she preaches the gospel from the time of the first advent to the end of the age (vv 6-16). Here John introduces the theme of Babylon, which will be developed in chapters 17-18. Finally, this vision closes with a picture of judgment on the earth at the end of history (vv 17-20). While John carries this theme of redemption and judgment to the end of the age, chapter 15 will revert back to the first century, describing the third and final set of judgments.

The crucial issue for the interpreter is the time frame of the events described. In this chapter the reference to the winepress outside the city, and the blood which flowed, refers to the atonement of Christ (Isa 63:1-6). *From now on* in v 13 refers to the blessing which flows from the cross. Verses 14-16 do not describe the return of Christ, but instead describe him as seated on his heavenly throne. *Firstfruits* is a reference to the beginning of the harvest. And the wrath of God, described in the closing verses of this chapter, as well as 19:15, comes upon those who reject the atoning blood of Christ. Jerusalem was destroyed in AD 70 because it did not recognize her time of visitation from God through Christ (Luke 19:43-44). John continues to assure the early church, persecuted by Rome, that "Babylon," too, is fallen.

And yet across history the everlasting gospel continues to be proclaimed. One generation after another victoriously makes it across to Mount Zion and join the 144,000 who worship before the throne. The harvest continues to be brought in and judgment continues to fall. Babylon, in whatever contemporary form, continues to fall (see Isa

21:9) and the church continues to preach and sing. As the church grows, her song gets louder.

Christ will come at the end of the age. The final harvest with be gathered and the full strength of judgment will be outpoured. The saints will rest eternally and the smoke of hell will rise forever and ever. In 4:8 the living creatures never cease to worship, while in 14:11 the unsaved never cease to suffer. While this chapter had specific relevance for the first century church, it provides an overview of God's plan which goes beyond the first century. Caird reminds us that John is expositing Psalm 2. The world is in rebellion against God, but God has installed his Son on Mount Zion as the ruler. Just as he was victorious, so we also overcome with him. Here John depicts us as standing with him on Mount Zion.[257]

1. The final victory of the church 14:1-5

As this chapter opens, the 144,000 are again introduced. We first encountered this number in chapter 7. Just as 13:16-17 described the mark of the beast, so the name of the Father and the Lamb are written on the foreheads of God's people. "The destiny of every person is determined by the mark that person bears. When judgment comes there will be no room for ambiguity; people will have by their 'mark' declared their master."[258]

The 144,000 were the first Jewish converts to Christianity and were the "firstfruits" of the harvest. "The converts of that day, on which the Holy Ghost descended, were the *first-fruits* of the Spirit."[259] At the time of John's writing they would have constituted the church in its entirety. Clarke wrote, "The reference appears to be to those

---

[257]Caird, *Revelation*, 178.

[258]Mounce, *NICNT,* 264.

[259]McClintock and Strong, *Cyclopedia*, 7:930.

Jews who were the *first converts* to Christianity."[260]

The firstfruits of crops were brought to the temple in the festival of Firstfruits, which was also Pentecost. Thus, for the early church the outpouring of the Spirit at Pentecost was the beginning and basis for their growth. The firstborn of cattle were brought to the temple as a sacrifice. The firstborn of the Jews also were set apart as the Levites. As the *firstborn* these early Christians, comprising the church of the Firstborn (Heb 12:23), are the new Levites serving God in the new temple, the New Jerusalem.

In chapter 7 they were sealed, protecting them from the great tribulation; in chapter 14 they have made it safely across to Mount Zion. Mount Zion is the location of Christ's throne, the heavenly Jerusalem which is above. It is a symbolic description of heaven. Of the seven references in the New Testament to Zion, five are quotations from the Old Testament. Of the two new references, one is found here and the other is Hebrews 12:22-23, which defines Zion as the heavenly Jerusalem, the city of the living God, and the church of the firstborn. While the reference in Hebrews incorporates the church on earth and in heaven, v 3 specifies that the church is "before the throne." The location of the events in vv 1-5 is not as critical as the finality and triumph of the church. This, then, is a reference back to the heavenly scene in chapters 4-5. Compare 14:1-5 with 5:6-11.

The symbolism of *firstfruits* is that there is more to follow (sec Exod 23:19; Rom 8:23, 11:16; 1 Cor 15:20, 16:15). Bauckham identified them as a remnant whose witness will lead to the conversion of more people later.[261] The gospel is to be proclaimed to every nation, tribe, language, and people. Verses 15-16 depict a worldwide harvest.

While the 144,000 are symbolic of the whole church and at the time of John's writing constituted the whole church, the description in 15:2-4 depicts a more general group who make it to heaven. The word *aparche* (firstfruits), can have the meaning of foretaste or

---

[260]Clarke, *Commentary*, 6:1029.

[261]Bauckham, *Climax of Prophecy*, 291-292.

pledge, similar in meaning to "earnest."[262] If the first group of believers survived the attack of Satan and made it safely to heaven — so can the rest of us! We will stand the storm and make it safely to the haven of rest.

They belong to the Father (v 1). The seal of the living God (7:2) contains the names of both the Father and the Son (14:1). This double name gives an exalted view of Jesus (see also vv 4, 12). The sealed have been redeemed or purchased by the Son (v 4). They have been sealed by the Spirit (2 Cor 1:22; Eph 1:13; 4:30). The text literally says they are virgins — symbolically they have not committed spiritual adultery with the harlot Babylon. Usually the church is described with feminine attributes. Although John is speaking corporately, the reason he uses male attributes here is that the church has come out of battle and only males were soldiers in Israel's army. Before Israel entered into holy war, there was a ceremonial consecration which included abstaining from sex (1 Sam 21:5; 2 Sam 11:11). John equates fornication with idolatry in 2:14, 20, so it is natural for him to connect the moral purity of the overcomer with abstinence from cohabitation with Rome, who is the beast and the prostitute.

In contrast to those who falsely profess to be Jews in 2:9; 3:9, and those who deny that Jesus is the Christ (1 John 2:22), no lie was found in their mouths. Verse 13 also denies the false teachings of purgatory and soul sleep. They are blameless — without blemish or faultless (v 5). This is Christ's purpose for the entire church (Eph 5:27). To be blameless refers to the inner purity of our character. Thus, the followers of the Lamb reflect the character of the Lamb, who had no deceit (Isa 53:9; 1 Pet 2:22) and was led to slaughter (Isa 53:7). John again helps the early church to understand their persecution and martyrdom. Just as Jesus offered himself as a sin offering, so the firstfruits were also an offering (Lev 23:9-14). And all sacrifices were to be without blemish.

In this life we will never know freedom from ignorance, mistake, temptation, or a thousand infirmities, but we can be blameless. Our

---

[262]Aune, *WBC*, 52B:817.

motives can be pure. To what extent can we be made blameless in this life? According to 1 Thessalonians 5:23 we are kept blameless unto the coming of the Lord. 2 Peter 3:10 teaches the day of the Lord will come unexpected, so we are to live holy lives now and be found without spot and unblemished (v 14). Jude 24 tells us that he is able to keep us from falling and present us blameless (not faultless). Our complete holiness is the provision of Christ and it is our responsibility to appropriate this provision and be found in this condition when the Lord returns.

The church is not only given a heavenly perspective, they are also given a task to accomplish. Worship is the agenda of the church. John heard a roar like rushing waters and like a loud peal of thunder, which was harpists playing their harps. Music in an integral part of this book. Heaven is the "homeland of music" and the city of unceasing song.

Bunyan wrote that as Christian and Hopeful entered heaven the celestial choirs filled heaven with melodious music. There was singing and shouting and the sounding of trumpets. And all the bells of the city rang with joy.[263]

Both trumpets and harps are mentioned as being in heaven. The Greek word *kithara* is the basis for our word *guitar*. Some churches are opposed to "mechanical" instruments in worship, but they were used in Old Testament worship and they will be used in heaven! Certainly it could not be wrong for the New Testament church to copy on earth what the heavenly church was doing at the time John saw into heaven.

We worship through music. Through music we are encouraged to stand and through worship in song we wage battle. It was said that the Roman Catholic Church feared Martin Luther's hymns more than his sermons. While we will sing when we get to heaven, may God help us sing along the way. Psalms 120-134 were called "songs of ascent." As the pilgrims traveled up to Jerusalem for the feasts they sang these psalms. As we march to Zion, the heavenly Jerusalem, we

---

[263]Bunyan, *Pilgrim's Progress*, 145.

go singing.

A new song was sung. Revelation 4 gave the old song — praise to God the Creator; Revelation 5 gives the new song — worthy is the Lamb. All of God's creation (represented by the four living creatures) should praise God as creator. *The elders* refer to God's people under both the old and new covenant, but only the redeemed could sing the new song to Christ. The 144,000 are the first ones, but not the only ones, to make it to heaven. At the time of John's vision they were the only ones who knew the new song. According to 15:3 the old song is the song of Moses; the new song is the song of the Lamb.

These new songs are in response to God's creative and redemptive acts in history. Although David and Isaiah admonished the people to sing a new song to the Lord, the people did not understand then that Christ was the Lord. After the coming of Christ we reached a new epoch in the history of redemption and this necessitated a new liturgy. According to v 13 from now on those who die in the Lord Jesus Christ are more blessed than those who waited in Abraham's bosom. The increase in blessing stems from the victory of the cross.

The emphasis here is on the spiritual state of those who have died, not the circumstances of their death. Those who are found in Christ when death comes are blessed in their rest (Job 3:17). In v 11 those who worship the beast have no rest. They are tormented forever and ever. "The wicked are like the tossing sea, which cannot rest" (Isa 57:20). But the church is blessed because it is promised rest. It is true that the church has no rest on this earth, but (v 13) there is coming a time when we will know rest.

George Whitefield burned out as an evangelist at 56 years of age. He said he did not grow weary of the work, but weary in the work. If we are in Christ when we die, we die in the Lord. We will rest from our labors, but our works keep on working (v 13). However, *rest* should not be conceived of as the cessation of all activity. This word *labor* means labor to the point of weariness and even pain. "Heaven is not so much a place where no work is done as one where pain has ceased."[264] Rudyard Kipling wrote,

> We shall rest — and faith, we shall need it —
> Lie down for an aeon or two,
> Till the Master of all Good Workmen
> Shall set us to work anew![265]

Those who die in the Lord are blessed "when they have lived to see the cause of God reviving, the peace of the church returning, and the wrath of God falling upon their idolatrous cruel enemies."[266] They are blessed because they are at home with the Lord (2 Cor 5:6). They are blessed because the influence of their works continue. Nothing we do for Christ is lost. No prayer is ever wasted. "You put my tears into your bottle when I cry out to you" (Ps 56:8; see also Rev 5:8; 8:3-5).

The Scriptures assure us our labor is not in vain in the Lord (1 Cor 15:58). Christ assured the church, "I know your deeds, your hard work, and your perseverance" (Rev 2:2). "He who goes out weeping carrying seed to sow, will return with songs of joy, carrying sheaves with him" (Ps 126:6). They are blessed in their reward. Even a cup of cold water given in his name will be rewarded (Matt 10:42). Therefore, in the fact of persecution, this beatitude assured the early church of rest and reward.

We have reason to worship and we have no higher priority than to worship. In 2 Chronicles 20 God instructed King Jehoshaphat to conquer their enemies by having the army sing. The church is a singing army. Notice that the angels received their trumpets in 8:2, but do not sound them in v 6 until *after* the prayers of the saints have been offered on the altar. Again in 15:1 the angels with the seven plagues are introduced, but they do not begin in chapter 16 until *after* the worship of vv 2-8.

---

[264]Morris, *TNTC*, 20:183.

[265]Kipling, "When Earth's Last Picture Is Painted" (1892).

[266]Tong, *Matthew Henry's Commentary*, 6:1166.

2. The message of the church 14:6-13

Evangelism is also the agenda of the church, even if it means martyrdom. In v 6 we hear an angel proclaiming the eternal gospel to every nation, tribe, language, and people (v 6; Matt 24:14). This angel is introduced as "another" of the same kind. This is probably a reference back to 12:7. The gospel is called everlasting because it has been preached in all past ages (Gal 3:8; Heb 4:2) and because it is based in the changeless character and purpose of God.[267]

Although things looked hopeless, this first angel "proclaims the ultimate and certain spread of the gospel throughout the world."[268] The angel commanded everyone on earth to worship God and warned that those who worship the beast will be judged. The full gospel contains three elements: a universal call to worship God, an announcement of the defeat of evil, and a warning to those who reject deliverance. This deliverance was articulated in 1:5-6. The whole world is called to worship. We are to fear God and give him glory for his creation and his judgment. The phrase "give him glory" implies repentance (see 11:13; 16:9). The warning that judgment is about to fall implies that it is not yet too late to repent.

We worship him who made the heavens, the earth, the sea, and fountains of water (v 7). Johnson observed that these four aspects of creation correspond to the four spheres affected by judgment in the first four trumpet judgments (8:7-12) and the first four bowl judgments (16:2-9).[269] The dual nature of the gospel as both salvation and judgment was also symbolized by the sweet and sour book in chapter 10.

The preaching of the gospel is committed to men, not angels. This gospel is communicated by men. Just as the dragon worked

---

[267]Caird, *Revelation*, 182.

[268]Stuart, *Apocalypse*, 2:291. Stuart also said v 7 teaches "the complete success of evangelization" [p. 295].

[269]Johnson, *Triumph of the Lamb,* 205.

through the Roman empire, so the heavenly angel directs the evangelism of the church. The preaching of the heavenly angel therefore is actually carried out through human *angels*. An angel is a messenger, whether supernatural or human, and the characteristic of a messenger is that they are sent. We are commanded to go into all the world and preach the gospel to all creation. The early church did just that (Rom 1:8; Col 1:5-6, 23).

The declaration of the second angel (v 8) anticipates chapters 17-18. This is the first reference to Babylon (see also 16:19; 17:6; 18:2, 10, 21). Wall defined Babylon as "any and every place where a congregation of believers struggles to live for God. The evils found there are found everywhere and at any time before Christ's return."[270] John Bunyan portrayed Babylon as Vanity Fair in *Pilgrim's Progress.*

Yet Peter used "Babylon," as a more specific code reference to Rome (1 Pet 5:13). Rome was the current, first century, manifestation of the original pagan empire. Leon Morris wrote that "to men of the first century there was no better illustration of what Babylon means than contemporary Rome."[271] Babylon had conquered Jerusalem in 587 BC and Rome conquered Jerusalem in AD 70. Although the symbol "Babylon" comprises more than Rome, John is assuring the early church that Rome, too, will fall.

Babylon corrupted all the nations by making them drink the wine of spiritual adultery (v 8; Jer 51:7-8). This adultery is in contrast to the description of the Christians in v 4, who kept themselves pure. Those who do not drink from the cup of the Lord (Ps 16:5; 116:13), will drink the bitter cup of his wrath (Ps 75:8). Those who drank Babylon's wine have also drunk the undiluted wine of God's wrath (v 10; see 15:7; 16:1, 19; 17:2; 18:3; 19:15). You cannot drink one cup without drinking the other. "God's wrath is not merely the outworking of impersonal laws of retribution built into the structure of reality, but the response of a righteous God to people's adamant

---

[270]Wall, *NIBC*, 18:157.

[271]Morris, *TNTC*, 20:180.

refusal to accept his love."[272] Ladd defined the wrath of God as the "settled reaction of his holiness to man's sinfulness and rebellion." God's wrath is a necessary correlative to his love and mercy. John repeatedly emphasizes God's wrath in this book (12:12; 14:8, 10, 19; 15:1, 7; 16:1, 19; 18:3; 19:15).[273]

Under the old covenant, there was a special type of warfare known as a holy war. It is also called *herem* warfare, after the Hebrew word *herem* for *ban*. That which was placed under the ban was set apart or devoted for complete destruction. The holy war was initiated by God to exterminate aggravated immorality, blasphemy, and apostasy. Israel was to completely eradicate such practices by aggressively destroying peoples given over to such practices so their practices would not be passed on to future generations. Fire was taken from the altar and carried by the priests to burn up the cities conquered under holy war. Since these cities were under God's judgment, his holy fire was to be used. Aspects of this ban are discussed in Exodus 32:20; Leviticus 20:14; 21:9; Numbers 21:1-3; Deuteronomy 7:5; 12:3; 13:12-18; Joshua 6:15-19; 8:19;11:11; Judges 1:17; 20:13, 40, 48; 1 Samuel 15:9; 30:1; I Kings 9:16; 20:42; 2 Kings 10:26; 25:9; Isaiah 34:5.

John tells the church that they are also involved in a holy war and that the kingdoms of this world are placed under God's ban. He will destroy the world by fire (2 Pet 3:10). The seal, trumpet, and bowl judgments described by John are, in fact, God's decisive war against evil. But while these judgments began in the first century, God withholds complete and utter destruction until the end of the age in order to allow the nations time to repent, turn to Christ, and come out of the system devoted to destruction. The holy war of the church, therefore, is not terrorism but the proclamation of the gospel which results in a great harvest.

The fall of Babylon is the result of the preaching of the everlast-

---

[272]Mounce, *NICNT*, 273.

[273]Ladd, *Commentary,* 195.

ing gospel. While the fall of Babylon is certain, it is not necessarily instantaneous. Stuart wrote that a comparison of 16:19-21 with 18:4-8 and 18:20-24 with 19:11-21 insinuates a gradual accomplishment of the destruction of Babylon.[274]

It is significant that at the end of the age, the angel who had charge of the fire (v 18) announced the final phase of judgment. Since the entire world system is placed under a ban, the gospel call includes a call to *come out* of its bondage (18:4). While God has predestined the fall of Babylon, her actual fall is not described until 18:21. For those who do not heed God's call to flee Babylon, there is a third message.

The warning of the third angel (vv 9-11) links back to 13:16-17. While it may appear to be economically advantageous to receive the mark of the beast (18:3-17), it results in spiritual judgment. The description of judgment in vv 10-11 alludes to the destruction of Sodom and Gomorrah (Gen 19:28) "for their unnatural crimes."[275] Yet the smoke of this torment rises forever and ever. The consequences of accepting or rejecting this eternal gospel are eternal, just as the intent of the ban, under the old covenant, was permanent eradication of evil. "The punishment of the damned is not a temporary measure"[276] (see also 19:3; 20:10). Beale concluded, "The notion of eternal punishment in vv 10-11 should not be diluted by affirming that the imagery of the verses have only a rhetorical function of warning, and does not convey any doctrinal idea of a future state of punishment."[277] Peterson wrote that annihilationists also appeal to the destruction of Babylon in 18:8, 18; 19:3 as proof that annihilation is taught here. "This argument fails because, in the nature of the case, the city of Babylon cannot survive the creation of the new heaven and

---

[274]Stuart, *Apocalypse*, 2:296.

[275]Clarke, *Commentary*, 6:1029. See also Deut 29:23; Ps 11:6; Isa 34:10; Jer 49:18.

[276]Mounce, *NICNT,* 274.

[277]Beale, *NIGNT*, 765.

new earth (Rev 21:1), whereas the damned do survive, as Rev 21:8; 22:15 bear witness."[278]

In contrast, those who follow the Lamb to final salvation persevere in obedience, keeping the commandments of God and the faith of Jesus — faith *from* Jesus and faith *in* Jesus (v 12). This statement corresponds to the statement of 12:17.

3. The harvest of redemption and judgment 14:14-20

Verses 14-20 describe the harvest of the earth. This description is not restricted to the second advent, but begins with the ascension of Christ into heaven and the period of harvest between his ascension and return. He is not described as coming, but as seated (v 14). He sits at the father's right hand (Dan 7:13). He said as he was leaving earth, "All authority in heaven and on earth has been given to me. Therefore go and make disciples of all nations." "The son of man" has a crown on his head and a sickle in his hand. The hammer and sickle of communism will never rule the world, but the crown and sickle of Christ will!

Verses 14-16 also correspond to Matthew 24:30-34. The Son of Man is seen ascending into heaven, arriving in clouds and glory. He sends his angels to gather the elect from the four winds. The generation to whom Jesus was speaking would not pass away until they saw a great harvest. Yet this harvest is constantly being reaped in every generation. Jesus launched a harvest of grace in his first coming which would continue through the gospel witness of the church. The final harvest would not come until the end of the age (Matt 13:40).

World evangelism is not primarily the responsibility of Christ or the angels — it is the work of the church. According to Hebrews 1:14 angels assist us in our ministry. From a spiritual perspective, demonic spirits inspire evil empires (chapter 9) and angels assist with the kingdom of God. Ultimately, however, we proclaim the gospel and pronounce judgment on the world system through binding and

---

[278]Peterson, *Hell on Trial*, 96.

loosing (Matt 18:18). However, there are six or seven angels speaking in this chapter (depending on whether the voice in v 13 is counted). It is reasonable to assume that the last three angels are speaking independent of men since they came out of the temple in heaven. But John was specifically told to convey the message of the angel in v 13. Since the church is God's voice to the world, it is reasonable to conclude that the church proclaims and acts in cooperation with the heavenly angels. Verse 13 and 22:17 are also the only two times in this book in which the Holy Spirit speaks directly, although he has inspired all Scripture.

Christ was the sower who came into the world with the good seed. In v 15 John said the time to reap has come. We are to sow the gospel seed (Matt 13:1-23) and reap. In Matthew 9:37-8 Jesus taught that there was a great harvest coming and that he was the Lord of the harvest. Yet we are his body and we are the ones who are sent to work in the harvest field. The final harvest is the end of the world (Matt 13:39). Binney wrote, "The whole description is symbolical, and refers to the consummation of all things, when the great harvest of the world will be reaped, when the righteous and the wicked shall be separated, and each receive their final appropriate reward."[279] Johnson wrote,

> If martyrs and other believers who have died in persevering faith constitute the first fruits, already gathered on Mount Zion to praise God and the Lamb, the rest of the grain to be gathered by the Son of Man is the complete harvest of his saints. The end of history, therefore, will bring not only a great grain harvest, as the saving sweep of Christ's sickle gathers his faithful followers, but also a great grape harvest, as Christ's enemies are gathered to be crushed in the winepress of God's wrath.[280]

---

[279]Binney, *Commentary*, 693.

[280]Johnson, *Triumph of the Lamb,* 212.

REVELATION 14:14-20

In the last verses of this chapter the image changes from harvesting grain to grapes. In Israel wheat was harvested in the spring and fruit in the late summer. In v 16 Christ swung his sickle *over* the earth; in v 19 another angel thrust his sickle *into* the earth. The grain harvest is the harvest of the righteous, while the grape harvest is the judgment of the wicked. Passages such as Joel 3:12-14; Isaiah 17:5; 63:1, and Matthew 13:37 use similar language to describe judgment.

Christ comes for his own in salvation, but his angel harvests the wicked at the end.

> The harvest of the good is gathered in by the Lord Himself, that of the wicked by His angel. Is there not a beauty and tenderness in this contrast? It is as though that Son of Man and Son of God who is judge of quick and dead, Judge alike of the righteous and the wicked, loved one half of His office and loved not the other. It is as though He cherished as His own prerogative the harvest of the earth, and were glad to delegate to other hands the vintage. It is as though the ministry of mercy were His chosen office, and the ministry of wrath His stern necessity.[281]

While the righteous are gathered first, then the wicked, John however, does not teach two judgments a thousand years apart (see Matt 13:30). Bauckham took the grain harvest(vv 15-16) in a positive sense as the conversion of the nations of the world and the grape harvest (vv 17-20) in a negative sense as the punishment of the unrepentant.[282] These two harvests restate the harvest of firstfruits (v 4) and the wine of judgment (v 10).

The angel in v 18 came from the altar of burnt offerings and had

---

[281]Kelley, ed. *Methodist Commentary*, n. p; comments on Rev 14:20.

[282]Bauckham, *Climax of Prophecy*, 238-337; Carrington, *The Meaning of the Revelation*, 254-255. Both Mark 4:29 and John 4:35-38 describe reaping as redemptive.

authority over fire and had brought judgment upon the wicked (see 8:3-5). Those who by faith offered the burnt sacrifice turned away the judgment of God. Those who had no atonement for their sins fell under God's judgment and his fire consumes them eternally.

The harvest grapes were thrown into the great wine press of the wrath of God (v 19). Those who drank the wine of Babylon (v 8), will now drink the wine of God's wrath. This winepress is outside the city (v 20), signifying the place of judgment (Heb 13:12). Here is an awesome picture of "the grapes of wrath." Outside Jerusalem were winepresses. Grapes were thrown in and trodden on in the making wine. Normally this was a joyous time, but Isaiah 63:1-6 depicts Jesus Christ treading the winepress alone. His garments are stained red symbolizing his blood shed outside Jerusalem. When we partake of communion, the grape juice represents his blood. But woe to those who reject his blood and trample it underfoot. Again in 19:15 Christ is depicted as treading the winepress of the fury of the wrath of God Almighty.

Hebrews 10:29 speaks of trampling the Son of God under foot and treating as unholy the blood of the covenant. "It is a dreadful thing to fall into the hands of the living God" (v 31). Those who reject the blood will themselves be trampled in the day of vengeance. Rushdoony wrote that winepresses usually were located outside the city. Those who refuse to find sanctuary in the City of God are cast out to the winepress of the vengeance of God. "Jesus once went outside the gates of earthly Jerusalem, sentenced to death by the City of Man. Now the condemned nations go outside the gates of the true Jerusalem, to be destroyed in the winepress of the vengeance of God."[283]

The nation of Israel rejected the blood of Christ saying, "His blood be upon us" (Matt 27:25). Now in 14:20 their blood flows as high as a horses bridle [4½ feet high] for 200 miles. The length of Palestine north and south is 200 miles. While this is not meant to be taken literally, symbolically the whole region is depicted as drowning

---

[283]Rushdoony, *Thy Kingdom Come,* 182.

in its own blood during the Roman invasion. It will be either his blood or our blood! Never mind the beast; beware of the wrath of the Lamb! Therefore knowing the fear of the Lord, we persuade men through evangelism (2 Cor 5:11). The time for judgment (v 7) *and* conversion (v 15) has come. Earthly Jerusalem will fall, but Christ stands with his own on Mount Zion, the heavenly Jerusalem.

Theologians refer to the church on earth as the church militant and the church in heaven as the church triumphant. Technically we are triumphant even on earth, but we have not yet won the final battle. In the hymn, "The Church's One Foundation" one verse says:

Mid toil and tribulation and tumult of her war
She waits the consummation of peace forevermore
Till with the vision glorious her longing eyes are blest
And the great Church victorious shall be the Church at rest.[284]

[284]Samuel J. Stone, "The Church's One Foundation," (1866).

Chapters 12-14 Summary

Interlude — War against the dragon and the beast 12:1-14:20

- A. The holy war 12:1-17
- B. The two beasts 13:1-18
  1. The beast from the sea 13:1-10
  2. The beast from the earth 13:11-18
- C. The church militant and triumphant 14:1-20
  1. The final victory of the church 14:1-5
  2. The message of the church 14:6-13
  3. The harvest of redemption and judgment 14:14-20

The heavenly perspective is given in chapter 12. Satan was thwarted in his attempt to prevent the coming of Christ. When he failed, he turned on the church. Chapter 13 provides the earthly perspective. After the dragon was thwarted in his attempt to abort the Messiah, he then empowered Rome to pursue the church of Christ. The beasts which Daniel saw have now gone through several mutations, but each tyrannical government was controlled by the same dragon, who is Satan.

The first century church was living during a time of intense spiritual struggle. Nero embodied the Roman Empire and he unleashed the first persecution of the church. If apostate Judaism was the first enemy of the church, the Roman beast became the second enemy. John explained to the people of God that Christ conquered at the cross and brought in a new world order. Chapter 14 portrays the church as victorious in the beginning and abundant in the end. Particularly chapters 12 and 14 go beyond the first century in order to encourage the church. We must prepare ourselves for a long battle.

REVELATION 15

9. Seven Bowls 15:1-16:21

The seals, trumpets, and bowls all describe God's judgment from different perspectives. The opening of the seals emphasize Christ our prophet who opened the new covenant to us. The sounding of the trumpets announced Christ our King. The pouring out of the bowls, or chalices used in the Old Testament ritual for drink offerings or libation, depict Christ as our priest. In this chapter John sees seven angels preparing to pour out the seven bowls of God's wrath. Then, just as he has done in chapters 4-5 and 7:9-17, John gives another description of heaven.

We are also told that after these seven plagues the wrath of God will be finished. Jesus had taught that at the time of Jerusalem's fall there would be great tribulation, unequaled from the beginning of the world until the time in which he spoke and never to be equaled again (Matt 24:21). John is describing the beginning of the end. He is not describing the last events of history, but the last series of judgments he saw. The old covenant was about to expire. Satan has been defeated. The world system was dying and being replaced by the kingdom of God.

In the temple worship, the lamb was slaughtered, then the incense offering was followed by the trumpet blasts. The last ritual act was the drink offering poured out. John follows the same sequence in this book.

A. Seven angels 15:1-8

Once again John specifies that this vision is symbolic (v 1). In 12:1 John saw the church symbolized by a woman and in 12:3 the devil symbolized as a dragon. Now here is "another sign." The symbolism of chapter 15 is based upon Old Testament liturgy. The temple was opened (v 5). This is a reference to the Holy of Holies accessible only to the High Priest.

The *testimony* (v 5) refers to the ten commandments, the covenant document. This testimony was kept in the ark of the covenant, which was the most important item in the tabernacle. John saw this ark in 11:19. Now the focus is on what is contained in the ark. The purpose of this emphasis is to interject the idea of covenant. The stone tablets in the ark were a witness or testimony to the covenant God made with Israel. Israel had broken covenant with God and now must face judgment.

In Hebrews 8:5 we are told that this tabernacle was a copy and shadow of the heavenly tabernacle. When Moses set up the old tabernacle he could not enter it because a cloud of the glory of God has filled it (Exod 40:34-35). The cloud of God's Shekinah presence had led Israel on their way (Exod 13:21; 14:19, 24). There had been a cloud of smoke at Mount Sinai (Exod 24:15-16).

Solomon built a magnificent temple which replaced the tabernacle. When it was dedicated, the glory of God filled the temple until the priests could not minister (1Kgs 8:10-11). Isaiah also saw a vision of this temple filled with smoke (6:3-4). Yet that temple was destroyed by an invasion of Babylon in 587 BC. Ezekiel saw that glory depart in 10:2-4. Ezra rebuilt the temple and although it was inferior to Solomon's temple, Haggai prophesied that "the desired of all nations will come [the Messiah], and I will fill this house with glory, declares the Lord Almighty. The glory of this present house will be greater than the glory of the former house" (2:7-9).

This temple was about to be destroyed by the Romans. No one could enter for the purpose of intercession because the old temple was under God's ban. The day of grace for Jerusalem was over, but the temple in heaven was about to open. Again, there is nothing to suggest a rebuilt temple on earth.

The glory of God was manifested or promised with each "grand opening" of the heavenly temple. The heavenly temple opened through the death of Christ (Mark 15:38). At the moment Christ died, the veil of the old temple was torn and we were allowed to enter into the presence of God. We have confidence to enter the Most Holy Place by a new and living way opened for us through the blood of

Christ (Heb 10:19-20).

The inaugural glory of the heavenly temple was the Holy Spirit poured out at Pentecost. When we read the account of Pentecost, Peter speaks of wonders in heaven above — blood, fire, and smoke (Acts 2:19). John said (15:8) that the heavenly temple was filled with smoke from the glory of God and from his power. No one could enter until the plagues were completed. While the smoke still symbolizes God's glory and holiness, in contrast to the smoke in the temple previously as a sign of God's presence and blessing, here the smoke symbolizes his wrath in response to the breaking of the covenant. According to Leviticus 26:21 seven plagues are promised for those who break covenant.

The use of the word *plague* (vv 1, 6, 8) connects with the Egyptian deliverance under Moses. We can also pinpoint the time when these plagues occurred, because with the atonement of Christ, the destruction of the old temple, and the outpouring of God's glory at Pentecost we can now enter the Most Holy Place with confidence (Heb 10:19-25). We can be cleansed by the Blood, purified by the fire, and experience the cloud of glory.

Those who refuse the blood do not enter the new temple and those who reject Pentecost faced the holocaust described in Revelation 16. Verse 2 makes it clear that the church went through the tribulation and emerged triumphant out of their conflict with the beast, his image (the false prophet), and the number of his name (see 13:17). The emphasis here is upon the victory of the people of God and vv 2-4 serve as a conclusion to chapters 12-14. These saints rejoice because of the judgment which is coming upon the beast. While the beast temporarily conquered the saints (11:7; 13:7), the saints ultimately conquer. God is glorified and they are vindicated by these judgments (16:5-7).

While the Bible teaches that the church went through the tribulation, it is also clear that the tribulation is past, not future. John gave to the persecuted church of the first century hope that they would make it across. He described seven plagues falling upon their enemies, while they stand beside a sea of glass (4:6), and sing the song of Moses and the Lamb.

The song of Moses in Exodus 15:1-18 was a song to the Lord. The circumstances of this song are similar to the occasion of Revelation 15. God delivered his people, took vengeance upon their enemies, and in so doing revealed his righteousness.

The song of Moses is also the song of the Lamb. The Lord God Almighty is praised for his great and wonderful works, as well as for the justice and truth of his ways. He is the king of the nations. Verse 4 begins with the rhetorical question, Who will not fear and glorify God? Three reasons are given: First, he alone is holy. This word for holiness (*hosios*) emphasizes the unapproachable majesty and power of God, which is illustrated in v 8. While *hosios* is used only here and in 16:5, the more common term is *hagios*, which occurs twenty-four times in Revelation. Bauckham wrote that while *hosios* is "the quality that characterizes God as the only true God," *hagios* is a quality that can be shared by the people of God.[285]

This song, which worships God through reverential fear and glory, is the response of God's people to the call to worship in 14:7. Bengel wrote, "When God pours out His fury it is fitting that even those who stand well with Him should withdraw for a little, standing back in profound reverence till by and by the sky becomes clear again."[286]

Second, all nations will worship him. Here John returns to the theme of world evangelism, first introduced in 5:9.

Third, his righteous judgments have been made manifest (Gen 18:25). The blood of the Lamb has purchased people from every tribe, language, people, and nation (5:9). Concerning "all nations," Wesley said,

> This is a glorious testimony of the future conversion of all the heathens. The Christians are now a little flock; they who

---

[285]Bauckham, *Climax of Prophecy*, 303-304.

[286]Quoted by Smith, *Wycliffe Bible Commentary*, 1514.

> do not worship God an immense multitude. But all the nations shall come from all parts of the earth to worship him, and glorify his name.[287]

This optimism is an essential part of John's message. Caird wrote that there are a few passages in this book in which John speaks unequivocally and not symbolically. These passages should control our interpretation of the symbolism.

Once Israel was under Egyptian bondage. They cried out to God for deliverance and God sent ten plagues on Egypt. Moses demanded that Pharaoh "let my people go that they may worship me."[288] They crossed over the Red Sea and sang the song of Moses. Once in the wilderness, they received the "testimony" at Mount Sinai and constructed the tabernacle. Now the new Israel of God is under Roman persecution, which will be referred to figuratively in chapters 17-18 as "Babylon." They cried out to God asking, "How long?" It is in worship that the answer to "how long?" comes. Worship provides the context for believing in justice while experiencing injustice. "Seven angels of judgment get ready for their work while the congregation sings a hymn."[289] God, speaking through John, assured them that he was about to pour out seven plagues and they, too, would pass over a sea mixed with fire. Christ, would be their Moses (Heb 3:2-6) and Joshua (Heb 4:8). Christ, who purchased our deliverance on the cross, will lead us out of Babylonian captivity.

When a body of water is calm, we speak of it as "smooth as glass." Both glass and calm water are transparent. However, what John saw looked *like* glass mixed with fire. Fire is generally considered to be red. Therefore, the new Israel also crossed over a red sea (compare to 12:15-16; 14:20). And once across to Mount Zion they sing the song of Moses *and* of the Lamb, with harps rather than Mir-

---

[287]Wesley, *Notes*, 709.

[288]Exod 7:16; 8:11, 20; 9:1, 13; 10:3.

[289]Peterson, *Reversed Thunder*, 136-139.

iam's tambourine. Just as Egypt lost horse and rider in the Red Sea, so Jerusalem's horses were bridle-deep in a red sea of blood. "The same 'great and wondrous deeds' of (Exod 15:1) at the exodus is seen again when he hurls the enemies of the people of God into eternal punishment (Rev 14:9-11, 17-20)."[290] Here we see the people of God singing in celebration of the victory after the battle.

We, too, will have to pass through the fire. Peter said our faith would be tried by fire (1 Pet 1:7). "Everyone who wants to live a godly life in Christ Jesus will be persecuted" (2 Tim 3:12). The hymn writer explained, "The flames shall not hurt thee, I only designed thy dross to consume and thy gold to refine."[291]

Modern prosperity teaching is defective because it does not acknowledge the place of trials in the life of a believer. They teach that anything negative is a lack of faith. The truth is that we are tested and persecuted *because* of our faith!

But while most Christians acknowledge they have trials, many forget the glory of the new covenant. The church, both militant and triumphant — on earth and in heaven, is under the new testament and constitutes the new temple of God. We are cleansed by the Blood and baptized with the fire of the Holy Spirit. We are the temple of God on the earth and when we enter the Most Holy Place through prayer, the glory cloud ought to saturate us like smoke. The devil has been defeated, his world system has been judged and has fallen, we are overcomers, and we sing a song of worship and victory.

The church is depicted in 5:8 as having a harp and a bowl. The harp is used for praise; the bowl contains our prayers. Wiley said that John's symbol, the harps of God, must not be spoiled by literalists. The harp symbolizes the harmonies of the heavenly life. Evil brought discord, but redemption restores harmony. The symbols of water and fire stand for renewal and purification. Thus, God is tuning us to be in unison with all the redeemed. "If you would stand upon the sea of

---

[290]Bauckham, *Climax of Prophecy*, 298-300.

[291]"How Firm a Foundation"(1787).

glass mingled with fire, with the harps of complete and perfect triumph, there must be the beginning of those harmonies here."[292]

Verse 7 depicts angels, dressed as priests, executing the judgment of God by pouring out the bowls. The judgments which come in chapter 16 fulfill God's promises to execute judgment upon the antichrist. These judgments come in answer to the prayers of God's people. The bowls cannot be poured out until they are filled up. If we would pray more, God would do more! These judgments avenge the honor and authority of Jesus Christ who came to open "a wider door of liberty for his people to worship him in numerous solemn assemblies, without the fear of their enemies."[293]

---

[292]Wiley, *Harps of God*, 11-19.

[293]Tong, *Matthew Henry's Commentary*, 6:1168.

REVELATION 16

B. Seven Last Plagues 16:1-21

John has described the seal judgments, the trumpet judgments, and now he moves to the bowl judgments. It is characteristic of John to make the same point repeatedly. As the seals are opened, a new day dawns and judgment is released upon the old system. The trumpets repeated the judgment of the seals, but sounded a call to repentance. With the trumpet warnings, judgment was intensified with the emphasis on the destruction of one-third. The bowls repeat the message but reveal God pouring out his judgment. Here the emphasis is upon total destruction of the old system, not the collapse of the physical universe.

John's emphasis is now that the prayers of the church have been heard. These prayers have filled up the bowls which will be poured out in response. In 5:8 our prayers, like incense, fill the golden bowls. Then in this chapter seven bowls are poured out. These seven bowl judgments were God's response to the prayers of his people.

The theme of chapter 15 was that God would lead the new Israel across the sea to victory, just as he delivered his people from Egyptian bondage. There are similarities between the ten plagues of Egypt and the seven bowl judgments which are called *plagues* four times (15:1, 6, 8; 16:9).

The plagues of Egypt were literal; the seven last plagues were symbolic (15:1). Beale argued that the pouring out of a bowl by each angel is certainly not literal, but a metaphoric representation of the execution of divine judgment from heaven. If the plague of darkness in 8:12 symbolized the spiritual darkness of idolatry, and if the declaration of woe which followed was metaphorically portrayed, then it is likely that the following descriptions of the effects of the woes are also metaphorical. The big picture is that those who shed the blood of the saints and prophets would be judged by God. No other city was as guilty as was Jerusalem. Jesus leveled this indictment against Jerusalem in Matthew 23:37. Therefore the judgment would come in particular against Jerusalem and against the generation that crucified

Christ (Matt 23:35-36). They caused economic hardship (2:9), suffering, imprisonment, and death (2:9-11) for the church. They will get what they deserve (vv 5-7). Thus, the warning is that those who commit violence unleash a cause and effect principle. Consequently, they get what they have given. "All who draw the sword will die by the sword" (Matt 26:52).

The first four seals described warfare and death. The first four trumpets described blood and death. The first four bowls also describe blood and suffering. While there is variation in John's description, there is this common theme of warfare, blood, suffering, and death. The sequence is the same for the trumpets and bowls: earth, sea, rivers, sun. There are differences,

> but the similarities between the trumpets and the bowls overshadow the differences. . . . The difference in effect does not necessitate seeing the trumpets as different judgments or as chronologically preceding the bowls. . . . There is not a one-to-one correspondence between each corresponding trumpet and bowl. But they are similar enough to be considered parts of the same overall program of divine judgments occurring during the same general period.[294]

Each time, the fifth judgment is varied, but things climax with the sixth. When the sixth seal opened there was an earthquake, the sun turned black and the moon became as blood and the stars fell. This sounds similar to the seventh trumpet. Then the seventh seal opened to the seven trumpets. The sixth trumpet described the release of four demonic spirits at the Euphrates River who went forth to inflicted injury. The seventh trumpet opened to the seven bowls. The sixth bowl describes three evil spirits at the Euphrates River. But unlike the previous pattern the seventh bowl is the conclusion of God's judgment.

---

[294]Beale, *NIGNT*, 808-812.

1. First bowl — sores on the land 16:1-2

The voice from the temple must be the voice of God, since 15:8 declared that no one could enter the temple until the plagues were completed. Just as boils were the sixth plague of Egypt, so those who worshiped the beast were plagued. The word for *sore*, found only here and Luke 16:21, carries the meaning of an ulcer. An ulcer is an outward manifestation of an inward corruption. This ulcer is described as bad and evil. Swete said it was as if the mark of the beast had "broken out in a deadly infection."[295] Moses had warned of this in Deuteronomy 28:27, 35 as a curse upon those who were guilty of idolatry and apostasy. Josephus described the stench of dead bodies and how Titus groaned when he saw valleys full of dead bodies and the thick putrefaction running about them.[296] Here the *sore* also represents suffering like the spiritual and psychological torment of the fifth trumpet (9:4-6, 10).

2. Second bowl — sea turned to blood 16:3

In 8:8 the second angel sounded his trumpet and something like a huge fiery mountain was thrown into the sea. The sea was turned to blood, just as was the Nile and all the water was turned to blood in the first Egyptian plague. Here the result is the same, but we are only told that the second angel poured his bowl into the sea and that all marine life died. At the close of chapter 14, the land of Palestine was figuratively covered in blood. Josephus did record an instance where thousands of Jews fled to the Sea of Galilee and so many were slaughtered by the Romans that the whole lake was stained with blood,[297] but we should not expect to find every detail fulfilled literally. Walvoord conceded, "It is possible that the sea does not become

---

[295]Swete, *Revelation*, 244.

[296]Josephus, *Wars of the Jews*, 5.12.3-4.

[297]Josephus, *War of the Jews*, 3.10.9.

literally human blood but that it corresponds to it in appearance and lothsomeness."[298] Stuart concluded that vv 2-3 means the enemies of the church would be annoyed everywhere — on the land and on the sea.[299] Since Rome was in the southern tip of Italy and land trade was limited, the sea was the lifeblood of the Roman Empire. Beale explained that the plague was basically an economic plague and should be understood in light of 18:17-19 where those who make their living on the sea are devastated.[300]

3. Third bowl — rivers turned to blood 16:4-7

In 8:10-11 a star fell on a third of the rivers and fountains, making them bitter and poisonous. Here the imagery is varied and the rivers and fountains become blood. Again, this symbolizes economic suffering (see 18:8-19). This figurative interpretation is based on Psalm 79:3, 10, 12 and Isaiah 49:26, from which John drew. The angel of the waters[301] praised the holy One, who is eternal, for his justice. His judgments are faithful and just. They shed the blood of the saints and prophets and so God has given them blood to drink. The threefold description of God implies his sovereignty over history. Since the description of God is virtually the same as that given in 6:10, the judgment of the third bowl is part of God's answer to the prayer of the saints in 6:10.

The response in v 7 involves a personification of the altar (see also 9:13). To this point, God's judgments have been blood and fire. Those who reject the blood of the Lamb are plagued with blood and those who reject Pentecost experience holocaust.

---

[298]Walvoord, *Revelation*, 233.

[299]Stuart, *Apocalypse*, 2:310.

[300]Beale, *NIGNT,* 815.

[301]Barclay explained that in the Hebrew worldview every natural force, whether the wind, sun, rain, or waters, had its directing angel [*Revelation*, 2:127]. Clarke made the same point [*Commentary*, 6:1033-1034].

4. Fourth bowl — sun scorched 16:8-9

The fourth trumpet resulted in a plague of darkness, which was also the ninth plague on Egypt. Deuteronomy 28:22 warned of such a judgment. This is a reversal of darkness, with the sun burning like fire. The fact that those who fell under these plagues refused to repent and glorify God, indicates that they could have done so. This "scorching" could refer to the terror caused by the zealots within the besieged city of Jerusalem. However, the blood-washed are ultimately protected from the scorching sun (7:16).

5. Fifth bowl — throne of the beast 16:10-11

Not only are the Jews "burned" for persecuting the church, but Rome, the throne of the beast (13:2; see also 2:13) was plunged into darkness. Just as darkness was the ninth Egyptian plague was directed against Ra, the Egyptian sun god, the kingdom of Satan was short-lived. God simply has to speak (v 1), and it is finished (v 17).

The sun was also darkened with the fifth trumpet, as smoke came out of the abyss (9:2). Darkness is a symbol of judgment in 1 Samuel 2:9; Amos 5:20; Joel 2:2; Zephaniah 1:15. It also symbolizes ignorance and wickedness in Psalm 82:5; Proverbs 2:13, Ecclesiastes 2:14. In such passages as Isaiah 13:9-10; Ezekiel 32:7-8, Joel 2:10; 3:15; Amos 8:9, and Habakkuk 3:11 darkness is a biblical symbol for political upheaval and the fall of rulers. Jesus warned in Matthew 24:29, "Immediately after the distress of those days 'the sun will be darkened, and the moon will not give its light; the stars will fall from the sky, and the heavenly bodies will be shaken.'" After Nero committed suicide in June 68, Rome was plunged into civil war. Rome had four emperors in the year 69.

The gnawing of tongues was the result of all the previous judgments: boils, thirst, and scorching heat (compare to the expression of 9:5-6). Again, John emphasized the fact that these judgments did not produce repentance. Their hearts, like the heart of Pharaoh, became hardened beyond recall. Josephus described the seditious within

Jerusalem who had become so hardened that they "were incapable of repenting of the wickedness they had been guilty of."[302]

6. Sixth bowl — invasion of demons 16:12-16

Verses 12-16 are a recapitulation of 9:13-21. The language of v 20 is similar to that of the sixth seal in 6:14. In vv 12-16 these evil spirits influence the kings of the earth to gather for "the war" (v 14). The Euphrates River was dried up so the kings from the east could cross. Just as Israel had been invaded by the Assyrians and Babylonians to their north and east, so now Babylon would be attacked from forces even further east. Cyrus led his Persian armies from the east and north (Isa 41:2, 25). "From the east I summon a bird of prey" (Isa 46:11). God cleared the way for him (Isa 44:27-28). Jeremiah also promised that God would dry up the waters (50:38; 51:36). The Romans feared an invasion of Parthia from their eastern border and they had often been driven back.

This drying up of the Euphrates is the antithesis of Israel crossing the Red Sea and later the Jordan River. "The drying up of rivers is one of the responses of nature to the coming of God (Isa 50:2; Hos 13:15; Nah 1:4)."[303]

This invasion of demons (v 14) was an invasion of darkness. Verse 13 describes frogs, corresponding to the second Egyptian plague. With the sixth trumpet, the demons were symbolized as locusts. These frogs come out of the mouths of the dragon, the beast, and the false prophet. This symbolizes their false teachings, which was accompanied by signs — imitating the work of Christ. Whedon described this battle as "a battle of ideas."[304] "The historical plague of frogs is now applied symbolically to deceptive spirits. The allusion is one of the clearest examples in the book of a literal exodus plague

---

[302]Josephus, *Wars of the Jews*, 5.12.4.

[303]Aune, *WBC*, 52B:891.

[304]Whedon, *Commentary*, 5:440.

reapplied to a new situation and spiritualized."

Christ came to do spiritual battle (vv 14-15). The results of this battle are described in chapter 19. John described this battle as "the great day of God Almighty" (v 14). According to Acts 2:16-21 "the great and notable day of the Lord" began at Pentecost. This "day" extends until Christ's second coming.

But during this time of his glory and judgment, there are special times when he visits the world in either glory or judgment (see Amos 5:17; Joel 2:11). Revelation 1:7; 2:5, 16, 25; 3:3, 11, 20; 22:7, 12, 20 also all contain promises that Christ would come. These references do not necessarily describe his second advent (see Matt 16:28).

The exhortation of v 15 borrows from John's words in 3:3, 18. The exhortation to *watch* means to be awake.

Verse 15 is not a promise that all who are saved will persevere. Instead it is a blessing reserved for those who do persevere. As soldiers we should be prepared to fight, because our commander may call unexpectedly (1 Thess 5:2-8). Mulholland wrote,

> The presence of this passage makes it extremely difficult to presume the "rapture" of the church prior to the supposed outpouring of God's wrath on sinful humanity. It also makes it highly improbable that any type of "tribulation map" or "blueprint of the future" can be taken seriously. If Christ tells the church that the end will come like a thief, unexpected, unforeseen, unprepared for, how can anyone have the temerity to presume to predict the events of Christ's coming.[305]

These demonic spirits gather at a place called Armageddon. Revelation 16:16 is the only place in the entire Bible the word *Armageddon* is found. Theologically, Armageddon signifies "the place of the final struggle between the powers of evil and the Kingdom of

---

[305]Mulholland, *Revelation*, 270.

God."[306] Therefore, if the interpreter believes the Kingdom of God has not yet been established, he will tend to interpret Armageddon as a future event. If, however, it is understood that the Kingdom came with Christ's first advent, then the great tribulation will be linked with the first century siege of Jerusalem. Thus, the climatic spiritual battle of Armageddon was also fought in the first century when the kingdom of Christ invaded this dark world. This concept does not imply the cessation of all conflict between the kingdom of darkness and light, but it does mark the turning point of the great war of the ages. In Matthew 24:29-31 it was immediately after the great tribulation that the sign of the Son of man appears in heaven. Then the gospel trumpet is sounded. John follows the same outline. After the great tribulation of Revelation 6-19, Christ appears in heaven on a white horse and conquers by the Word which precedes from his mouth.

By concluding this is a spiritual battle, I am not denying its reality. The most real battles we fight are in the spiritual realm. Armageddon was the spiritual battle fought between the kingdom of darkness and the kingdom of light. As Dwight Wilson documented in *Armageddon Now!* futurists have consistently failed in their speculation concerning a coming world conflict. There is no such geographical place. There is no mountain of Megiddo. The best scholars recognize this and conclude this is not a literal reference to a geographic site. There is a *valley* of Megiddo which is entered on the West at the port of Haifa. About twenty miles from Haifa is the plain of Jezreel and the city of Megiddo is located on the edge of this plain. This valley is about thirty-six miles long and has an average width of fifteen miles. The valley of Megiddo is 15 miles x 15 miles x 20 miles.[307] Such an area is not large enough for the armies of all the world. Thus, a stronger case can be made for understanding Armageddon as a *spiritual* battle which was fought between the kingdom

---

[306]Ladd, *Commentary*, 216.

[307]Tenny, *Zondervan Pictorial Dictionary,* 1:259-260.

of darkness and the kingdom of light in the first century when the kingdom of Christ invaded this dark world.

7. Seventh bowl — fall of Babylon 16:17-21

The seventh bowl is described in vv 17-21. The seventh angel declares, "It is done."We have been brought to this point in 8:5 and 11:19. Notice also the similarity of the language of v 20 with 6:14.

Commentators differ concerning the identity of *the great city* in v 19. In 11:8 *the great city* is Jerusalem. Those who interpret the city as Jerusalem tend to connect the description of this city, split into three parts from the great earthquake, with Zechariah 14:3-5. However, the book of Revelation centers around two great cities. In this context, John is introducing the fall of Rome, which will be the subject of chapters 17-18. Rome is called *the great city* five times in the next chapter. *Babylon the Great*, therefore identifies *the great city. The cities of the nations*, also referenced in v 19, describes all of the Roman provincial cities which were affected by the fall of Rome. Rome was split into three factions contending for control, after the death of Nero in AD 67, and a large portion of Rome was burned in battles between rival factions.[308] I see no need to decide whether this earthquake brought down Jerusalem or Rome. Actually apostate Jerusalem had become part of "Babylon." The triumph of Christ brought both to an end. First, the Jewish system was brought down, then Rome, and ultimately all the kingdoms of this world.

Babylon drank the cup of wine, which was God's furious wrath (see 14:10; 18:6). The basis of God's wrath was that Babylon drank and served the wine of adultery (14:8; 17:2, 4; 18:3). This bowl was poured into the atmosphere because that is where the lightning, thunder, and hail occur. Lightning, rumblings, peals of thunder and a great earthquake parallel the manifestation of God at Mount Sinai (Exod 19:16-18). The hailstones described in v 21 link this plague with the seventh Egyptian plague (Exod 9:18-26). During the final

---

[308]Mulholland, *Revelation*, 273.

five months of the siege of Jerusalem, after Titus had urged the inhabitants to surrender and they refused, Josephus described the catapults which were used to launch 100-pound stones over a quarter of a mile. These white stones rained on the city like hailstones.[309]

At the sixth *seal* the old world order rolled up and the new order unrolled. At the inauguration of the new covenant on the day of Pentecost, Peter explained that the outpouring of the Holy Spirit constituted a spiritual shakeup. John said as the seals of the new covenant were broken there was a spiritual earthquake (v 18). It was prophesied in Haggai 2:6 and explained in Hebrews 12:26-28. There was no earthquake like it. It brought down Babylon. At Mount Sinai, when the law was given, the earth shook. Pentecost was the commemoration of the giving of the law. At Pentecost God shook the whole world by unrolling his new covenant. The establishment of the kingdom of God deposed every king, prince, general, rich, and mighty man (6:15) and overthrew our enemies. This description corresponds to the seventh *trumpet* and the seventh *bowl.*

Terry noted that at 11:15, at the seventh trumpet, the beginning of Christ's reign was announced. But the sounding of that trumpet was delayed by the revelation of many things which must come to pass before the end. Here John is not yet ready to introduce the coming of the kingdom of Christ. Instead he depicts the judgments by which the end of the pre-Messianic age was consummated.

The first reference to Babylon the Great was in 14:8. The second is in 16:19. Now chapters 17-19 will focus on the fall of Babylon. We are through the seals, trumpets, and bowls. Judgment has come and the enemies of the church have been defeated. Babylon is defeated and Jerusalem is victorious. Historically, Babylon has fallen. Historically, Rome fell in AD 476. But Babylon still exists and many people are still captivated by its system. What they do not know is that Babylon has no future. The future is with the new Jerusalem (see 21:2).

---

[309] Josephus, *Wars of the Jews*, 5.6.3.

Chapters 15-16 Summary

V. Seven bowls 15:1-16:21
- A. Seven angels 15:1-8
- B. Seven last plagues 16:1-21
  1. First bowl — sores on the earth 16:1-2
  2. Second bowl — sea turned to blood 16:3
  3. Third bowl — rivers turned to blood 16:4-7
  4. Fourth bowl — sun scorched 16:8-9
  5. Fifth bowl — throne of the beast 16:10-11
  6. Sixth bowl — invasion of demons 16:12-16
  7. Seventh bowl — fall of Babylon 16:17-21

The pouring out of the bowls or chalices used in the Old Testament ritual for drink offerings or libation, depict Christ as our priest. After these seven plagues the wrath of God will be finished. Jesus had taught that at the time of Jerusalem's fall there would be great tribulation, unequaled from the beginning of the world until the time in which he spoke and never to be equaled again (Matt 24:21). John is describing the beginning of the end. He is not describing the last events of history, but the last series of judgments he saw. The old covenant was about to expire. Satan has been defeated. The world system was dying and being replaced by the kingdom of God. The old system has met its "Waterloo" — its Armageddon. Those who refuse the blood do not enter the new temple and those who reject Pentecost faced the holocaust described in Revelation 16. But a new and living way opened for us through the blood of Christ (Heb 10:19-20).

REVELATION 17

Interlude — Babylon the harlot 17:1-18:24

Babylon was first mentioned in 14:8, then again 16:19. Now it becomes the major theme of chapters 17-18. Alan Johnson wrote that these two chapters "form an extended appendix to the seventh bowl, where the judgment on Babylon was mentioned."[310]

We first encounter *Babel* in Genesis 10-11. The word *babel* means "confusion" and Genesis 11:9 contains this play on words. Babel was the first great city of man. About 150 years after the flood, God told them in Genesis 9:1 to spread out and replenish the earth. Instead the people rebelled against God and decided to "build ourselves a city, with a tower that reaches to the heavens, so that we may make a name for ourselves and not be scattered over the face of the whole earth" (Gen 11:4). This constituted the first act of organized rebellion in recorded history. But rebellion against God meant the *loss* of freedom. The city was founded by Nimrod (Gen 10:9-10). Josephus wrote that Nimrod "gradually changed the government into tyranny — seeing no other way of turning men from the fear of God, but to bring them into a constant dependence upon his power."[311]

The tower was also an observation tower used in astrology. Although the stars were created as signs to mark seasons and days and years (Gen 1:14), this astronomy was first perverted into astrology at Babel. This represented the first rival religion to the true worship of God and marked the beginning of paganism. There are really only two religions in the world: Christianity and paganism. One teaches that we are separated from God by sin and that God became man to die for our sins. The other option teaches that man is not separated from God, but in fact has the power within himself to become god. The Bible teaches God had to come down; Babylon was man's first attempt to lift himself up.

---

[310]Johnson, *XBC*, 12:554.

[311]Josephus, *Antiquities*, 1.4.2.

After Adam and Eve sinned, they hid. When Cain sinned, his face was downcast. But Babel was proud and wanted to make a name. God restrained the s in of ancient Babel and the tower was never completed, but the spirit of pride and rebellion lives on. In v 5 Babylon is called a *mother*. If she is a mother, who are her children? Every city built by man without God is Babylon.

Egypt was the first great city of man politically. However, Egypt adopted the astrology of Babylon. Then Assyria was the next great world power, but the Chaldeans drove the Assyrians out of Babylonia in 625 BC and the Babylonian empire became the world power. It is significant that Babylon conquered Israel and led them into captivity. While Daniel was in Babylonian captivity, he saw a vision of a man, whose feet represented Rome and head represented Babylon.[312] Although Babylon was politically replaced as the world power by the Medes and Persians, Greece, and finally Rome — symbolically every world power built upon the foundation of Babylon. By the first century the evil empire is no longer Egypt; it is Rome. While John writes during the time of the final Roman empire, the kingdoms of man are a beast which has gone through numerous mutations. Thus, John makes symbolic references to Egypt, Babylon, and Rome, which are all connected spiritually. Rome was the current embodiment of the beast.

By the time of John's writing Babylon symbolically is Rome — the city of seven hills (17:9). Some commentators feel that John's writing would have been banned by the Roman empire if he attacked them directly, so he spoke of Rome almost in a code, referring to her as *Babylon*.[313] However, John's description of *Babylon* corresponds to the *Dea Roma* coin which was minted in AD 71 under Vespasian. On one side of the coin there is a depiction of Vespasian. On the

---

[312]According to Beale, well over half of all the Old Testament allusions in this chapter come from Daniel, and most of them are from Daniel 7 [*NIGNT*, 890].

[313]Augustine mentioned this possibility in *City of God*, 20.19; Stuart, *Apocalypse*, 2:319; Metzger, *Breaking the Code,* 85.

reverse side is Roma, the pagan goddess of Rome, sitting on seven hills with the river god Tiber at the right. Thus this political symbolism reflects the same symbolism used by John and links the beast, the Roman Caesar, with the harlot.[314]

While we can trace political changes across history, John also uses *Babylon* to represent religious abuse. All world dictatorships rule by appealing to religious authority. And religion gains acceptance by compromising with political power. This is depicted by John as the impure woman (false religion) riding on the beast of Roman political power, which we saw in chapter 13.

The Jews sold out to Rome by accusing Jesus of opposing taxation and claiming to be king. They shouted out, "We have no king but Caesar" (John 19:15). There is a no more dangerous combination than political ambition justified by religious vocabulary. Most of the wars that have ever been fought have started on this basis. There is always a temptation for the church to compromise with the world. The terrible irony is that Israel, which on three occasions was invaded by Babylon, later decided to cooperate with *Babylon* in order to persecute the Christians. There is a sense in which Jerusalem had become Babylon.

The best interpreters divide over whether John is connecting Rome with Babylon or Jerusalem with Babylon. Although the focus of the second half of Revelation is on Rome, I do not think it is necessary to pick between them; John's point is that they had become one in the same. The church had become so much like the world that it was part of the world system. A common theme of the Old Testament prophets is that Jerusalem had been unfaithful to God and had become a prostitute committing spiritual adultery by loving the world (see Isa 1:21; Jer 2:20-24, 39-33, 3:1-3; Ezek 16:1-63; 23:1-49; Hosea 1:2-4:15; Mic 1:7). Thus, the woman in 17:1 is Israel. She sits on the beast of Rome and they *both* constitute "Babylon."And yet Rome attacked Jerusalem (v 16). Satan's kingdom is divided against itself (vv 16-17).

---

[314]Aune, *WBC*, 52C:920-922.

Any religious organization which compromises truth in order to gain power is *Babylon*. We are to "come out" and be separate from *Babylon*, regardless of the organization. The word *church* literally means "called out ones" (*ekklesia*). We are not to be unequally yoked together with unbelievers (2 Cor 6:14-18). Too often, like Achan who brought a Babylonian garment into the camp of Israel and caused the defeat of the entire nation (Josh 7), we are guilty of bringing the culture and values of Babylon into the church. Babylon today is Paris fashion, Las Vegas gambling, Hollywood entertainment, San Francisco perversion, and Washington, D.C. corruption. We should not be a member of a secret society which has mixed together Zoroaster's ancient magic, the zodiac and pagan astrology, Jewish superstition, Muslim teaching, Hindu philosophy and Christian terminology. Whether it is called Freemasonry or Mormonism, scripturally it is *Babylon*.

In essence all false religions are one. Whether we are looking at cults, the occult, secret societies, new age philosophies, humanism, communism, or apostate Christianity, there is a common denominator found within all error. It is an appeal to human pride and a rebellion against God's law. It is a faith in something other than or in addition to the blood of Christ.

The spirit of Babylon rules politically (17:18). It controls the world's commerce (18:11-13). It governs the entertainment industry (18:22). But it deals in more than pleasure, power, and wealth — it buys and sells the *souls* of men (18:13).

God has pronounced judgment upon Babylon. Although some have speculated that Babylon would literally be rebuilt, they have missed the whole meaning of John's vision. According to Isaiah 44-48 Cyrus the Persian would conquer Babylon. Isaiah 13:20 and Jeremiah 51:26 specifically declare that Babylon "will be desolate forever." From the time that Cyrus conquered Babylon in 539 BC, Babylon never again became an independent political power — although it continued to exist for another three hundred years.

REVELATION 17:1-18

A. The influence of Babylon 17:1-18

One of the seven angels showed John the punishment of the harlot. John was carried away in the Spirit to the desert, where the true church was being protected (12:6,14). But here John sees another woman in the desert, representing the apostate church, Judaism the counterpart to the faithful church in chapters 12, 21-22. Because this woman has committed spiritual adultery against Christ, she is depicted as a harlot who is "in bed" with political rulers. This harlot is symbolically upheld by the beast, which was first introduced in 13:1-3. Yet the harlot and the beast are one. "Babylon refers both to the pagan world and the apostate church that cooperates with that world."[315] She is identified in v 18 as the great city that has a kingdom over the kings of the earth. In 18:23 this *Babylon* is accused of leading all the nations astray.

The gaudy harlot is dressed in purple and scarlet. She is covered with gold and precious stones. In the hand of the harlot was a golden cup, full of obscenities and filth. She caused the earthly to get drunk (v 2; 14:8; Jer 51:7) and is herself continually drunken (v 6) with abundance, power, pride, violence, idolatry, and the blood of the saints, that is, those she has martyred (see 18:24). Osborne summarized Babylon as: idolatry, immorality, luxury, and persecution.[316]

It is obvious from the description of a prostitute sitting on a scarlet beast with a title on her forehead, that *Babylon* symbolizes something. Verse 5 calls this symbolism a *mystery*. *Mystery* is not part of the name. Again we are reminded that the description given is not to be taken literally. The mystery is a secret revealed in the form of symbols which is explained to John (v 7; see also 1:20). The term *great* carries the connotation of "notorious." To call this harlot *great* is a statement of sarcasm. The term *mother* means archetype, "the parent, ringleader, patroness, and nourisher of many daughters that

---

[315]Beale, *NIGNT,* 885-886.

[316]Osborne, *BECNT*, 613.

closely copy after her."[317]

Verse 8 is a parody on 1:4, 8, where God's eternity is emphasized. "That the beast 'is not' refers to the continuing effects of his defeat by Christ at the cross and resurrection. . . . Therefore, the application of the threefold formula for divine eternity to the beast is intended to ridicule the beast's vain efforts to defeat the *true* eternal being and his forces."[318] The beast repeatedly comes up from the abyss, but is headed for destruction (19:20). It has seven heads and ten horns. Also, in v 8 is another reference to the book of life.

The biblical symbolism of the beast is fluid. Daniel saw four beasts, as four world empires in Daniel 7. Then John saw the last of Daniel's beasts with seven heads. The seven-headed beast can refer collectively to the Roman Empire or the seven heads can refer chronologically to the succession of Roman emperors. 13:18 refers to the beast as one individual emperor.[319] 13:18 and 17:9 are parallel passages, both of which call for wisdom. This seems to connect them as having the same subject, which is Nero.

The seven heads of the beast were first mentioned in 12:3, then 13:1. Based on Daniel 7, the beast was Babylon, Medo-Persia, Greece, and then Rome. Here the focus moves from the history of the beast to his current form as Rome. The seven heads in vv 3, 9 carry a double meaning dealing with both geographic place and chronological time. First they represent the seven hills of Rome. No one in the first century would have connected this reference to any other city.

Since the first interpretation of the seven heads corresponds to the seven hills of Rome, the second interpretation should be related. Thus, John is describing seven Roman emperors. Swete wrote that if the beast is the Roman Empire, his seven heads are emperors.[320]

---

[317]Wesley, *Notes*, 714.

[318]Beale, *NIGNT,* 864.

[319]Gentry, *Before Jerusalem Fell*, 310.

[320]Swete, *Apocalypse*, 217.

REVELATION 17:1-18

While the book of Revelation is symbolic, here John uses symbolic language to describe first century events. There would be no point in describing the beast which *was*, which *is not*, and which *will come* if John is not trying to convey the concept of time. How can five of seven be fallen (v 10) without some historical framework? "When John talks of the five kings who have fallen, he is talking of history. When he talks of the one who 'is', he is talking of current events. When he talks about the ones who are to come, he is making genuine prophecies."[321]

Starting with Julius Caesar, there were a total of five who fell before Nero. Nero was the sixth emperor. The seventh head refers to consolidated reign of Galba, Otho, and Vitellius who were each emperor for only a matter of months. An "eighth" which followed was Vespasian. Thus, Revelation was written before June 68. The message of Revelation to the early church was that in the years which lay ahead, although the Roman empire would wane, then come back and appear invincible, it was doomed to destruction.

The seven heads in vv 9-10 include all the Roman emperors up to the time of John's revelation. John is writing during the reign of the sixth emperor, Nero. Starting with Julius Caesar, there were a total of five who fell before Nero. According to Foxe's *Book of Martyrs* Nero was the sixth emperor and thought to be the antichrist.[322] With the death of Nero, the Julio-Claudian line of Roman emperors ended and the Roman Empire was plunged into civil war.

The seventh head refers to consolidated reigns of Galba, Otho, and Vitellius who were each emperor for only a matter of months. Galba ruled from June 68-January 69. In January 69 allegiance was switched from Galba to Otho and Galba was slain. Otho ruled from

---

[321]Wilson, "The Problem with the Domitianic Date," 603.

[322]Foxe, *Book of Martyrs*, 1:100. See "The Identity of the Sixth King," chapter 10 of Gentry, *Before Jerusalem Fell*, 146-164; Sproul, *Last Days According to Jesus*, 146-147; Mulholland, *Revelation*, 281.

January 69 until his suicide on April 17, 69. Then Vitellius was declared emperor. He died in battle with Vespasian on December 20, 69. Thus, from June 68-December 69 was the "Year of the Four Emperors." This accounts for the "little while" of v 10.

Then v 11 refers to an eighth. Yet the beast has seven heads (compare the seven-eight formula to Eccl 11:2; Mic 5:5). The Greek text of v 10 referred to "the five," "the one," and "the one." Yet v 11 refers to "an eighth." While it could be argued technically that Otho was the eighth, John gives us a clue that he is not counting "the eighth."

Here John uses a "seven-to-eight-equals-one" pattern. Johnson explained, "The eighth day was the day of the resurrection of Christ, Sunday. It was also the beginning of a new week. The seventh day, the Jewish Sabbath, is held over, to be replaced by the first of a new series, namely Sunday." In this book each of the series of sevens, except for the seven churches, follows a pattern of the seventh of the old series becoming the first of a new series.[323] The beast was, is not, but will revive (13: 3, 12, 14).

An eighth, Vespasian, would follow and the Roman empire would be "healed" under his leadership. The Roman empire nearly collapsed after the suicide of Nero. It was not Nero who came back to life, although some commentators refer to the Nero redivivus myth. Instead, it was the beast, the Roman empire which revived under Vespasian. Verses 8, 11 refer then to the Roman empire which *was* from Julius to Nero, which *was not* during the year of the three short terms, and which *would come* back under Vespasian. It is also significant that the Greek text uses the neuter case to refer to the beast, but the masculine case to refer to the eighth king. Thus, the eighth emperor is a person, but his significance is that under him the Roman Empire revived.

1. Julius Caesar 49-44 BC
2. Augustus 31 BC - AD 14

---

[323]Johnson, *XBC*, 12:560-561.

3. Tiberius AD 14-37
4. Gaius or Caligula AD 37-41
5. Claudius AD 41-54
6. Nero AD 54-68
7. [Galba AD 68-69; Otho AD 69; Vitellius AD 69]
8. Vespasian AD 69-79

Yet this "revived" Roman empire was still part of the old monster that was slain by Christ at the cross. John's point is stated in vv 8 and 11 — while it may appear to the persecuted church that the Roman Empire was invincible, it was actually headed for destruction. The cross of Christ was the fatal wound to the beast (13:3). It may have appeared to be alive and well, but it was under God's ban and was scheduled for destruction. "Every power which sets itself up against God shall in the end break itself on the Cross."[324]

John assured the early church that Babylon would fall. Because Jerusalem had identified with Babylon, it fell in AD 70. Jordan wrote that while the Roman empire did not cease to exist in AD 70, it did fall and ceased to exist as a spiritual power.[325] I would prefer to say that "Babylon" came under God's ban, that it is cursed and has no future. Nor is Rome "eternal," but God allows the spirit of Babylon to remain in his world as a means of testing his people.

In vv 15-17 John gives some insight into the internal tension or power struggle within the Roman empire.[326] Wall described its self destruction as "evil turns upon itself in order to 'accomplish God's purpose.' . . . The destiny of the anti-God kingdom is self-destruc-

---

[324]Caird, *Revelation*, 221.

[325]Jordan, *A Brief Reader's Guide to Revelation,* 42.

[326]Aune recalled the hostility that many Jews from Palestine had toward Rome, which led to open revolt in AD 66, when Jewish insurgents seized the Roman garrison at the Antonia fortress, as well as Masada [*WBC*, 52C:931]. It is reasonable to assume this resentment was shared by other provinces.

tion."[327] God causes the wrath of men to praise him (Ps 76:10). Swete wrote that the ten kings "will not fall out, for their unanimity is of God, Who has chosen them as instruments of His Will; and it will continue until His words . . . shall be fulfilled."[328] However, he is not the author of evil.

While the church felt Roman persecution, the kingdom of the beast suffered from ambition, jealousy, squabbling, and hatred. The harlot attempted to sit on many "waters" (vv 1, 15; Jer 51:13), which constitute peoples, multitudes, nations, and languages and they all want to be God.This reference to languages in this context reminds us of the original confusion of languages or babel in Babylon (Gen 11:6-9). Only Christ can unify such diversity (5:9; 7:9). Literal Babylon fell. Jerusalem fell. Rome fell. But the spirit of Babylon continues to operate in the realm of darkness. Babylon will be destroyed, but the church will be delivered.

In vv 12-16, ten kings were involved. These kings correspond to the ten horns mentioned in vv 3, 7. Osborne connected them to the kings of the earth in 16:14.[329] According to 17:2 the harlot committed adultery with the kings of the earth and v 18 concludes that through this illicit relationship Babylon reigned over the kings of the earth. The Roman empire divided itself into ten provinces.[330] These ten kingdoms, which were subject to Rome, had no real autonomy. They were not significant enough to be remembered, but the regions over which they ruled were Italy, Achaia, Asia, Syria, Egypt, Africa, Spain, Gaul, Britain, and Germany.

John's purpose is to give the early Christians assurance that God knows the future of the Roman empire. They have no way of knowing

---

[327]Wall, *NIBC*, 18:204-205; 209. See also Mark 3:23-26.

[328]Swete, *Apocalypse*, 222.

[329]Osborne, *BECNT*, 592.

[330]Osborne, *BECNT,* 621. Notice also that on this basis Herod (Matt 2:1, 3; Mark 6:14; Luke 1:5; Acts 12:1) and Agrippa (Acts 25-26) were called *kings*. Osborne called this an honorary title.

that by AD 313 Constantine would convert to Christianity. They are simply told that the Lamb will overcome. According to 12:7 the dragon lost the battle against Christ and so now he makes war against the rest of the woman's seed (12:17), the followers of Christ.

The followers of Christ are called, chosen, and faithful (v 14). Wesley noted that those who finally overcome with Christ were called by his word and Spirit, were taken out of the world, when they were enabled to believe in him, and were faithful unto death.[331] It is such followers who are able to make war against the beast (13:4). In this war against the beast, these followers of the Lamb will prevail as surely as Christ prevailed at the cross.

[331]Wesley, *Notes,* 715-716.

REVELATION 18

B. The fall of Babylon 18:1-24

While 14:8 announces the fall of Babylon and 16:19 describes its fall, chapter 17 does *not* describe its destruction. Babylon is introduced and described in chapter 17 and her destruction is described in chapter 18. The fact that this destruction has already been mentioned simply reflects John's tendency to recapitulate. It is common for John to introduce a concept, then return to it, giving further explanation.

The correct *interpretation* of this chapter is that Rome has fallen. Verses 21-23 establish the fact that the Roman empire will not be reestablished. However, the *application* is that *Babylon*, as a philosophy, is always bankrupt, but still alluring, attractive, beautiful, tempting. Yet her doom is so certain it is spoken of as having already happened. Those who sell their soul for what she offers will be punished with her (v 4). Spiritual Babylon has fallen, but sinful man keeps trying to rebuild her in different forms. Rebellious man will never succeed in establishing the city of man permanently. God will always sent confusion and division. There will always be more than one leader struggling for control. However, God has established a new order which will succeed. False religion will always oppose the exclusive claims of Jesus Christ, but he will overcome (17:14).

1. The pronouncement of judgment 18:1-3

After the angel had shown John the true nature of Rome, in chapter 17, another angel of the same kind, but with great authority, begins another vision by declaring that Rome has fallen. The aorist verb, which is repeated, emphasizes the certainly of the event, even though it had not yet occurred. The declaration of the angel is similar to that of Isaiah 21:9, when Cyrus had captured Babylon. Since Rome is already the habitation of evil spirits, when she falls demons will be all that remain. John describes fallen Babylon as the home of demons, a haunt (v 2) for evil spirits and unclean vultures. Compare to the desolation described in Isaiah 13:19-22; 34:11; Jeremiah 50:39. In fact, Aune catalogued fourteen verses from Jeremiah 50-51 which are incorporated in this chapter.[332]

Verse 3 explains three reasons for her fall (see Isa 23:17). First, Rome fell because she made the nations drink the wine of her adulteries (14:8). Second, the kings of the earth fornicated with her. Third, the merchants of the earth became rich from her excessive luxury. This illicit relationship is driven by power, sex, and money. Kings compromised with her for political gain and merchants compromised for greed. Verses 11-13 will expand on the luxury of Rome.

2. The call to evacuate 18:4-8

In vv 4-8 another angel of the same kind calls the people of God out of Babylon. His words are a quote from Jeremiah 51:45. Just as Abraham was called out of Babylon (Gen 12:1), Lot came out of Sodom (Gen 19:14-15), and just as God's people fled to Pella during the siege of Jerusalem (Matt 24:15-18), so we are called to separate ourselves from sin (2 Cor 6:17). While the early church could not flee the Roman Empire, they were instructed not to compromise with Rome, just as we are not to love the world (1 John 2:15-17).

Specifically the early church was warned that it must maintain separation from Rome so that it would not share in her sins which are piled up to heaven (see Gen 18:21). God will punish her "double" and those who are implicated with her will also share in her plagues. Kline argued that the word *double* carries the idea of "duplicate" or "equivalent." Thus, "Babylon's inequities were to be balanced by their equal weight of punishment in God's scales of justice."[333]

Binney wrote that v 4 implies that there may be found some of God's true people even in a community, civil or ecclesiastical, as corrupt as that described in vv 2-3 and that by remaining there they incur the double danger of sharing in its sins and consequent

---

[332]Aune, *WBC*, 52C:983.

[333]Kline, "Double Trouble," 177.

plagues.[334] Those seduced by the harlot to abandon their loyalty to Jesus will be blotted from the book of life and included in the plagues designed for Babylon.

Verse 7 describes the brazen arrogance of Rome. She sits as a queen and does not intend to vacate her throne. The harlot's words echo Isaiah 47:7-8. She refuses to mourn, because her soldiers have been victorious not killed. But the judgment of God will be so devastating that she will be forced to acknowledge the reality of her condition. She will be burned by fire (see 17:16).

3. The lament of grief and loss 18:9-20

Verses 8-20 describe the reaction of three groups who have compromised in order to share in Babylon's power and wealth. Compare this description of lament to Ezekiel 27:28-33. Each group stood far off, each wept and wailed, "Alas, alas, you great city" (vv 10, 16, 19)[335] over the suddenness of the destruction "in one hour" (vv 10, 17, 19). Metzger wrote that while Rome's decay and degeneracy persisted for centuries, during a fateful week in August, 410 Rome was pillaged and laid waste.[336] While the decline was gradual, the fall was sudden.

Those who associated with Rome, like any other harlot, paid for the privilege. They were seduced by the wine of her fornication (14:8; 17:2; 18:3) and they were deceived by her sorcery (v 23). Now those who have made the "investment" react with horror when they see it "go up in smoke" as judgment came. The kings of the earth reacted with horror in vv 9-10. Yet they remained at a safe distance, afraid of losing their own power if they got involved.

---

[334]Binney, *Commentary*, 697.

[335]This Greek word *ouai* is the same word which was used three times in 8:13. However, it was a pronouncement of judgment there. Here it is an expression of grief and mourning.

[336]Metzger, *Breaking the Code,* 87.

Then the reaction of the merchants is described in vv 11-20. They also mourned at a distance, afraid of going down with their investments. Twenty-eight luxury items are listed in vv 12-13. This list is modeled on the list of forty products traded by Tyre in Ezekiel 27:12-24.

This list may be divided into six categories: precious metals and gems, expensive fabrics, ornamental pieces, aromatic substances, foodstuffs, animals and people. "The purpose of the long list is to impress the reader with the tremendous flow of trade that poured into Rome."[337] These imports come from India, China, Africa, Arabia, Armenia and beyond.

In v 14 the costly and splendid things, which were the desire of Babylon's soul, can literally be translated "bright things." But the splendor of the angel in v 1 is more awesome than the glitter of Babylon. Materialism will never satisfy the hunger of our soul for God's glory. The description of Rome in v 16 compares with her description in 17:4.

Bauckham called the book of Revelation "one of the fiercest attacks on Rome and one of the most effective pieces of political resistance literature from the period of the early empire." Babylon must fall in order to make way for the arrival of the New Jerusalem. Of particular emphasis in this chapter is Rome's economic exploitation of her empire. Roman civilization, as a corrupting influence, rode on the back of Roman military power, which produced the unity, security, stability, and prosperity which was referred to as *pax Romana*. Tacitus described the "peace of Rome" as "peace with bloodshed." The city of Rome grew great through military conquest, which brought wealth and power to the city and spread its economic and cultural influence throughout the world. Rome believed that she could not fall.

The satanic nature of Roman power was most clearly demonstrated in the deification of the state which created a state religion. Thus, economic exploitation and the corrupting influence of the state

---

[337]Mounce, *NICNT*, 333.

religion went hand in hand. The luxuries which Rome imported, were often obtained through plunder or produced through economic exploitation. They were the price which the kings of the earth have paid for the favors of the harlot. But, Bauckham pointed out, the price was actually paid by their peoples in taxation and slavery. John's cargo list ends in v 13 with a reference to slavery, revealing the inhuman brutality and the contempt for human life, on which the whole of Rome's prosperity and luxury rests.[338] This verse constitutes the only outright condemnation of slavery in the New Testament. The actual Greek word used in v 13 simply means *bodies*. But the word *soma* was used to refer to a slave.[339] Perhaps 20% of the population in the Roman Empire were slaves in the first century and Rome was the greatest of all slave markets.[340]

Those who mourned the fall of Babylon included the client kings, as well as the local ruling class (17:2; 18:3, 9; see Ps 2:2), the merchants of the earth who did business with Rome (vv 3, 11, 23), and those employed in the maritime transport industry (v 17). The third category may include not only shipowners, but sea pilots, sailors, and fishermen who were simply trying to make a living as part of a crew. The rhetorical question in v 18 corresponds to the rhetorical question in 13:4 (see also Ezek 27:32). Yet their grief is obviously for their own lost revenue. They, too, stand afar off to mourn and casting dust on their heads.

Those who sold their soul to gain a share in this wealth, as well as those who depended upon this commerce for their livelihood, were in anguish over their loss. But the people of God, whether saints, apostles, or prophets, rejoiced that she has been judged. The author John would fit all three categories. See also 19:1-4 for heaven's

---

[338]Bauckham, *The Climax of Prophecy*, 338-371.

[339]Schweizer, "σῶμα," *TDNT*, 7:1058. See Ezek 27:13. The usual word for *slave — doulos* is the word commonly used for a servant of God. Perhaps for this reason John employs other language [Michaels, *IVPNTC*, 206].

[340]Aune, *WBC,* 52C:1002-1003; see also Barclay, *Revelation*, 2:162-163.

reaction. However, it is possible that good people may depend upon such commerce for their livelihood without selling their soul in the process (for example, Lydia in Acts 16:13-15). Aune wrote that the Old Testament contains denunciations of merchants, "not for their wealth but for the dishonest practices they used to gouge the poor."[341]

Chapters 2-3 reveal that Christian congregations existed in prosperous communities and they struggled to make a legitimate living within a corrupt society without committing spiritual adultery. In such cases they may suffer economic hardship when God judges the world system, but they do not necessarily lose their soul. The test is whether they are more concerned with their loss of income or whether they are more in tune with heaven and can rejoice over the justice of God — even in the face of material loss. Heaven shouts with joy over this downfall in 19:1-3. Thus, the people of God on earth ought to be more in tune with heaven's priorities, than with their own economic prosperity. They still have an obligation to provide for their own (1 Tim 5:8), while living in this world, yet they are warned to "come out" of the evil world system and not submit to the control of Babylon (v 4; see also John 17:15).

According to v 20 the sentence of death which Babylon passed on God's people has been appealed to God and God has reversed the sentence, finding Babylon guilty.

4. The enactment of destruction 18:21-24

Verses 21-24 describe the actual fall of Babylon (compare to Jer 51:63-64). This is what John was promised to be shown in 17:1. The city of man is now silent. Entertainment has ceased. Commerce has stopped. Even domestic tranquility is a thing of the past (see Jer 25:10). Six times in vv 21-23 the phrase *never again* is used. According to Josephus, Rome killed over 1,100,000 Jews during their seven

---

[341] Aune, *WBC*, 52C:990.

years of revolt.[342]

This fall describes a *spiritual* reality. The people of God in all times are to live with the mindset that there is no future in Babylon — although all leading economic indicators may give an entirely opposite forecast. Again, the concept of now and not yet is applicable. God has judged many rebellious empires and across history they have fallen. Yet *Babylon* continues to mutate, taking new shapes and forms. But this spiritual Babylon is under the ban of God. It was stripped of its usurped authority by Christ when he triumphed over it by the cross (Col 2:15). The kingdom of the world *has become* the kingdom of our Lord and of his Christ (11:15). "Yet at present we do not see everything subject to him" (Heb 2:8). John is teaching the church to see that which is invisible to the natural eye (Heb 11:27). Thus, the new Jerusalem, not Rome, is eternal.

---

[342]Josephus, *Wars of the Jews*, 6.9.3. These numbers are disputed. See Gentry, *The Divorce of Israel*, 2:1410.

Chapters 17-18 Summary

Interlude — Babylon the harlot 17:1-18:24

- A. The influence of Babylon 17:1-18
- B. The fall of Babylon 18:1-24
  1. The pronouncement of judgment 18:1-3
  2. The call to evacuate 18:4-8
  3. The lament of grief and loss 18:9-20
  4. The enactment of destruction 18:21-24

John depicts two cities — Babylon is the city of man and Jerusalem is the city of God. John also depicts two women. In Revelation 12 the pure woman is the true church; in Revelation 17 the impure woman is false or corrupt religion (compare 17:1 and 21:9).

The Old Testament prophecies concerning a literal rebuilt Babylon have been fulfilled. Symbolically, *Babylon* represents the world system of idolatry, immorality, luxury, and persecution.

However, the confusion of Babel was reversed at Pentecost. We preach a universal gospel which will establish the city of God upon this earth. Babylon may be the mother of all that is false, but we are the children of the new Jerusalem "that is free and is our mother" (Gal 4:26). Abraham left Ur of the Chaldees, located within Babylonia, for Salem, the city of peace (Gen 14:18). We must do the same.

REVELATION 19

VI. The conquering Christ — 19:1-20:15

In chapter 16 there was a description of the spiritual forces which gathered at Armageddon. Christ then came to do spiritual battle (16:14-15). Chapters 17-18 were an interlude explaining the epic conflict between Babylon and Jerusalem: the city of man and the city of God. This chapter describes the battle which was introduced in chapter 16.

To understand John's description in these chapters we must grasp three concepts: the decisive victory of Christ at the cross; the progressive victory of Christ across history; the final victory of Christ at his second advent.

The emphasis of chapter 19 is on the progressive victory of Christ across history. Thus, as we come to John's last climatic vision (19:1-22:21) the past, the present, and the future begin to blur as the kingdom is described both in terms of already and not yet. The present victory of Christ is based upon his reign; his future victory based upon his return.

History is more than names, dates, and records. History must be interpreted. Too many Christians have accepted a pagan interpretation of history which is pessimistic. This chapter gives a Christian interpretation of history from heaven's perspective. It exalts Christ as the central figure of human history. According to v 10 the purpose of prophecy is to exalt Christ.

In this chapter the Christian life is portrayed as a meal and a war. Peterson wrote, "The moment we walk away from the Eucharist, having received the life of our Lord, we walk into Armageddon, where we exercise the strength of our Lord."[343] But the same Christ who is spiritually present at his table, has also triumphed over the evil one by the cross. Thus he prepares a table before me in the presence of my enemies (Ps 23:5). But whether we are eating at the Lord's table or evicting the evil one wherever he attempts to establish a

---

[343]Peterson, *Reversed Thunder,* 161.

stronghold in God's creation, we should sing *hallelujah*.

A. Heaven rejoices at Babylon's fall 19:1-5

Chapter 18 closed with weeping and mourning from those who invested their lives in the city of man. Smoke continues to rise from Babylon forever and ever (see Gen 19:28; Isa 34:10). If this destruction occurs at the end of the world, it would mean nothing to say that the smoke from it rises eternally. According to 2 Peter 3:10-12 the whole earth and everything in it will be destroyed at the end. Therefore, the imagery of Babylon's smoke rising describes the spiritual impact of a first century event. While there is always fuel being added to the fire, Babylon cannot ever be rebuilt so long as it is burning forever.

In contrast, we hear the triumphant song of victory continue to rise from the church. In 18:20 heaven, along with the saints, apostles, and prophets were told to rejoice. The sacrifice of praise from God's people rises just as the smoke of Babylon also ascends. While John introduces five visions with the phrase "after this I saw," this is the only time he begins with the phrase *after this I heard*.

The multitude in heaven is probably the church triumphant of 7:9-17. Mounce argued that this was the church because they specifically mention salvation and are concerned for avenging the blood of the martyrs, as in 6:10.[344] Furthermore, the description of this choir as a "multitude" in the singular occurs only here in 19:1,6 and in 7:9. This choir shouts *hallelujah*. This is the only time it is used in the New Testament and it occurs four times in succession (vv 1, 3, 4, 6). The additional *amen* and *praise our God* together sound like a great roar. It is proper to lift up our voices in praise to God.

Amen, hallelujah in v 4 occurs nowhere else in the New Testament, but is found in Psalm 106:48. *Amen* means "so be it." It "concludes the doxology of 1:6, affirms the prophecy of 1:7, concludes the series of praise songs in 5:9-14, frames the praise song of 7:12, and

---

[344]Mounce, *NICNT*, 341.

concludes the book (22:20-21). . . . Thus the 'amen' in some sense confirms the worship of the previous hymns, and the 'hallelujah' continues the praise established in 19:1, 3 and leads into the call to praise (v 5)."[345]

The twenty-four elders represent the church (see 4:4). The four living creatures represent nature (see 4:6-8). This is the last time they appear in John's vision. Like a great drama, John has first introduced the cast and now they begin their exit. At the end of this chapter the beast and false prophet also take their exit. This literary structure is a chiasm, in which characters are introduced into the drama and then dismissed in the opposite order.

The call to worship in v 5 comes from Psalm 135:1, 20. At v 5 the church on earth, comprising his servants who fear him (11:18), is invited to join in and the invitation to praise God is in the present tense. We are to keep on praising him. We should praise Christ for his glory, for his salvation, for his power (v 1). We also ascribe to him praise for his righteous judgments; they are just and true (see 15:3; 16:7). God is also exalted for avenging the blood of the church. The verb *ekdikeo* (to avenge or vindicate) occurs only in 6:10 and 19:2, linking these two passages. This then is the celebration of God's answer to the prayer in 6:10 for justice. According to Luke 21:22 these days of vengeance occurred in the first century.

In 5:12-14 Christ was worshiped as worthy to open the seals. There was a praise service in 11:15-19 after the seventh trumpet sounded. Now after the seven bowl judgments we come to the same point in time. Babylon has fallen and the kingdom of God established. Both 11:15-17 and 19:6 use the same language to describe the initiation of Christ's kingdom.

B. The marriage of the Lamb 19:6-10

As the church on earth responds, echoing the sound of heaven, she rejoices, is glad, and gives God glory because he is almighty, his

---

[345]Osborne, *BECNT*, 666.

reign has begun, and her relationship with him is personal — he is the Lord *our* God. The aorist tense of the verb *reign* signals the initiation of God's rule and the establishment of his kingdom. Because these realities are true now, there is no need to project the worship of the church into the future. We should be singing now in preparation for the heavenly choir.

In (vv 7-8) the church, the bride of Christ, has made herself ready. She was given clean white robes and she maintains her purity through faith in the blood (1 John 1:7; 3:2-3). She prepares herself by remaining faithful (2:10, 13; 13:10; 14:12; 17:14), maintaining her testimony for Jesus (1:9; 6:9; 12:11, 17; 20:4), enduring hardship (1:9; 2:2-3, 19; 3:10; 13:10; 14:12), and obeying God's commands (12:17; 14:12).

While she was given clean white linen garments were given her to wear, yet she must make herself ready (vv 7-8). In Ephesians 5:26 Christ cleansed his wife; in 2 Corinthians 7:1 the church is exhorted to cleanse herself. The righteousness of the church was not only imputed to her, but her actions are also to be righteous. These good works are the evidence of a living faith. Clarke explained that the fine linen is not the righteousness of Christ imputed to believers, but "that which the grace and Spirit of Christ has wrought in them."[346]

Verse 9 is one of six benedictions in this book (see also 1:3; 14:13; 20:6; 22:7, 14). Those who are blessed are those who respond to God's invitation. Yet Ladd rightly said, "The initiative to salvation is always the call of God."

There were two major events in a Jewish marriage. The betrothal and the wedding were normally separated by twelve months. The two individuals were considered husband and wife, and were obligated to faithfulness, at the time of the engagement (Gen 29:21; Deut 22:23-24). The betrothal was a covenant agreement which was considered binding and was only broken by divorce. Notice that in v 7 the bride is already called the *wife*, even before the marriage ceremony and supper. In Matthew 1:18-20 Mary is called the wife of Joseph and

---

[346]Clarke, *Commentary*, 6:1051.

Joseph is called her husband, even though they were only betrothed. In the same way, the church is the betrothed wife of Christ (2 Cor 11:2), but the wedding does not take place until 21:9.

In one sense the church is already the wife of Christ, but in another sense she has not yet seen him. Bahnsen said the Marriage Supper of the Lamb is the weekly celebration of the Lord's Supper.[347] I would prefer to call the Lord's Supper the appetizer, while we await the full banquet. Terry wrote that the marriage of the Lamb is the union of Christ with believers and essentially refers to spiritual life. This marriage of the Lamb is a process continually going on, as such unions of Christ and his beloved and elect ones continue to be consummated. The glory and blessedness of life with Christ in heaven are but the perpetuation of the union formed by faith and love in this world. However, this progressive corporate relationship between the church and Christ is portrayed as the union of one believer with Christ and the entire process of ages is conceived as complete. "Things future are conceived as already complete."[348]

While John introduces the marriage supper here, he is not writing in chronological sequence. The marriage actually comes in 21:2, 9. John interjects it here to draw a contrast between two suppers: the supper of destruction (v 17) and the supper of fulfillment (v 9).

Yet the present state of the church, even under persecution, is her communion with Christ. And Christ is really present with his church through his Spirit. Thus, the feast has already begun. Isaiah 25:6; Matthew 22:2-14; 25:1-13; Mark 2:19; Luke 12:35-40; 13:22-30; 14:7-24 all describe some aspect of the kingdom as a feast, which is a present reality, but also anticipates a climax in which all will be present, including Abraham, Isaac, and Jacob, all the prophets, and those from the east, west, north, and south. Christ will eat with us.

Before Christ's return we are to compel as many as we can to

---

[347]Bahnsen, *Victory in Christ*, 20. See also Chilton, *Days of Vengeance*, 473; 489.

[348]Terry, *Biblical Apocalyptics*, 441.

accept the invitation and prepare to attend (Luke 14:15-24). Every time we partake of the Lord's Supper we anticipate the Marriage Supper and every time we evangelize we are inviting sinners to supper. Someday the entire church of all races, languages, nations, and periods of history will gather at one table. On that day we will come from the north and the south, the east and west and sit down at his table and all eat and drink (Luke 13:29). Christ himself will be the host. He will be our bread and his blood will be our wine (John 6:53-56). We will be sustained eternally through the merits of the atonement. John 6:58 teaches that we will live eternally as we feed on Christ.

The first time the Lord's Supper was observed there were only eleven; the last time there will be a number too great to count. The first time it was called the last supper because it was the last time Christ was physically present; but he is always spiritually present. It was the last time Passover was observed. Passover looked back to deliverance. The Lord's Supper not only looks back, but it looks forward. We are to continue to do this until he comes. At Passover, they ate the lamb, but at the Marriage Supper the Lamb will eat with us.

When John mistakenly worshiped the angel (see also 22:8; Gen 18:2), he was instructed to worship only God. Then, lest we also become distracted, we are told the true spirit of prophecy is always evidenced in the fact that it bears witness to Jesus Christ (v 10). Walvoord wrote, "This means that prophecy at its very heart is designed to unfold the beauty and loveliness of our Lord and Savior Jesus Christ." Christ is the central theme of prophecy.[349] The Holy Spirit inspires all true prophecy and he glorifies Christ (John 16:13-15) and the spirit of the prophets is characterized by their testimony concerning Jesus.

The interpretative question is whether *the testimony of Jesus* is *about* Jesus or *from* Jesus. This phrase has already been used once in v 10 as a subjective genitive — hold to the testimony borne by Jesus.

---

[349]Walvoord, *Revelation*, 273.

However, in 6:9; 11:7; 12:11; 17:6 the testimony is borne by Christians about Jesus and thus this second phrase in v 10 should be understood as an objective genitive as it is in 20:4.

The spirit of prophecy is a genitive phrase. Taken objectively it would refer to the prophecy inspired by the Holy Spirit. Bauckham wrote, "The Spirit speaks through the prophets to the churches and through the churches to the world."[350] While this is true, in 22:9 there is a reference to the prophets, of which John is a brother. Therefore, this phrase may refer to the spirit of the prophets, much as 1 Corinthians 14:32. A third possibility is "the spirit of *the* prophecy," a reference to the book of Revelation itself. In 1:3; 19:10; 22:7, 18-19 the Greek text in each instance has the definite article *the*. Thus, in the case of 19:10 the spirit of this book is the revelation about or from Jesus Christ.

Bruce wrote that the prophets of old bore witness to Jesus in advance. The same witness is still borne, in the power of the same Spirit, not only by a prophet like John but by all the faithful confessors who overcome the enemy by the blood of the Lamb and the word of their testimony.[351]

What follows in vv 11-16 is a prophetic testimony concerning Jesus. Almost everything John describes in this vision matches some earlier description, but as John recapitulates previous visions he reaches the climax of the book. This is the most glorious of all revelations of Christ.

C. The ride of the king 19:11-21

In v 11we see Christ riding above all the earthly conflicts. Here Christ is depicted as a warrior against the forces of evil. This is truly a just and holy war. The warrior bridegroom was also described in Psalm 45. However, neither his weapons nor ours are carnal (2 Cor

---

[350]Bauckham, *The Climax of Prophecy*, 161-162.

[351]Bruce, *The Canon of Scripture,* 264.

10:4). It is significant that the only weapon Christ has is the sword, which is not in his hand but proceeds from his mouth.

Jesus comes in revival for his church. Jesus comes in judgment on this world. And Jesus will come at the end of the world to raise the dead and judge the world. But this account does not describe his second advent. Although Walvoord called vv 11-13 "one of the most graphic pictures of the second coming of Christ to be found anywhere in Scripture,"[352] this is no more a description of the return of Christ than 4:1 is the rapture of the church. While John sees Christ riding, nothing in the passage tells us that he is returning. David Brown wrote that the detailed character of the vision convinced him that this was *not* the second advent.[353] Although it is necessary to premillennialism to locate the return of Christ here, prior to chapter 20, the word *come* is not used in this chapter with relationship to Christ. None of the usual Greek words which describe the second advent are found in this chapter: *parousia*, *epiphania*, *apokalupsis*, *erkomai*, or *horao*. Verses 11-16 say nothing about a "last" battle. Apart from the citation in v 15 from Psalm 2:9 which is in the future tense, no other verb in vv 11-16 is future. The emphasis is not on what Christ will do, but who he is.

MacArthur entitled 19:11-21 "The Glorious Return of Jesus Christ," but never pinpointed at what verse he returns to earth. He also conceded that this chapter does not mention "either a translation (rapture) of living believers, or a resurrection of dead believers."[354] Mounce conceded that the imagery reflects the Jewish tradition of a warrior Messiah more than the New Testament teaching of the second

---

[352]Walvoord, *Revelation*, 274.

[353]Brown, *Christ's Second Coming,* 472-476. Brown was one of the three commentators in the Jamieson, Fausset, and Brown Commentary. See also Stuart, *Apocalypse*, 2:479.

[354]MacArthur, *Revelation 12-22,* 213.

advent of Christ.[355]

Instead this chapter describes the coming of Christ's kingdom as Christ riding forth from victory to victory through the course of history. Descriptions of the second advent always include the general resurrection and final judgment. Christ will not return on a horse, but on a cloud. According to Acts 1:11, he did not leave on a horse, nor will he return on one. One day Christ will come in the clouds. The actual time of his return is located in 20:11-15 and the general resurrection and judgment follow. John Jefferson Davis wrote that 19:11-21 describes the progressive triumph of the risen Christ in heaven over the forces of evil prior to the parousia, while 20:11-15, referring to the last judgment, implies the presence of Christ on earth. The fact that heaven is opened (v 11) so that the embattled church on earth can gain a true perspective, as well as the fact that what is seen is the armies of heaven following Christ (v 14), both imply that the scene in 19:11-16 is a heavenly one.[356]

The Scriptures are clear that the reign of Christ began with his ascension and v 6 identifies the time frame of chapter 19. Literally *the Lord God Almighty has begun to reign.*[357] As a result of the victory of the cross, the beast and false prophet were captured. With the establishment of Christ's kingdom, Rome and the Roman emperors fell. Rome was not only the fourth and final phase of Daniel's beast, but it was symbolically called *Babylon.*

1. The revelation of Christ 19:11-16

The emphasis of John's vision is not on the battle, but on the General. He is given four titles in this section: Faithful and True (v 11), a secret name (v 12), the Word of God (v 13), and King of Kings and Lord of Lords (v 16; 17:14). He is portrayed by three Old Testa-

---

[355]Mounce, *NICNT*, 351.

[356]Davis, *Christ's Victorious Kingdom,* 88-89.

[357]Beale, *NIGNT,* 931.

ment pictures: he conquers through his Word (Isa 11:4), he rules with an iron scepter (Ps 2:9), he saves through his atonement at the wine-press (Isa 63:1-6).

Throughout this book the battle has raged. The judgments began in chapter 6 under the leadership of the rider of the white horse. Now destruction is complete and we see the white horse riding on. The victory of the church is implicit in the person of Christ, the head of the church. At a point in time the eternal Son of God took upon himself a human body and also became the Son of Man. For thirty-three years he walked the dusty roads of Palestine. Toward the end of his ministry, he rode a donkey into Jerusalem. He left this world on a cloud, but he is still involved in human history. Now he rides a white horse. He is still in the saddle and still holds the reins. He still rides across time and with each generation he accumulates a larger army. Someday he will return in clouds of glory.

Christ rides between the first and second advent. While some people get absorbed in the identification of the four horsemen, let us listen for hoof beats of this white horse. The path of the rider of the white horse is the history of revival. We must keep our eyes on the white horse and assemble with the expectation that the horse and rider will pass by our assembly.

David Brown wrote that the capture of the enemy (v 20) happens through the authority of the church.

> This symbolic *seizure* and *chaining* of the enemy — is it the effect of mere sovereign power carrying off the field a troublesome foe, out of pity to a Church unable to cope with and cast him out? Is it something done for the Church's *relief*, and altogether without the Church's *instrumentality*? . . . It is Christ's doing, doubtless; but it is his doing in and by his Church.[358]

Christ rides in conquest. His kingdom progressively advances.

---

[358]Brown, *Christ's Second Coming,* 411.

His name is Faithful and True (v 11). Christ is called *Faithful* because he keeps his promises (Jer 10:10); he is called *True* because he is the source of truth. Truth means both reliability and correspondence to reality. But in v 12 also declares, "He has a name written on him that no one but he himself knows." We have not exhausted the nature of Christ by reciting a creed. There is an incomprehensibility about God (see Gen 32:29). His eyes are like blazing fire (v 12). This same description was also given in 1:14; 2:18. He is light and in him there is no darkness at all. He sees all things in a clear light. Nothing can be hidden from his penetrating vision. On his head are many crowns (v 12). This is the only time any one head is said to have more than one crown. In v 13 he is called "the Word of God." Words are an expression of our personality. Christ is the expression of God's character and will. Stuart called him the great executor and communicator of the will of God. He has been the Word from the beginning (John 1:1).

The sword of the Spirit is the Word of God (Eph 6:17). The Word of God is living and active (Heb 4:12). "Out of his mouth comes a sharp sword with which to strike down the nations" (vv 15, 19; 1:16; 2:12, 16). This is the only weapon with which Jesus is armed, but according to v 21 the Word of God is sufficient to defeat all of Satan's host. "Thus the only weapon the Rider needs, if he is to break the opposition of his enemies, and establish God's reign of justice and peace, is the proclamation of the gospel."[359]

When we preach the Word of God with the anointing of God's Spirit, it becomes the message of Christ from his own mouth. His Word has absolute authority and nothing can stand before it. The kingdom of Christ is established and the world is converted through the preaching of his gospel. He rules with a rod of iron. Literally, he shepherds them with a staff of iron. His rod is both gentle and firm. We will either submit willingly or come under his judgment. Swete wrote,

---

[359]Caird, *Revelation*, 245.

> He smites the nations not by judgments only, but by the forces which reduce them to the obedience of faith. . . . The whole course of "the expansion of Christianity" is here in a figure: the conversion of the Empire; the conversion of the western nations which rose on the ruins of the Empire, the conversion of the South and the far East, still working itself out in the history of our own time.[360]

Verse 16 describes his robe which was dipped in his own blood (v 13) before the battle begins. John has already emphasized the blood of Christ in 1:5; 5:9; 7:14; 12:11. Isaiah 63:1-6 depicts the Savior with his garments stained crimson. Calvary was the winepress where he shed his blood to turn away God's wrath. But for those who do not trust in his shed blood for salvation, their own blood is poured on the ground as judgment (Isa 63:6). There is no middle ground. According to Isaiah 63:4 we either experience redemption or vengeance. We will either eat or be eaten.

Christ trod the winepress alone (Isa 63:3) because salvation is through no other name. This theme is picked up in v 15, "He treads the winepress." In 7:14 that our robes are washed and made white in his blood (v 8; see also Isa 61:10). However, as our High Priest, his robe will always be stained and his body scarred (John 20:27). They were permanently stained at the cross prior to this battle (see 5:6). Christ overcame by shedding his blood, before any battle is mentioned.

In v 16 he is called *King of Kings and Lord of Lords*. This inscription is located on his outer garment, that is, where his robe fell open across his thigh. Since God is the only Ruler, the King of kings and Lord of lords (1 Tim 6:15), this passage asserts the deity of Christ. This declaration was written on his thigh. The thigh was the place where the sword hung. Since his sword is his word, Christ is victorious through his sovereign lordship, decreed by his Father. The fiat decree of the Almighty in Psalm 2:7-9 explains why there is no

---

[360]Swete, *Apocalypse*, 250.

battle here. Thus, *King of Kings and Lord of Lords* is another statement of his absolute authority and also explains why he has many crowns.

Verse 14 also describes the armies of heaven following Christ. According to 17:14 this army consists of "his called, chosen, and faithful followers." They are dressed in the white linen which was described in v 8. There is no record that they actually engage in any combat. Their earthly days of spiritual struggle have ceased; they are at rest (14:13). They are overcomers because they are with the victorious Christ. Reginald Heber wrote,

> The Son of God goes forth to war, a kingly crown to gain;
> His blood red banner streams afar: Who follows in His train?
> Who best can drink his cup of woe, triumphant over pain,
> Who patient bears his cross below, he follows in His train.[361]

2. The victory of Christ 19:17-21

Those connected with the bride of Christ, the new Jerusalem, will experience fulfillment. They are both the invited guests (v 9) and the bride at the marriage supper in v 9. Individually, believers are *guests*; collectively they are the *bride.*

A second supper is described in v 17 and is a parody on the first supper. The invited guests at this second supper are vultures and the main course will be the flesh of the kings of the earth and their army who will be destroyed (see Matt 24:28). This incorporates all those connected to the harlot Babylon. According to v 18 the destruction of Satan's kingdom is total. Yet in 21:24 the kings of the earth are described as bringing their tribute into the city of Jerusalem. This description provides a further indication that this battle is spiritual warfare and that Christ conquers at least some of his enemies through conversion.

The battle imagery was drawn from Ezekiel 39:17. Notice that

---

[361]Heber, "The Son of God Goes Forth to War," (1812).

the invitation goes out before the battle is ever fought. According to v 19, the Roman beast, the kings of the earth (16:12-16) who were the ten Roman provincial rulers of 17:12-16, and their armies gathered to make war against Christ; "to oppose the progress of his gospel, and the enlargement of his kingdom."[362] Literally, v 19 calls it "the war." However, John says nothing about the battle. The decisive battle was won long ago at the cross. John moves from the description of the armies which are drawn into battle to the conclusion of the battle, when the beast is seized. Leon Morris concluded that John "may mean that there was no battle. Though the forces of evil appear mighty they are completely helpless when confronted by the Christ."[363]

Contrary to the expectations of Jewish apocalyptic literature, which envisioned a literal military battle, the battle was won on the cross (5:5, 9). Satan was defeated by the blood of the Lamb. Stuart argued, "To look for a specific and literal battle, as a fulfilment of chapter 19, would be like looking for individual facts in history, as the fulfilment of the symbols indicated in chapter 14, or in 18:21-24, and in 19:1-10."[364]

The Roman beast and his false prophet, the emperor Nero, were captured and cast alive into the lake of fire (see also 20:10, 14-15; 21:8). This is a reference to Gehenna (*geenna*), an abbreviation for "valley of the son of Hinnom." This name was given to the valley south and west of Jerusalem where human sacrifices were offered (2 Kgs 16:3; 23:10; Jer 7:31). Because it was denounced as a place of wickedness in Jeremiah 7:32; 19:6 it was equated with hell and became a description of hell. By the time of Jesus it was the city dump and the fires of burning garbage never went out. Thus, Jesus used it as a word picture for eternal punishment.

Verse 20 should be connected with 14:10-11, as well as 20:10;

---

[362]Benson, *Notes*, 5:792.

[363]Morris, *TNTC*, 20:232-233.

[364]Stuart, *Apocalypse*, 2:352.

21:8. These descriptions refer to eternal conscious torment, not annihilation. Robertson wrote that "the fact of hell is clearly taught here, but the imagery is not to be taken literally any more than that of heaven in chapters 4, 5, 21, 22 is to be so understood. Both fall short of the reality."[365]

The *false prophet* was last mentioned in 16:13-14 where he was identified as the second beast of chapter 13; the "mouthpiece" of the Roman Empire. Yet John is not here providing a detailed account of Nero's end nor attempting to describe the Fall of Rome. "Rather, the Lake of Fire is his symbolic description of the utter defeat and complete destruction of these enemies in their attempt to seize the Kingdom." Like Sodom, Rome is destroyed by fire and brimstone.[366]

This then was the turning point, but not the end of the conflict between good and evil. In 20:10 the devil will join Nero and Babylon, his "puppets" who have been in hell since their demise. Not only did the early church triumph over the Roman Empire, but the people of God are led forward from victory unto victory "till every foe is vanquished and Christ is Lord indeed."[367]

---

[365]Robertson, *Word Pictures*, 6:456.

[366]Chilton, *Days of Vengeance,* 491.

[367]George Duffield, Jr, "Stand Up, Stand Up for Jesus" (1858).

REVELATION 20

D. The Millennial Kingdom 20:1-6

Although the early church was under persecution, the revelation of John gave assurance that Rome would fall. And as Christ leads his church from victory to victory, the kingdom of Christ will expand. Now John tells them that Satan will be bound for a thousand years. In 9:1 Satan fell from heaven and was given the key to the Abyss. While Satan was given a key (9:1), Christ holds the keys (1:18). Here an angel descends from heaven having the key to the Abyss in order to bind Satan.

Neither the key, the chain, the seal, nor the dragon in vv1-2 can be taken as literal. A spirit cannot be bound with a physical chain. Although John writes in symbolic language, he clearly identifies the dragon with the ancient serpent, who lied to Eve in the beginning, as the devil, meaning *slanderer* and Satan, meaning *adversary* or *accuser*. This identification was also made in 12:9.

The devil is also symbolized as the ancient serpent. He is the one who lied to Eve in the beginning. He is the father of lies (John 8:44). And where he has control, darkness clouds the minds of men. But the light shines in the darkness and the darkness has not overcome it (John 1:5).

The figure of the dragon builds on the two monsters in Job 40-41. The land monster was called *Behemoth* and a sea monster called *Leviathan*. In John's vision in Revelation 13 he saw a dragon coming up out of the sea and another beast coming out of the earth. All this symbolized Satan's work behind the scenes in world empires and pagan governments.

Babylon, Egypt, Assyria, the Medes and Persians, Greece, and Rome all had a beastly nature because they were controlled by the dragon. But while Satan is the prince of this world system (John 12:31; 14:30; 16:11), we proclaim that unto us a son is born, to us a son is given, and the government will be on his shoulders. He will be the prince of peace and of the increase of his government and peace there will be no end (Isa 9:6-7).

The word *millennium* itself is not used in Scripture. The term *millennium* is from two Latin words *mille*, meaning a thousand and *annus*, meaning year. The phrase *a thousand years* is used six times in this chapter, but nowhere else in Scripture. The Greek word used is *chilias*. It always occurs in the plural, except in 5:11, but is always translated in the singular.

John established the fact in the opening verse of his revelation that his vision is symbolic; that it was signified or given in signs. In the Greek language *chilioi* was the highest number. To go beyond a thousand, you had to say "thousands and thousands." In 5:11 John attempted to describe an innumerable host of angels by writing, "thousands upon thousands and ten thousand times ten thousand" (see also Eccl 6:6). Rob Staples, recognizing that John did not have a numerical concept higher than a thousand, concluded that the term *thousand* in Rev 20 may simply mean "our future in Christ, which words cannot adequately describe, will be the most glorious thing we have ever experienced. . . . It will be magnificent, and it will be forever!"[368]

Mulholland observed that the phrase "thousand years" occurs without the definite article in vv 2, 4. The remaining instances where a definite article is used (vv 3,5,6,7) are all references back to the same subject previously introduced. Therefore, the emphasis is not upon a precise period of time, but upon the quality of the time.[369]

Five times in this chapter the word *thousand* is plural. John is conveying to us that the reign of Christ will be a long time. In 2:10 he warned the early church that they would have ten days of tribulation. Now he says they will have a thousand years of peace. I take neither number literally, but I take the contrast seriously. Therefore, I conclude that *thousands*, as used in this chapter, means an indefinite period of time.

My own conclusion is that the millennium began with Christ's first advent because v 2 ties the beginning of the millennium with the

---

[368]Staples, *Words of Faith*, 116.

[369]Mulholland, *Revelation*, 307-308.

binding of Satan. If the first resurrection is a present possibility, then the millennium is also a present reality. Thus, the millennium is a symbolic expression for the kingdom age, which began with Christ's first advent. I cannot justify creating a distinct category or dispensation for the millennium based on only one passage of Scripture which is difficult to interpret.

Binney explained that during an indefinite period known as the millennium Satan will be bound, or his influence greatly restrained, and the reign of Christ and righteousness generally prevail. "This does not imply a *total cessation* of Satanic influence during that period."[370] It does imply that the world stage has been cleared of beastly world empires. Satan can no longer continue to orchestrate world empires, as he did in 13:1. This binding also implies that as Satan is cast out, all men will be drawn to Christ (John 12:31-32). And it implies that the saints, and not Satan, have dominion.

The crucial question of this passage again relates to time. When is Satan bound? He experienced his first restraint when he was kicked out of heaven. Apparently this fall occurred prior to Genesis 3 because at that time we see the serpent deceiving Adam and Eve. Revelation 12:4 describes the fallen angel cast to the earth. According to 2 Peter 2:4 God did not spare angels when they sinned. They are now bound in chains. However Wesley wrote, "Though still those chains do not hinder their often walking up and down, seeking whom they may devour."[371] Bahnsen explained,

> The fact that the demons are enchained does *not* mean that they are completely devoid of power and utterly without influence in the world. They have been committed to chains

---

[370]Binney, *Commentary,* 700.

[371]Wesley, *Notes*, 626. Wesley wrote, "It is plain Satan, the murderer and the deceiver of mankind, is in a great measure bound already; he is not now permitted to deceive the nations, as in the past ages. And even in the Romish countries scarce any are now called to resist unto blood" [Letter to Mary Cooke, 21 Dec 1787].

> from the time of their fall into sin, and yet the gospel records show them to have been extensively active, just as Revelation 9 teaches that God makes them serve His purposes in history. Thus, being enchained does not imply being destroyed or immobilized; it simply signifies that the demons are under God's control and restrained in their activities. Their operations never set them free from the ultimate end to which God's chains have assigned them. God observes a kind of *lex talionis*: the angels who did not *keep* their first position are now being *kept* by God — for eternal damnation.[372]

Jude also states that angels which did not keep their original position of authority are now kept by God until the day of judgment (v 6). They still operate, but under restraint. The fact that they are bound with everlasting chains does not mean they are completely without power or influence. It means that God is in control and he only allows them to go so far.

If Christ has taken authority over hades and death, symbolized by the Abyss, through his own death and resurrection, then the binding of Satan is the direct result of the resurrection.[373] However, this binding does not totally incapacitate him. The verb "to bind"— *deo* is used three times to describe the bonds of matrimony (Rom 7:2; 1 Cor 7:27, 39). The point is that while marriage does involves some restrictions, it is not absolute bondage. Luke 13:16 and Acts 20:22 also use this verb in a figurative sense, allowing limited activity.

Although he is bound in the Abyss, his influence still continues. Passages such as Acts 5:3; 2 Corinthians 4:4; 11:14; Ephesians 2:2, 1 Thessalonians 2:18, and 1 Peter 5:8 may all be cited to show that Satan is active. And some who saw the light of the gospel, choose to remain in darkness (John 3:19-20).

While Satan could have been bound by the direct sovereign

---

[372]Bahnsen, "The Person, Work, and Present Status of Satan," 18.

[373]Beale, *NIGNT*, 985.

power of God, God has ordained that he be bound instead through the influence of the gospel. As we enforce the victory of the cross, the church progressively also binds Satan. In Matthew 16:19 Peter was given the keys of the kingdom, to bind and loose. In Matthew 18:18-20, the *you* pronoun is plural and the promise in v 20 indicates that the church as a whole has this authority, not simply Peter.

In Revelation 20:4-6 the saints are seated, reigning with Christ, and exercising authority, in contrast to Satan's bondage. Bloesch wrote,

> The millennium in Revelation 20 must be understood as a symbol of divine manifestation in history, not a literal thousand-year period within history. The binding of Satan in Revelation 20 does not mean the decapacitation of the devil and his legions but seeing through his subterfuges and thereby reducing his power to deceive (Isa 24:21-22; Rev 20:1-3). This binding, moreover, is to be construed not as an act fully realized in the past but as a process that will be completed in the future. Satan is dethroned not only by the crucified and risen Christ (Rev 12:10) but by the preaching of the gospel by the church under the cross (Rev 12:11).[374]

The kingdom of Satan is built on deception (v 3). He masquerades as an angel of light (2 Cor 11:14). He prowls *like* a roaring lion (1 Pet 5:8). But Jesus Christ is the true lion (5:5). The verb *deceive* in vv 3, 8, 10 is *plano*, which means to cause to go astray or deceive. According to 12:9 Satan is the one deceiving (the same Greek word - *plano)* the whole world. But this ability to deceive has been thwarted through the preaching of the gospel.

Athanasius wrote *On the Incarnation of the Word of God* in the fourth century.

> Since the Savior has come among us, idolatry not only has

---

[374]Bloesch, *The Last Things*, 109-110; 136.

> no longer increased, but what there was is diminishing and gradually coming to an end: and not only does the wisdom of the Greeks no longer advance, but what there is is now fading away: And demons, so far from cheating any more by illusions and prophecies and magical arts, if they so much as dare to make the attempt, are put to shame by the sign of the Cross. And to sum the matter up: behold how the Savior's doctrine is everywhere increasing, while all idolatry and everything opposed to the faith of Christ is daily dwindling, and losing power, and falling. And thus beholding, worship the Savior "Who is above all" and mighty, even God the Word; and condemn those who are being worsted and done away by Him. For as, when the sun is come, darkness no longer prevails, but if any be still left anywhere it is driven away; so, now that the divine Appearing of the Word of God is come, the darkness of the idols prevails no more, and all parts of the world in every direction are illuminated by His teaching.[375]

Since the result of the binding of Satan is that he cannot deceive (v 3), this suggests that he is bound through the message of the gospel. Satan's power to deceive fades in direct proportion to the preaching of the gospel (Acts 13:47; 26:18, 23). Where the light shines, the darkness is dispelled (Isa 49:6; Luke 2:32; John 1:5), and disciples will be made of all the nations (Matt 28:19).

He was bound so that he might not deceive and dominate the nations any longer (Acts 14:15-16). Every ancient civilization was polytheistic and the gods they worshiped were not only actual demons (Deut 32:16-17), but this false religion with its idolatry was interwoven with the political structure. The dictator was appointed by the god and the nation was under the stronghold of that demon-god.

---

[375]Athanasius, *Incarnation of the Word*, §55; *NPNF*2 4:66. John of Damascus recorded a similar statement in the eighth century [*On the Orthodox Faith*, 4.4; *NPNF*2 9:75].

Until the coming of Christ, only Israel had a true knowledge of God. And with the coming of Christ, there was an unprecedented flurry of demonic activity. The fact that the kingdom of God had come was demonstrated by the fact that Christ cast out demons (Matt 12:28; Luke 11:20). Daniel foresaw that when the kingdom of God was established, it would bring to an end all those former satanically-controlled kingdoms (2:44). The Gentiles no longer sit in this darkness (Matt 4:14-16; Luke 2:32; 4:18). The gates of death and darkness cannot hold back this kingdom of light (Matt 16:18).

Furthermore, 2 Timothy 2:9 says that regardless of our circumstances, the Word of God cannot be bound or chained. As the church declares the Word of God and exercises its authority, Satan will be progressively bound. The truth of God's Word sets free and breaks the deception of Satan.

God has heard the cry of the martyrs (6:10). Swete wrote, "The main point is that the souls under the altar at last have their reward."[376] Even though they were persecuted and beheaded for their testimony, they had resisted the beast of Rome. The Romans executed by crucifixion and decapitation. The verb *pelekizo* occurs only here in the New Testament and it means to behead with an axe. The axe was later replaced by the sword. Yet the reference to those beheaded is figurative, encompassing all who have maintained the faith regardless of their cause of death (see 6:9) since the promise in v 6 is that they are not under the penalty of the second death. All who die in faith constitute part of the triumphant heavenly church.

Now they were actually given authority to sit with Christ in the heavenlies and reign with him a thousand years. But v 4 does not state the subject. Suspense builds as we read through to v 6 and still not subject is stated. Then in v 6 John discloses that those who are seated with authority are those who have been born again, having been raised from spiritual death to life.

The Greek text in v 4 describes those who had been beheaded because of their testimony for Jesus and because of the word of God

---

[376]Swete, *Revelation*, 288.

and who had not worshiped the beast or his image and had not received his mark. While they were still alive on earth, yet they had not worshiped Caesar. They were living martyrs in the sense that they had been crucified with Christ (Gal 2:20) and had experienced the first resurrection through the new birth. Both groups are blessed and holy. The second death has no control over either group. The entire church is a priesthood of believers (1:6; 5:10). Both groups live and reign with Christ for a thousand years. This does not imply that those on earth lived the full thousand years, but that the church, whether on earth or in heaven, collectively reign throughout the entire church age.

Verse 5 introduces the first resurrection. It is implied that there is a second resurrection at the end of the millennium. The use of *protos* does not necessarily indicate simply a first and second resurrection in sequence. In 1 Corinthians 15:3 the same term *protos* is used to declare that the doctrine of Christ's resurrection is of *first* or primary importance. Our eternal destiny hinges on this spiritual resurrection, which is regeneration.

Verse 6 also speaks of the second death. It is implied in v 4 that the early church experienced a death which was not the second death. And so this passage *seems* to be teaching two deaths and two resurrections a thousand years apart. Premillennialism holds that the first resurrection coincides with the return of Christ at the beginning of the millennium. However, this interpretation contradicts 1 Corinthians 15:20-55, which states that Christ is to reign until all enemies are put under his feet. A more consistent interpretation realizes that the first resurrection is linked to the second death and that both are figures of speech, describing spiritual realities. If the second death is spiritual separation from God, then surely the first resurrection is spiritual life with God.

The first resurrection is best understood as the resurrection of the Lord Jesus Christ (1 Cor 15:20-23; Col 1:18; Rev 1:5). Through saving faith we also participate in Christ's resurrection (Col 2:12). Not only have we been raised up with Christ, but we have also been seated with him (Eph 2:5-6) and we reign with him (Rev 5:6-10). Thus, we are the church of the firstborn (Heb 12:23). The church consists of those who have received this spiritual resurrection and are reigning with Christ, whether on earth or in heaven.

All verbs in vv 4-6 are in the aorist (past) tense. Kik explained, "The time of sitting on the thrones and reigning with Christ is the same as that of not worshiping the beast. It was while the saints were actually seated upon the thrones that they were refusing to worship the beast and to receive his mark."[377] Thus, while the saints advance God's kingdom on earth, even the martyrs who died become God's triumphant army in heaven and are alive and reigning with Christ. And all these who have been raised spiritually will also be raised bodily at the general resurrection, but will not be subject to the second death.

Thus, the teaching of 19:6 is that God reigns and that he, not Caesar is Almighty. At his resurrection the kingdoms of this world became the kingdom of our Lord and his Christ (11:15). Jesus Christ now reigns and has reigned since his resurrection (Acts 2:34). Colossians 1:12-13 refers to the kingdom of Christ as a present reality. Therefore, the teaching of 20:4-6 is that the church, his body, has also been resurrected and now reigns with Christ. Because we have been resurrected we have entered the coming age; the kingdom has come and we now reign with Christ for a thousand years.

John 5:24-29 brings together in one passage both spiritual and physical resurrection. Spiritual resurrection *has now come* and a time *is coming* when physical resurrection will occur. Therefore, the first resurrection should be understood as spiritual; the second resurrection is physical. The first death is physical; second death is spiritual. Jesus taught us in Matthew 10:28 not to be afraid of those who kill the body (the first death), but to fear God who can destroy both soul and body in hell (the second death; 21:8).

Bloesch wrote that the idea of two resurrections is alluded to several times in the New Testament (John 11:23-26; 1 Cor 15:20-23; Rev 20:4-6). "The first resurrection is the spiritual resurrection of the dead through faith. The second is the physical or bodily resurrection

---

[377]Kik, *An Eschatology of Victory*, 45; 212-213.

at the consummation of world history."[378]

Thus, this passage does not teach two physical resurrections a thousand years apart. John is telling the early church that death is not defeat. As the millennium unfolds, they reign with Christ in heaven. Verse 4 states that they reigned a thousand years. In other words, death does not terminate the authority of the church. The church reigns with Christ, both on earth and in heaven. Again, v 6 declares that they are all priests and kings who will reign for a thousand years.

While this was a comforting thought to the early church, they struggled to put in proper perspective all those who have been martyred. John said he saw their souls or lives (v 4). The word *psuche* has already been used by John in 8:9,12:11, and 16:3 (perhaps also 18:13) in the sense of *life*. Verses 4-5 teach that they too are victorious; they overcame the beast (Rome) and the image (Nero) and did not receive his mark. Because they were born again, which is the first resurrection, they lived and reigned a thousand years. "They lived and reigned with Christ a thousand years" (v 4) indicates that because they had been born again they too were reigning and sharing in the kingdom. Thus, they are depicted as seated on thrones, having been given the authority to judge.

The thrones symbolize the spiritual dominion of the Christian over the world, the flesh, and the devil. All true believers have this authority—whether dead or alive (see 5:10). Jesus had promised this in Matthew 19:28 and Luke 22:30. But the verb *krino* can also mean to govern. While Christ is the final judge, in 4:4 and 11:16 we find that the twenty-four elders sat on thrones. In 3:21 the overcomer is promised the right to sit with Christ on his throne. Here the martyrs are promised in vv 4, 6 that they will reign with Christ. Thus, the picture is that the church reigns with Christ.

But how can it be said they reigned a thousand years if they were martyred? How can we reconcile their martyrdom with their authority? Their martyrdom is irrelevant; it amounts only to physical death. Because they had experienced spiritual life, they reigned with Christ

---

[378]Bloesch, *The Last Things*, 130.

on earth and will continue to reign with Christ in heaven while the rest of the church reigns on earth. It does not say they reigned *on earth*. John does not say these saints in heaven return to earth during the millennium. Jesus does not physically reign on earth, but he is reigning nonetheless over earth. He returns *after* the thousand years. So these martyred Christians also reign, *but not on earth*. While we cannot avoid the curse of sin, death does not have any bearing upon our position with Christ. Thus, whether dead or alive, whether on earth or in heaven —the church reigns.

Verse 5 teaches that in contrast to the saints who live now with Christ, whether in heaven or on earth, the rest of the [spiritually] dead are not part of this spiritual resurrection and will not come to life at all until the end of the millennium. Their physical resurrection will be part of the second or general resurrection. Swete explained that John's reference to the rest of the dead in v 5 "merely guards against the impression that he had referred to the General Resurrection."[379] "The rest of the dead" (v 5) refers to those who did not die in the faith. They are not raised physically until after the millennium is over, Christ returns, and there is a general resurrection. The dead in Christ have not yet been physically raised either, but they are with Christ and where Christ is there is life. Their spiritual state is more important than their physical condition. Therefore, John does not include them with the rest of the dead.

Again is not in the Greek text. It falsely implies that the martyrs *do* return to earth with Christ to live again. When Christ returns, the sea will give up its dead; hades will give up its dead. "The accidents of death will not prevent any from appearing before the judge."[380] There will be a general resurrection — the *second* resurrection. At that time all will be raised to life, but not necessarily to reign.

The books are then opened (v 12; see Dan 7:10). Another book was opened which is the book of life. All the dead were judged on the basis of their works. "This makes the judgment include both classes,

---

[379]Swete, *Apocalypse,* 263.

[380]Swete, *Apocalypse,* 272-273.

saint and sinner. The Book of life was also open, which proves that the righteous, as well as the wicked, were judged." Those not found in the Book of Life will be cast into the lake of fire. "This implies that some were found written in the book of life in that judgment, which makes it sure that the righteous were judged at the same time."[381]

In v 14 John tells us that the lake of fire is the second death. The second death is eternal death. In hell the damned will live forever, but it is called *death* not *life*. The essence of death is separation. In the first death, the body and soul are separated. In the second death the sinner is forever separated from God. What greater punishment than to be eternally separated from love, from goodness, from mercy, from grace, from hope. Contrary to Pinnock , who defined the second death as "extinction and total oblivion,"[382] the damned live forever but the quality of their life is so wretched it is an eternal death.

But the good news is that those who have experienced first resurrection are exempt from the second death (v 6). Verse 6 should begin with *This is the first resurrection*. We can base no interpretation on chapter and verse divisions. The antecedent of *this* is found in v 4 — "they lived and reigned with Christ a thousand years." Thus, "this [spiritual regeneration] is the first resurrection."

According to v 6 those who have been born again are blessed and holy. This is initial sanctification. The new birth saves from eternal death. The born again are not under the authority of the kingdom of darkness. We will die once, but that is merely the separation of the soul and body. When we die our soul will return to God and we will live forever with him (see 14:13).

But does this mean then that once I am saved, I can never lose it? According to 2:11 it is the *overcomer* who is not hurt at all by the second death. And we overcome through the blood of the Lamb. Like the early church we must not love life so much that we avoid standing for Christ (12:11).We must hold to the testimony of Jesus, keep the commandments of God, and remain faithful to Jesus (6:9; 14:12).

---

[381]Luther Lee, *Elements of Theology*, 298.

[382]Pinnock, "The Conditional View," 158.

Clarke admonished his readers, "See that thy name be written in the sacred register; and, if written in, see that it never be blotted out."

E. Final Overthrow of Satan — Gog and Magog 20:7-10

In 1 Chronicles 5:4 *Gog* was a personal name. *Magog* was a person's name in Genesis 10:2 and 1 Chronicles 1:5. These words do not appear elsewhere in Scripture until Ezekiel 38-39. There they are used symbolically to describe ungodly forces. The context of Ezekiel was describing the uprising of the Maccabees in the second century before Christ. John picks up this expression for ungodly forces and uses it symbolically of this future revolt. Stuart explained, "That the names of these enemies will literally be *Gog* and *Magog*, and that they are literally to come from the four corners of the earth, and besiege the literal Jerusalem, no one versed in the language of the prophecy will attempt to contend."[383]

Ralph Woodrow gave five reasons why Ezekiel and John are not describing the same battle. Basically, Ezekiel described Gog as coming against Israel from the north (38:15; 39:2). John describes Gog and Magog gathering against God's people from the four corners.[384] The phrase *four corners of the earth* is a Semitic expression referring to the entire earth.

Some have questioned where such an army as described in v 7 could come from, if the kings of the earth and their armies were killed in 19:19-21. But 19:11-21describes a spiritual battle which is won by the Word of God. Chapter 20 continues this same battle. Satan is bound through the Word of God. Then vv 7-10 describe the end of this millennial period. After many have professed faith in Christ and the world has known its greatest prosperity, then Satan will be released, deceive the nations and gather together a rebellion numbering

---

[383]Stuart, *Apocalypse*, 2:364.

[384]Woodrow, *His Truth is Marching On,* 41-42. Josephus referred to Magog as those the Greeks called Scythians [*Antiquities*, 1.6.1]. Paul refers to the Scythians in Col 3:11. This is another generalized term for barbaric people.

as the sand of the sea. Although this last battle is described in military terms, some commentators have suggested that it may be a battle of ideas and doctrine (see 2 Thess 2:9-12).[385] The millennial period does not constitute a perfect world. If sin could enter a perfect environment causing Adam and Eve to fall, certainly sin could cause believers to fall in an imperfect world. That will only come after Jesus returns and we enter heaven. When the restraints are removed, evil will break forth. Paul writes in 2 Thessalonians 2:8 that this rebellion will be overthrown with the breath of his mouth and their lawlessness destroyed by the splendor of his presence. Paul's *man of lawlessness* in 2 Thessalonians 2:3 resembles John's description of Satan loosed in v 7. Both are deceivers, both lead a revolt against the Lord, and both are destroyed by the coming of Christ.

The one whom Paul calls the *man of sin* (2 Thess 2:3-8), John simply calls Satan. The beast and the false prophet were previously thrown alive into the lake of fire (19:20). Finally, after all Satan's puppets have been eliminated, it seems that the man of sin himself will be revealed at the last stage of world history. The Bible, however, contains no statement concerning a future world ruler called "The Antichrist."

The end of v 3 declares Satan will be set free for a short time. This implies that he had previously been bound. Verses 7-9 expand upon this event. Jesus said that some believe for a while, but in the time of testing they fall away (Luke 8:13). "See to it, brothers, that none of you has a sinful, unbelieving heart that turns away from the living God" (Heb 3:12). 1 Timothy 4:1 says that in the later times some will abandon the faith.

But why would God cause things to improve, then release Satan? "The whole period of human life is a *state of probation*, in every part of which a sinner may repent and turn to God, and in every part of it a believer may give way to sin and fall from grace; and that this possibility of rising, and liability to falling, are essential to a state of

---

[385]Brown, *Christ's Second Coming*, 445; Whedon, *Commentary*, 4:395; Davis, *Christ's Victorious Kingdom*, 111.

trial or probation."[386]Binney explained, "As Satan was permitted to tempt and deceive our first parents in paradise, so he will have like permission in this millennial state to show that no state or condition on earth, however perfect and holy, is exempted or secured from his evil designs."[387]

There will come a time when oppression, injustice, impurity, false teaching, and corruption will largely disappear. Although the human race will ultimately experience the blessings of Christ's kingdom, they have not lost their freedom to choose. It is only fair that they also be tested, just as the early church was tested.

Even though the enemy without is bound, we still have an enemy within. The believer will still be tempted by his own sinful nature. Luke 17:26-30 describes eating, drinking, buying, selling, planting, and building. Complacency, worldliness, materialism, the pursuit of pleasure will cause many to say "peace and safety" (1 Thess 5:3; see also 2 Tim 3:1-5).[388] Many will have a form of godliness, but no longer have the power. God will release the devil for a short time, so that their faith, like that of Christians of all other ages, will be tested. Many will fail the test. There will be a great falling away. Because they did not continue to believe the truth, they will open themselves to deception. Jesus asked, "When the Son of Man comes, will he find faith on the earth?" (Luke 18:8). The answer is *yes*, but that faith will have been tested by the period of apostasy and decline immediately prior to the return of Christ.[389]

Paul explained to the Thessalonian church that Christ had not already returned. The day of his return will not occur *until* there comes a falling away (2 Thess 2:1-12). Any yet two and a half billion

---

[386]Clarke, *Commentary*, 6:1069.

[387]Binney, *Commentary,* 701.

[388]Davis located the time frame of Luke 17:26-30; 1 Thess 5:3; 2 Tim 3:1-5 as after the millennium and before the second advent [*Christ's Victorious Kingdom*, 98; 111-112].

[389]Davis, *Christ's Victorious Kingdom*, 114-116.

people who currently have never heard the name of Christ cannot fall away from faith in Christ. Thus, this falling away will come *after* they have turned to Christ. There will be a short-lived rebellion, in contrast to a thousand-year age of blessing, which will come after a Christian civilization has been established.

Therefore, there must be a great turning to Christ before there can ever be such a departure from the faith. After the human race has seen what the grace of God can do, Satan will be allowed one last time to test the faith of those who trusted in Christ when things were prosperous. But God will not allow those who rebel to reverse the establishment of his kingdom. Yet if Christ were physically present on this earth and imposing his will by force, as premillennialism contends, how could such a rebellion ever get off the ground? Christ will not be humbled again (Phil 2:9-11). He will never be dethroned. He will not have to fight the devil again. This is not a reversal that sends us back to square one. Christ, whose reign began at his session at the Father's right hand, will continue to reign until all his enemies are defeated (Ps 110:1; 1 Cor 15:25). This Gog and Magog finale will demonstrate conclusively the righteous judgment of God, the victory of Christ, the defeat of Satan, the irrationality of sin, as well as magnify the sufficiency of God's grace in the lives of the overcomers.

Verse 9 describes this rebellion as surrounding the camp of the saints, even the city God loves. In this verse the church is depicted as a military camp. This picture is borrowed from Moses and Joshua, when the twelve tribes camped on all four sides of the tabernacle. The church is also referred to as the beloved city (see Heb 12:22). This theme will be developed in the last two chapters of Revelation.

"But they shall not succeed in their attempts; they shall not able to hurt the church and city of God."[390] Although this battle is yet future, it was written to encourage the early church, as well as us, that Satan will never be successful in defeating the church — although it often appears that we are defeated.

John describes the coming of Christ as "blazing forth in devour-

---

[390]Benson, *Notes*, 5:796.

ing fire" which falls from heaven and consumes them (v 9). Consuming fire from heaven is described in 2 Kings 1:10-12; Ezekiel 38:22; 39:6; Zephaniah 1:18; 3:8. An army of backsliders will look up to see Christ coming in all his majesty and there will be no contest. It will be judgment day. Satan will be cast into the lake of fire where he will remain forever and ever. God will have no further use for him. Satan was defeated at the cross, but allowed to continue a little while longer. At the end of the millennial period he will try one last time to incite a rebellion against God. This, too, will end in failure. Often when we have confronted him he has slithered away into the darkness, but when Christ returns there will be no hiding place. "Then the lawless one will be revealed, whom the Lord Jesus will overthrow with the breath of his mouth and destroy by the splendor (*epiphaneia*) of his coming (*parousia*)" (2 Thess 2:8).

The saints have all been tested and their probationary period is now over. Satan's challenge against the Almighty has been successfully answered. The world has seen God's best and Satan's worst. A number beyond any ability to count have chosen God's way. They have come out of great tribulation and have washed their robes in the blood of the Lamb.

F. The second advent and general judgment 20:9-15

The second coming of Christ is not a major theme of this book. While the actual return of Christ is not emphasized in this passage, it must occur at this time because the events which are emphasized, the general resurrection and general judgment, are events which accompany the second advent. Daniel Steele said, "There is no hint of the second advent of Christ till the general judgment in verse 11."[391] Benjamin Field argued against the view that Revelation 19 portrayed the second coming of Christ. Instead, he argued for Revelation 20:11,

---

[391]Steele, "Why I Am Not," 406.

compared with 2 Pet 3:10.[392]

Apparently John does not emphasize the coming of the Bridegroom because his focus is on the Bride, which will be the theme of the final two chapters. And John does not dwell on future events. Most of his revelation has dealt with events which happened shortly thereafter. Throughout this book there are time indicators in the text which place the events in the first century. But the last half of this chapter looks to the future. This is indicated by v 7, "Whenever the thousand years are finished." Then there is the general resurrection and judgment. We know from other passages of Scripture that these events come at the *end* of time.

But if John is trying to encourage the first century church, why does he project out into the distant future? After spending much of the book dealing with God's immediate response to their tribulation, he closes by dealing with God's ultimate response. If everything in this book was future, it would give the early church no immediate hope. If everything in this book is past, it would give no ultimate hope.

While v 11 does not specify who sits on the throne, passages such as John 5:22-27; Acts 10:42; 17: 31; 2 Corinthians 5:10, Philippians 2:11; 2 Timothy 4:1 are clear that Christ will be our judge. Christ will literally and physically return to raise the dead and judge the world. 2 Peter 3:10-12 indicate heaven and earth are to be destroyed by fire. Here the earth and sky are personified as fleeing from his presence (v 11; Ps 114:3, 7). 21:1 describes heaven and earth as passed away.

When the Son of Man comes in his glory, he will sit on his throne and judge the nations. He will separate the sheep and the goats. Those on his right hand will be brought into their inheritance and they will enter the joy of our Lord. To those on his left, he will say, Depart into eternal fire prepared for the devil and his angels (Matt 25:31-46).

John describes the return of Christ symbolically as fire from heaven. It should come as no surprise that the second advent is de-

---

[392]Field, *Student's Handbook of Christian Theology*, 264.

scribed symbolically, since that is the form of literature that John is writing. At the coming of Christ Satan will be thrown into the lake of fire (v 10).

Satan is often described as ruling in hell, but this is a misconception. It was John Milton who spoke of him as reigning in hell.[393] David wrote, "If I make my bed in hell, behold You are there" (Ps 139:8). God rules over the entire universe, including hell. At the coming of Christ, the dead will be resurrected. Christ will reign until he has put all enemies under his feet. After Satan has been thrown into hell, the last enemy, death will be conquered (1 Cor 15:25-26). Death will give up its hostages (1 Cor 15:52-55; 1 Thess 4:14-17). There will be a general resurrection.

Verse 13 informs us that "each person" will be judged. Therefore, it is valid to assume that each person will first be resurrected. John said that at the coming of Christ, death gave up the dead. This describes a general resurrection when the sea and death and hades (the grave) surrendered every person back to life. David Brown exclaimed, "If ever language expressed the doctrine of *a simultaneous and universal resurrection*, surely we have it here. Who would ever imagine that all mankind were not in this august scene, in their resurrection-state, and that himself would not form part of it?"[394]

This description alone destroys the teaching of conditional immortality and annihilation. While conditional immortality teaches that immortality is a gift given only to those who belong to Jesus Christ, v 13 teaches that whether buried on land or at sea, the dead will all be raised to life. The believer will be raised to eternal life; the sinner to eternal death.

At the coming of Christ all will stand at the judgment. "He has set a day when he will judge the world with justice by the man he has appointed. He has given proof of this to all men by raising him from the dead" (Acts 17:31). There will come a great day when every

---

[393]Milton, "Paradise Lost,"(written around 1650-1660) Book 1, Line 260— "Better to reign in Hell than serve in Heaven."

[394]Brown, *Christ's Second Coming*, 206-217; 286.

wrong will be righted, every mystery resolved, every hidden sin exposed, every faithful believer rewarded. If God is just, there must be such a day. The only logical time for this judgment is at the end of this present world. "The day of judgment is not to make God better acquainted with the character of man, but to make men better acquainted with the character of God."[395]

The Scriptures teach a general judgment: "Those who have done good will rise to live and those who have done evil will rise to be condemned" (John 5:29). "We will all stand before God's judgment seat . . . each of us will give an account of himself to God" (Rom 14:10-12). This doctrine made Felix tremble (Acts 24:25). "For we must all appear before the judgment seat of Christ, that each one may receive what is due him for the things done while in the body, whether good or bad" (2 Cor 5:10). "And I saw the dead, great and small, standing before the throne, and books were opened. Another book was opened, which is the book of life. The dead were judged according to what they had done as recorded in the books. . . . Each person was judged according to what he had done" (vv 12-13). "I will reward everyone according to what he has done" (22:12).

This book of life is metaphoric language for God's unfailing memory. Verse 15 implies that all who are listed in the "book of life" are spared from eternal punishment. This hope is stated in positive form in 3:5 and 21:27.

Here the throne of Christ is described as a great white throne because it is greater than any earthly throne and because of the magnitude of the issues which will come before this throne. Eternal destinies will be sealed. White depicts the absolute purity of the Judge. His hair is white as snow (1:14). He who sat upon a white horse now he sits upon a white throne.

The judgment will follow Christ's return (1 Cor 4:5; Rev 22:12). We will all be judged according to our works. "Then he will reward each person according to what he has done" (Matt 16:27). These passages make it clear that there will be a general judgment.

---

[395]Field, *Handbook of Christian Theology*, 277-278.

We will also be judged by our words. "But I tell you that men will have to give account on the day of judgment for every careless word they have spoken. For by your words you will be acquitted, and by your words you will be condemned" (Matt. 12:36-37). Our motives will be exposed (1 Cor. 4:5).

John warns that only those whose names are written in the book of life are admitted into heaven. In v 15 he concludes with a first class conditional statement which affirms the reality of the condition. There, in fact, will be people whose names are not found in the book of life and they will be cast into the lake of fire. Death is the last enemy to be destroyed (1 Cor 15:26) and hades is superceded by hell.

While Scripture does not elaborate on *where* or *how*, it is very specific concerning *who* will end up in hell. The Bible has more to say about hell than about heaven. In 21:8 John catalogs sin which will keep people out of heaven. If we accept the authority of Scripture we cannot deny the existence of hell. John Wesley wrote to William Law,

> Now this much cannot be denied, that these texts speak as if there were really such a place as hell . . . I would then ask but one plain question: If the case is not so, why did God speak as if it was? Say you, "To affright men from sin?" What, by guile, by dissimulation, by hanging out false colors? Can you conceive the Most High dressing up a scarecrow, as we do to fright children? Far be it from Him! If there be any such fraud in the Bible, the Bible is not of God. And indeed this must be the result of all . . . So that if we give up the one, we must give up the other. No hell, no heaven, no revelation![396]

It is often asked how a loving God can send people to hell. But God is not only a God of love, but of holiness (Hab 1:13), justice (Rev 15:3), and mercy (Mic 7:18). Those who go to hell have rejected God's mercy and his offer of salvation. God's love is not uncondi-

---

[396]Wesley, *Letter* to William Law, 6 January 1756.

tional in the sense that he will always say, "I forgive." The Spirit will not always strive with man. Just as God once loved the angels and now no longer loves the devil, so Tozer said the time would come when God would no longer love lost men.[397] Sinners in hell continue to rebel. They continue to curse and blaspheme God. Even if Revelation 16:9-11 is describing torment on earth, the same principle applies.

In 1861 Methodist theologian William F. Warren explained that just as libertarian freedom explains the existence of sin, so it also vindicates the benevolence of God although he permits the full, eternal fruition of sin's consequences. God's final treatment of the sinner does not imply a vindictive spirit. The conditions for the exercise of pardoning mercy would no longer subjectively exist as sinners persist in their lack of desire for salvation. Is hell hopeless? Warren explained that it is hopeless because its inmates have been so loved, and yet have rejected that love, that no new or higher manifestation is possible in which to hope.[398]

While the Hebrew *sheol* and the Greek *hades* usually refer to the grave, sometimes they specifically means a place of torment. The Greek words *gehenna* and *tartarus* are also translated *hell* and these words describe a place of torment. *Gehenna* is used twelve times in the New Testament and always refers to a place of torment.

While *hades* is used four times in this book (including vv 13-14 of this chapter), hell is also symbolically described as the lake of fire and the second death. Yet these symbolic references do not deny the reality of hell.

While hell is a real place of everlasting punishment, it is described symbolically in Revelation as the "lake of fire" and "the second death." To say these expressions are symbolic in no way tones down the awfulness of eternal punishment. Martin Luther said that no

---

[397] *The Tozer Pulpit*, 1:21-23.

[398] Scott, "Methodist Theology in America," 272-273.

picture of hell could be as bad as the reality.[399]

The lake of fire and brimstone (or sulfur) is mentioned six times in chapters 20-21. It is not literal, since Satan, who is a spiritual being with no body, was cast into this lake (v 10). The Bible does not explain how the fire can burn forever but not consume. We are only told in Matthew 3:12 that this fire is *unquenchable.* The phrase *lake of fire* brings together the imagery of water and fire. *Lake* speaks of water that is confined. While God's holiness covers the universe in blessing, since all sin is confined to one place, his holiness flares up in judgment and burns against sin. The lake of fire is not extermination but separation.

Peter Head wrote that John knows of no difficulty in the continuing existence of the wicked under the judgment of God (21:27; 22:14); the final triumph of God is not deemed incompatible with a continued exclusion and punishment of the godless. In fact, the final triumph of God's justice is seen in the salvation of the saints and the punishment of the wicked. There is no escaping the fact that Revelation clearly teaches and assumes the continued existence of the wicked in a destructive punishment primarily intended for Satan and his operatives. The eternal fire was designed for the devil and his angels, but human beings experience this judgment by virtue of their association with the Devil as children of wrath and their opposition to Jesus Christ. "The fiercest New Testament language is reserved for outspoken and blatant opponents of the gospel and persecutors of Christians."[400] Therefore the emphasis of the early Methodists was on warning sinners to flee the wrath to come (Luke 3:7).

Verse 10 says those in the lake of fire will be tormented day and night for ever and ever. This phrase "for ever and ever" is the strongest term in Greek.[401] It is also used to refer to the duration of God's

---

[399]Quoted by Oden, *Life in the Spirit*, 452.

[400]Head, "Duration of Divine Judgment," 226-227.

[401]Arndt and Gingrich defined αἰώνιος (*aionios*) as "without beginning or end" [*Lexicon*, 28].

own existence in 1:18; 4:9-10; 10:6; 15:7, the eternal power and glory of God in 1:6, 5:13, 7:12, and the length of Christ's reign in 11:15. According to Matthew 25:46 the duration of heaven is the same length as the duration of hell because the same adjective *aionios* is used to describe both. Compare also 20:10 and 22:5.

John uses words such as fire and death to describe something worse than physical pain. The uncontrolled fire that burns within the lustful, the jealous, the proud, the greedy led them to hell and now nothing in hell can satisfy that burning.

Jude 7 speaks of *eternal fire* and v 13 speaks of *blackest darkness*. If literal fire produces light and hell is a place of outer darkness, it follows that the fire is not literal but a metaphor describing divine judgment and human suffering which never burns out. Here John borrows the imagery of the destruction of Sodom and Gomorrah. After that judgment from God, Abraham arose the next morning and looked down toward the plain. He saw dense smoke rising from the land, like smoke from a furnace (Gen 19:28). See Revelation 14:10-11, which speaks of this smoke rising forever.

The second death symbolizes eternal separation from God. Just as there is a new and higher life in the Spirit, so there is also a second and deeper death. "The essence of hell is final exclusion from communion with God because of one's own fault."[402]

---

[402]Kasper, *The Church's Confession of Faith*, 347.

Chapters 19-20 Summary

VI. The Conquering Christ 19-20
- A. Heaven rejoices at Babylon's fall 19:1-5
- B. The marriage of the Lamb 19:6-10
- C. The ride of the king 19:11-21
  1. The revelation of Christ 19:11-16
  2. The victory of Christ 19:17-21
- D. The millennial kingdom 20:1-6
- E. Final overthrow of Satan — Gog and Magog 20:7-10
- F. The second advent and general judgment 20:9-15

The emphasis of chapter 19 is on the progressive victory of Christ across history. As this chapter opens, heaven rejoices over the fall of Babylon. The marriage supper of the Lamb is prepared, but the marriage does not happen until 21:9. In contrast to Babylon the whore, the bride makes herself ready. The bridegroom has provided her atonement; she is cleansed by his blood. As the general, he directs the battle on earth. The church declares the gospel, which binds Satan. Whether on earth or in heaven, the church is victorious. After humanity has experienced the prosperity of the gospel, Satan will be released for one last, brief hurrah.

Then Jesus returns. The dead are raised to live and a general judgment follows. The wicked are cast into an eternal hell and the righteous enter an eternal heaven.

REVELATION 21

VII. The revelation of the bride of Christ 21:1-22:5

These last two chapters describe the New Jerusalem. John has portrayed two women. Babylon is the harlot and Jerusalem is the bride, the wife of the Lamb (vv 2, 9). While it is described in terms of a city, the new Jerusalem is the church. These chapters portray the church in both her present and future glory.

It is easy to emphasize either part of this picture to the exclusion of the whole vision. The kingdom of Christ has been described as both *already* and *not yet*. Therefore, it is a mistake to interpret the entire chapter as either present or as future. If we take the progression seriously, these two chapters follow after the millennium and the coming of Christ.

These two chapters symbolize ten present aspects of the church:

- God presently dwells with us (21:3; 1 John 3:24; 4:13-16). If he himself is with us, then we are the temple of God. This is a present reality according to 2 Corinthians 6:16. The old temple was destroyed in AD 70 because it had been replaced with this new temple.

- We are a new creation. "I am making everything new" (v 5). "If anyone is in Christ, he is a new creation; the old has gone, the new has come!" (2 Cor. 5:17). Yet everything is not yet new. While the Christian is under the new order; much of the world is still under the old order of sin and death.

- We have drunk the water of life. "To him who is thirsty I will give to drink without cost from the spring of the water of life" (21:6). This theme of living water is found in Isaiah 55:1, "Come, all you who are thirsty, come to the waters; and you who have no money, come, buy and eat!" Jesus told the woman at the well, "Everyone who drinks this water will be thirsty again, but whoever drinks the water I give him will never thirst again. Indeed, the water I give him will become in him a spring of water welling up to everlasting life" (John 4:13-14). Jesus said, "If a man is thirsty, let him come to me and drink" (John 7:37). The water is available now, and the church is evangelistic as she invites all to drink it now (22:17).

- The river of life flows from the throne of God through the church (22:1-2). In Ezekiel 47 the church is symbolized as the temple of God and the river of life is the Holy Spirit who flows from it in ever increasing volume until the whole world is blessed.

- This symbolic city was built upon twelve foundations, which were the twelve apostles (21:14). Ephesians 2:20 says that the church is built upon the foundation of the apostles and prophets, with Christ Jesus himself as the chief cornerstone.

- The bride is portrayed as adorned with jewelry (21:11; 18-21). The garments of salvation and the robe of righteousness is the adornment of the church (Isa 61:10). Our adornment is a gentle and quiet spirit (1 Pet 3:4). See Psalm 45:13.

- The twelve gates (21:13) symbolize the universal composition of the church. People of all races and nations are coming into the church from the north, south, east, and west (Gen 28:14, 17; Luke 13:29). The high wall symbolizes the exclusion of all that is unholy. Taken literally, why build a wall 1500 miles long and 200 feet high and then leave all the gates open! Kik argued there would be no need for a wall in the consummate state if all the enemies of the church are in hell. Therefore, he concluded the gates are open to those who have not yet entered. This, then describes the gospel era.[403] All are invited to wash their robes and

---

[403]Kik, *An Eschatology of Victory,* 244; see also Sutcliffe, *Commentary*, 2:1121.

enter the gates (22:14).

- The church is the city of light (21:22-25; 22:5). John wrote that the darkness is passing and the true light is already shining. We are children of the light and we walk in the light (1 John 2:8; John 12:36; 1 John 1:7; Rom 13:11-12). The church is the light of the world; a city set on a hill (Matt 5:14; compare to Isa 60:1-22). "The nations will walk by its light and the kings of the earth will bring their splendor into it" (v 24) could depict a millennial, not an eternal condition.

- The cross of Christ is the tree of life (22:2). He is the true vine and we are the branches (John 15:1-8). We are to bear leaves and fruit. If we bear nothing we are removed. The healing of the nations is our task. There will be no need of healing or reconciliation in heaven. Furthermore, if there is no moon (21:23), the time cannot be marked in months such as 22:2 describes. Literalists have a real problem explaining how time can be thus measured in the eternal state.

- We are overcomers now (21:7). We need not live a defeated life. We can be sons of God now (1 John 3:1). We have the Holy Spirit now and he is the deposit guaranteeing our inheritance (Eph 1:13-14). The inheritance, however, is future and we have not yet arrived at our Father's house.

Yet while these truths are a present reality, there are some aspects which point ahead to a future state:

- There will be a new heaven and a new earth (21:1). The original earth and sky will be purged and renovated by fire (Ps 102:25-26; Isa 51:6; Luke 21:33; 2 Pet 3:10; Rev 20:11).

- There will be no more death (21:4). There will still be death during the millennium. Isaiah 65:17-25 describes a new heaven and a new earth. There will be no more the sound of weeping and of crying. Never again will an infant live but a few days. A man who dies before he reaches a hundred will be thought a mere youth. While this passage is a beautiful description of the millennial period, in which conditions are greatly improved, death is still present. However, in Revelation 21-22 John is describing a new heaven and a new earth in which there is no more death (v 4). According to 1 Corinthians 15:26, "The last enemy to be destroyed is death." Therefore, we are now looking into the future.

- There will no longer be any curse (22:3). The curse was pronounced in Genesis 3:14-19. The whole creation groans for release from the curse (Rom 8:18-23). Presently even the most godly are not free from these afflictions. Pain is part of the "former things."We are adopted into God's family now, but the redemption of our bodies comes with the general resurrection (Rom 8:23).

- There will be no more tears (21:4). While some commentators point out that the forgiven no longer shed tears of repentance and that we grieve not as those without hope, we still lived in a sin-cursed world and even Jesus himself wept over the human condition.

- This state is contrasted with the lake of fire which is the final state of the damned (21:8). But John describes a deliverance from tears, the curse of sin, and death. Therefore, this must be the final state of the saved.

While much of the book describes events which are now past, yet John brings his message of encouragement to a close by projecting the future of the church. Christ conquered Satan at the cross. That victory is historic. There is also a present victory that the church knows. But the Bible also promises a future triumph. The *no more* references are future. Where these references occur, they are describing the eternal state of the redeemed.

God takes up his abode with the saints (v 3). Thus, the indwelling God parallels the indwelling of his Spirit in the realized eschatology of John 14-17. This new Jerusalem is holy. It is something new and its descent out of heaven means that it does not belong to the old creation which is referred to as "earth-dwellers." Its walls and guards at each gate mean that, although they were then being persecuted, nothing can touch the people of God. The huge dimensions of the city means that there will be a large amount of converts coming into the city of God. Although the early church was poor, the rich material described in the chapter is meant to convey that the eternal wealth of the saints will be untainted like the Babylonian selfishness, greed, dishonesty, and oppression.

Thus, the emphasis is really upon the church, but heaven is the gathering place and final destination of the church. However, John does emphasize that heaven is a *place* (John 14:2), not simply a state of mind in which our consciousness is lost, having been absorbed into God. Therefore, it is legitimate to draw information about heaven from these chapters.

A. The new creation 21:1-8

There will be a new heaven and a new earth. The elements of the first heaven and earth will be destroyed by fire. "That day will bring about the destruction of the heavens by fire, and the elements will melt in the heat. But in keeping with his promise we are looking forward to a new heaven and a new earth" (2 Pet 3:10-13). This "destruction" is not annihilation, but purification and transformation. Peter compared it to the universal flood in Noah's day. Yet the earth was not destroyed in substance by the flood. Combustion does not annihilate but redistributes and rearranges the particles of matter. While only God, and not matter is eternal, passages such as Psalm 78:69; 104:5; 148:6 seem to teach the conservation of matter.

There will be no sea, no sun or moon (21:1, 23). If there is a new heaven and earth, it seems unnecessary to add that the sea is no more.

However, John is writing symbolically. Since the sea represented the source of the beast (13:1) and the place of the dead (20:13), it will be gone. John is not speaking geographically, but spiritually. There will, however, be a river of life and a lake of fire.

John sees the holy city descending from heaven. This theme was first introduced in 3:12. Abraham looked forward to this city with foundations (Heb 11:10). While the old prophets anticipated a rebuilt Jerusalem, this is the *new* Jerusalem. The AD 70 fall of Jerusalem accentuated the hope of a new Jerusalem. In v 2 this city is compared to a bride; in vv 9-10 the bride is symbolized as a city. There are not two separate descents.

The glory of the church is that God dwells with his people and the hope of the church is that they will dwell with God. John 1:14 says that the Word became flesh and tabernacled among us. Jesus is the manifestation of God's glory. Yet after finishing his mission he ascended back to heaven. But John uses that same word here to convey that God will tabernacle with us forever. This had been promised in Leviticus 26:11-12 (see also Jer 31:33; Ezek 37:27; Zech 8:8). And where God dwells, his glory is manifested.

The Father will wipe every tear from our eyes when we move into his house (see 7:17). There will be no more homelessness! All pain and crying, death and mourning will cease because they were part of the old order; the first earth. Earth is only the shadow land of heaven. C. S. Lewis wrote that earth is the shadow land of heaven. Heaven is going to be much more like earth than we realize—but without the presence of sin—much like our new body will correspond to our old body.

God, speaking directly for the first time in v 5, declares that he is making all things new (Isa 43:19) and death is not part of the new world. Death passed away at the general resurrection. But the God of truth has guaranteed a new creation.

John is commanded to write down these words which are trustworthy and true (see 19:9). Every word which proceeds from the mouth of God is true and this command to write his words down covers the entire book (see 1:11, 19).

In v 6 God speaks again, declaring "they are done." This is a statement of consummation. What Christ set in motion when he cried, "It is finished," has now been accomplished. The completion is described in 1 Corinthians 15:24-28.

God identifies himself as alpha and omega, the first and last letters in the Greek alphabet (AΩ). Thus, he is the beginning and the end. "That God is the beginning and end of history means that he rules over all events in between."[404] Christ made this same claim in 1:8 and 22:13. The word for *beginning* carries the meaning of *source* and the word for *end* means *purpose* or *fulfillment*. Thus everything was created by him and for him (see Col 1:16). God promises to share this purpose with us.

Those who are thirsty are promised divine satisfaction. Here John borrows from Isaiah 55:1. According to 22:1 God is the source of this water of life. Once more in 22:17 the thirsty are invited to drink freely. Perhaps this picture of drinking the water of life may be an intended contrast with 14:8, 10; 16:9; 17:2, 4; 18:3 where men drank the wine of Babylon.

God also gives us purpose by promising a father/son covenant relationship, which includes an inheritance, to all who overcome. The overcomer will inherit these things (v 7); the things described in this chapter.

At the beginning of this book John conveyed promises to the overcomer. They are fulfilled at the close of the book in the New Jerusalem. The overcomer eats from the tree of life (2:7; 22:2), is exempt from the second death (2:11; 21:7-8), eats at the Lord's table (2:17), rules with Christ (2:27, 3:21; 20:4, 22:5), has the morning star (2:28; 22:16), is dressed in white (3:5; 19:7-8), is named in the book of life (3:5; 21:27), is included in the new Jerusalem (3:12; 21:2), the name of God is written upon him (3:12; 22:4).

In contrast to the bliss of heaven, in v 8 John describes the inhabitants of hell. Robert Mounce commended on all eight classes of people, saying they all may refer to professing believers who have

[404]Beale, *NIGNT,* 1055.

apostatized, although he believes some descriptions can refer to pagans also. This is primarily a warning to Christians who considered turning back (see Heb 10:38-39).[405]

Here John gives a register of the other city, Babylon. The *cowardly* feared the threats of the devil more than they trust the love of Christ and therefore put personal safety and comfort ahead of faithfulness. Many to whom John initially wrote ended up as martyrs. The *unbelieving* does not describe those who have never heard, but those who denied their faith under pressure. God requires more than a one-time profession of faith; he requires a life of continued repentance and confessing Christ. Thus, the opposite of cowardice is an overcomer.

The *vile* refer specifically those who defiled themselves by participating in emperor worship. This same word is used twice in 17:4-5.[406] It is spiritual treason and spiritual adultery for God's people to compromise themselves by adopting the mind set and lifestyle of the world.

Murderers would include those who have persecuted the church. The *sexually immoral* are also indicted. The reference to those who practice *magic arts* uses the word *pharmakia*. In sorcery the use of drugs was generally accompanied by incantations and appeals to occult powers. The sin is occult involvement, but illicit drugs are often used in the process. *Pharmakia* was also used with reference to abortion. Augustine said that *idolatry* is worshiping anything that ought to be used or using anything that ought to be worshiped.[407] Finally *all liars* are included. It is especially grievous to pervert the word of truth, through false doctrine, pagan practices, or denying the faith (see 2:2; 3:9; 21:27; 22:15; Titus 1:16).

---

[405]Mounce, *NICNT,* 386; see also Stuart, *Apocalypse*, 2:377; Michaels, *IVPNTC*, 239-240.

[406]Wesley said the abominable were Sodomites [*Notes*, 726]. See also 22:15.

[407]Augustine, *On Christian Doctrine*, 1.3; *NPNF*1 2:523.

B. The new Jerusalem 21:9-14

Then John is invited to see the bride of the Lamb (v 9).Within 21:9-22:5 the Lamb is mentioned seven times. John specifies that the angel who gave him the invitation was the same angel who had the seven last plagues. Seven angels were involved and John does not specify which angel of the seven spoke. However, one of the seven had also invited John in 17:1 to see the judgment of the great harlot. John was carried away in his spirit and taken to see the bride coming down out of heaven.

The bride was introduced in 19:7. In 20:9 Satan's army came against her and in this battle she was represented as the beloved city. After her final victory, she now comes down out of heaven (v 10) as a bride comes down the aisle to be given to her husband (see Gen 24:62-66).

The holy city radiates with the glory of God, like the jewels sparkling on a bride. The Greek word translated "clear as crystal" suggests transparency, but the real point is the brilliance and sparkle of the city. Ladd observed that in 4:3 and here when John attempts to describe God's glory, the best he can do is to describe it as radiant precious stones.[408] Thus, the bride's adornment is actually the glory of God. She is clothed with the sun. The moon is under her feet and a crown of twelve stars on her head (12:1). It is significant that the very words used in 4:3 to describe the throne of God have all been borrowed to describe the church. Christ died for the church in order to make her holy so that she might be presented to him as a radiant church (Eph 5:26-27). The only way we can radiate the holiness of God is for God to indwell us (see v 3).

The Hebrew word for holiness is *qodesh* and one aspect of this word means brilliance. As God makes us holy, we radiate his glory. The adornment of Babylon is only external; the beauty of Jerusalem comes from the One who lives within her. The glory of God is de-

---

[408]Ladd, *Commentary*, 281.

scribed as weighty (2 Cor 4:17). Perhaps these heavy jewels in vv 19-21 also symbolize the weight of God's glory.

The twelve gates symbolize the universal composition of the church. People of all races and nations are coming into the church from the north, south, east, and west (Luke 13:29). The high wall symbolizes the exclusion of all that is unholy. Taken literally, why build a wall 1500 miles long and 200 feet high, then leave all the gates open! The gates of hades cannot remain closed (Matt 16:18), but must surrender the righteous dead to a city whose gates stand open. Isaiah 60:18 declares that the walls will be called *Salvation* and the gates *Praise*. The twelve angels at the gates remind us of the cherubim who guarded Eden's gate (Gen 3:24).

The concept of twenty-four elders was introduced in 4:4. The addition of twelve apostles (v 14) to twelve tribes (v 12) maintains the continuity of the Old Testament and the Christian church.

C. The walls of the city 21:15-21

If we grasp John's symbolism, we will not take literally the dimensions given in 21:16-17. Apparently the angel had to take the measurement since no human could measure something that vast. Since the wall is measured at a height of about 215 feet, but the city itself is 1500 miles high, it is obvious that John did not intend these measurements to be understood literally. By stating in v 17 that this human measurement is to be understood as that of an angel, John may be conveying the fact that these numbers are to be understood in a heavenly sense.

The city is literally said to be "four-cornered" in v 16. The square or cube symbolizes completeness, perfection, and symmetry. This corresponds to the Holy of Holies in Solomon's temple which was also a perfect cube (1 Kgs 6:20). We now can enter this most holy place, just as we enter the heavenly Jerusalem, through the blood of Jesus (Heb 10:19; 12:22).

Nothing in this new Jerusalem is out of order or balance. The emphasis is on the perfection and vastness of the bride. The dimensions given correspond to the approximate size of the known world in the first century. "This suggests further that the temple-city represents not merely the glorified saints of Israel but the redeemed from all nations."[409]

The arrangement of the twelve gemstones on the breastplate of the high priest were considered to be a miniature replica of the earthly tabernacle. The breastplate was also considered to be a small-scale version of the holy of holies, where the *Shekinah* glory of God dwelt. The breastplate was made of the same material and formed in the same square shape as the holy of holies. Thus, the twelve jewels symbolized God's glory. The earthly tabernacle was itself considered to be a model of the heavenly tabernacle (Heb 8:2; 9:11).[410]

Even the four horns of the altar may represent the four corners of the world. Thus, in 11:1-2 only the inner court of the temple was measured, because the outer court had been given to the Gentiles. Here the entire four-cornered city, which as a whole amounts to the house or temple of God, is measured. The significance is that here the Gentiles are included. Thus, the symbolic measurements emphasize the inclusion of all peoples within the church.

John used first century language to describe heaven. Today we would not describe a great city as having walls and gates. But ancient cities had them, therefore John uses walls and open gates metaphorically to convey no need for protection. To people who lived in dark houses, heaven was a place of light. To those who worked from dawn until dusk to make a living, heaven was a place of rest and abundance. These walls symbolize the *shalom* of God surrounding the community of overcomers (see Isa 26:1-2; 54:11-12; Zech 2:5).

The wall was made of jasper, while the city itself, even the street, was made of gold. All the gold and jewels are symbolic of the beauty of the bride. Clarke wrote,

> This description has been most injudiciously applied to

---

[409]Beale, *NIGNT,* 1074; see also Mulholland, *Revelation*, 325.

[410]Beale, *NIGNT*, 1081.

> heaven; and in some public discourses, for the comfort and edification of the pious, we hear of heaven with its golden walls, golden pavements, gates of pearl, etc., not considering that nothing of this description was ever intended to be literally understood; and that gold and jewels can have no place in the spiritual and eternal world.[411]

To the extent that this description of the bride may be applied to her place of residence, it is even a greater mistake to describe heaven in materialistic terms. To walk on gold is a statement of how little gold will be valued. Our descriptions of heaven are often in terms of finally attaining all the privileges of wealth and luxury. Many gospel songs focus on what our "mansion"[412] will be like. When the poor Christian attains more in this life, the less interested he tends to be in heaven. However, to tell carnally minded people that heaven is not the fulfillment of their greed would result in their loss of interest.

While John symbolically described the church and heaven in materialistic terms, yet this symbolism is too often misinterpreted literally. In Revelation 18 John was critical of Babylon's misuse of wealth. Here John uses symbols of wealth to convey the value of the church. If the list of jewels in vv 19-20 corresponds to the arrangement of the twelve gemstones on the breastplate of the high priest, then we are a kingdom of priests (see 1:6: 7:15; 1 Pet 2:5).

The twelve foundations were made of various shades of blue: sapphire, jacinth and amethyst; green: jasper, chalcedony, emerald, beryl, topaz, chrysophrase; red: sardonyx, carnelian or sardius; and yellow: chrysolite or yellow topaz. Since all the primary colors are

---

[411]Clarke, *Commentary*, 6:1060. See also Wesley, *Notes*, 728.

[412]Earle wrote concerning John 14:2 that the idea of mansions came from the Latin *mansiones* in the Vulgate. "In today's language a 'house' cannot have many 'mansions'; it has many rooms. The mistranslation here has led many people to get excited about having a mansion in heaven — for which there is no biblical basis" [*Word Meanings*, 2:48]. See also Daniell, *William Tyndall*, 136.

present, the luster of each would combine to create every color in the rainbow.

The twelve gates were each made of a single pearl, which would necessarily be the same height as the walls which were 216 feet high. The pearl is the only jewel produced by suffering and pain and these gates of pearl symbolize the fact that the entrance to heaven is through suffering (Acts 14:22).

D. The light of the city 21:22-27

Ezekiel 36-37 describe the first resurrection and revival; Ezekiel 38-39 describe Gog and Magog; and Ezekiel 40-48 describe the temple of God. Revelation follows the same outline, but then makes a radical change in John's blueprint: 19:11-20:6 also describe the first resurrection and revival; 20:7-10 describe Gog and Magog, but 21-22 does not have a temple. This is progressive revelation. Ezekiel had accommodated the final hope of God's people to old covenant terminology.

Ladd wrote that Ezekiel described the eternal new order in terms of a rebuilt temple in the new Jerusalem.[413] However, in terms of the new covenant, there is no temple at all (v 22). There will be no place set apart as holy and consecrated to the worship of God because heaven, in its entirety, is the temple of God and is permeated with the presence of God. Wall wrote that John relocated Ezekiel's new Jerusalem from the temple of a restored Jerusalem to a restored people who are the new Jerusalem.[414] Ezekiel's temple is the presence of God with his people. "The primary reason that John throughout 21:9-22:5 excludes most of the detailed descriptions of the Ezekiel 40-48 temple and its ordinances is because he understands it as

---

[413]Ladd, *Commentary*, 269-270.

[414]Wall, *NIBC*, 18:245-246. While 7:15 says the church serves God in his temple, this simply means that God's people will serve him in heaven (see 22:3). If the pillars in 3:12 are symbolic, so is the temple which they support.

fulfilled in God and Christ's presence and not in a physical structure."[415]

The church is a city of light (see also 22:5). John wrote that the darkness is passing and the true light is already shining.We are children of the light and we walk in the light (1 John 2:8; John 12:36; 1 John 1:7). The church is the light of the world; a city set on a hill (Matt 5:14; compare to Isaiah 60:1-22). There will never be another age of darkness.

The prophets anticipated the day when all nations would go up to Mount Zion (Isa 2:2-5). Israel was to be a light to the nations that would reach to the ends of the earth (Isa 49:6). The nations, who were once in darkness and came into the light of the gospel during the millennium, will continue to walk in the light of Christ. The kings of the earth, while no longer ruling, have bought their tribute into this city (Isa 60:3-5; Hag 2:7-8). However, it is not literal wealth that they bring; instead they themselves are the spoils which are given back to the one who alone deserves it (see Ps 96:7-9). While the "kings of the earth" had been aligned with the beast (17:2, 18; 18:3, 9; 19:19) and were ultimately destroyed (19:21), God in his mercy redeemed some from every tribe, tongue, people. They are no longer outside the city.

According to 22:15 sinners are still on the outside. Just as the physically unclean could not enter the old temple, so the spiritually unclean will not be allowed to enter the eternal temple. Heaven is a place of sanctity and security. Nothing profane will be allowed inside its sacred space. No pagan who engaged in abominable practices will be allowed. Neither will anyone who lies through a false profession of faith be granted entrance.

Since the devil will be tormented forever in hell, the gates can always be left open (v 25). Since heaven is a place of holiness (v 27), the unsaved would be miserable in such an atmosphere of holiness. The greedy materialist would also be disappointed. John Fletcher wrote,

---

[415]Beale, *NIGNT*, 1091.

> But suppose it were possible for thee, O sinner, to enter into heaven without having experienced the new birth. What wouldst thou do there? Drunkard! there is no strong drink in heaven. Sensualist! thou must leave flesh and blood behind, and how great would be the disappointment to be deprived of all the means of thy present happiness. Heaven itself would be no heaven for thee, and thy discontent would even prove a kind of hell.[416]

Wesley concluded that those whose names are on heaven's register are holy, persevering believers.[417] John has armed the church with hope that God will dwell among his people. The center of this holy city will be the throne of God and from this throne holiness and goodness will fill its walls. John has also portrayed Jesus Christ as the universal light by which the redeemed from all nations will walk. They will occupy this city from every tribe, tongue, and people. Thus, we are challenged to be overcomers and share in this hope.

---

[416]Fletcher, *Works*, 4:144.

[417]Wesley, *Notes*, 729; Benson, *Notes*, 5:803.

REVELATION 22

E. The river of life 22:1-5

The last chapter of the Bible connects with the first chapter of the Bible. In Genesis 2:8-17 God had planted a garden in the East. The word *Eden* means delight. The garden of Eden was filled with trees which were pleasing to the eye and good for food. In Revelation 2:7 this garden of Eden is called "the paradise of God." This Greek word for *paradise* means an enclosed garden.

In chapter 21 John portrayed the entire city as a temple. Here he portrays this paradise as covering the whole earth. The original garden was the first temple in which the first man worshiped God. Apparently Adam was to subdue the earth and thus extend the boundaries of the garden until Eden covered the whole earth. The dimensions of the New Jerusalem, as given in 21:16 was the approximate size of the known world in John's day and also suggests that this temple-city would also cover the whole earth. In Jewish tradition, their temple was considered a microcosm of heaven and earth. John is shown the reality of these expectations.

Four rivers flowed through the first garden (Gen 2:10-14). Here John saw one river, the river of the water of life, flowing from the throne of God *and* of the Lamb, through the church. This is the river described in Ezekiel 47. It flows from the temple of God and we are that temple. We were all given the Spirit to drink (1 Cor 12:13). Whosoever is thirsty may come and drink of the water of life (21:6). The bride says "Come, whoever is thirsty let him come and take the free gift of the water of life" (22:17).

Ezekiel measured the temple, then described it being filled with the glory of God (Ezek 43). In chapter 47 he saw water flowing from under the threshold of the temple and the further the stream went the bigger it got, until it flooded the whole earth. Jesus interpreted this passage for us in John 7:38-39 and we have access to this water of life. When Jesus ascended to the Father, he asked the Father to send the Comforter, the Spirit of truth. Jesus said after the Spirit came, whoever believes in him will have rivers of living water flowing from within him. We are the temple of the Holy Spirit and rivers of living water flow out of us individually. Collectively, we are the temple of God and through the church, God will flood the earth with his Spirit.

There had to be Calvary before there could be Pentecost. From the cross flows this mighty river. "There is a river whose streams make glad the city of God, the holy place where the Most High dwells." God dwells in the midst of his people. God is within her, *she will not fall*; God will help her at break of day. Nations are in uproar, kingdoms fall; he lifts his voice, the earth melts. The Lord Almighty is with us; the God of Jacob is our fortress. Come and see the works of the Lord . . . He makes wars cease to the ends of the earth; he breaks the bow and shatters the spear, he burns the shields with fire. Be still and know that I am God; *I will be exalted among the nations* (Ps 46).

And in the midst of the garden was the tree of life. This tree is referenced in vv 2, 14, 19; see also 2:7. Both the water of life and the tree of life symbolize everlasting life. According to Genesis 3:22 those who ate regularly of this tree would live forever. Liberal commentators are quick to explain that this was a mythical tree. It did not exist literally, but was used in this ancient literature as a symbol of life. On the other hand dispensational writers often argue that there will be literal trees in heaven.

We do not have to decide between a literal tree or a symbolic meaning because God takes ordinary things and uses them as a means of conveying spiritual truth. If God can use the ordinary communion elements of bread and wine and make them a means of spiritual blessing, God could have used an ordinary tree in a similar way.[418] The eating of this tree symbolized the continual giving of life. Adam Clarke wrote that it was placed in the midst of the garden as an emblem of that life which man should ever live, provided he continued in obedience to his Maker. And the use of this tree was probably intended as a *means* of preserving the body of man in a state of continual vital energy, and an antidote against death. This seems strongly

---

[418]Pope, *Compendium*, 2:10-11.

indicated from Genesis 3:22.[419]

Adam and Eve ate as an act of faith that God would preserve their lives. Apparently they had to eat of this tree regularly in order to maintain their quality of life both physically and spiritually. Just as one meal will not fill us permanently, so Adam and Eve, who had no doubt previously eaten of this tree were barred from continuing to partake of it and thus were subject to spiritual death. Therefore, the tree represented man's constant dependence upon God. We must continually eat of the tree and drink from the water.

Once paradise was lost, mankind decided to return and eat of the tree of life. But Genesis 3:24 depicts our plight. We cannot go back to the Garden of Eden. Yet for all who have tasted sin and found it bitter, and for those who have eaten from the wrong tree, the good news is that the tree of life reappears in the last book of the Bible and is accessible by faith. What was forfeited by Adam and thus denied to his descendants will be fully realized when paradise is restored. A river flows through it and the tree of life is on both sides of its banks. In this chapter the tree, the river, and the street are all singular, but perhaps all should be understood to be collective singulars. Thus, the single tree of life in Genesis has multiplied into a quantity of trees which line the river (see also Ezek 47:12). Their leaves are for the healing of the nations.

The good news is that the cross of Jesus Christ is the tree of life. Anselm observed that the enemy conquered humanity by tasting of a tree; Christ conquered the enemy by bearing suffering on a tree.[420]

When we believe on the Lord Jesus Christ and trust solely in his finished work on the cross to reverse the effects of sin, we eat of the tree of life. When we believe, we receive eternal life. The promise is, "To him who is overcoming [present participle], I will give the right to eat from the tree of life, which is in the paradise of God" (2:7). Since we overcome by the blood of the Lamb, we are now eating of the tree of life.

---

[419]Clarke, *Commentary*, 1:43.

[420]Quoted by Oden, *The Word of Life*, 106.

While the curse has not yet been lifted, nor have we yet seen the face of God, while we still need the sun and even though Christ has not yet returned — he has already come once and as a result we have access to this tree of life. We are branches who are dependant upon the tree for our very life (John 15:1-17).

However, it is not the trunk that bears fruit; the fruit is found on the branches. God saves *us* so that we will bear fruit. The church ought to export spiritual fruit all over the world! Just as the twelve spies came back from the land of Canaan with produce on their shoulders, so we cry out to a world who is searching for the lost tree of life, "Taste and see that the Lord is good" (Ps 34:8).

But the tree of life not only produces the fruit of the Spirit within us, this tree produces healing or health for the nations. If there is not sickness or death in heaven, why do the nations need healing? God's ultimate plan of salvation includes healing, not only of individuals, but nations of people. If Christ is the tree of life, his people are the leaves (compare to Ps 1:3). The healing of the nations is the task of the church and this restoration is initiated as we preach the gospel.

If there is no moon (21:23), time cannot be marked in months such as 22:2 describes. Literalists have a real problem explaining how time can be thus measured in the eternal state. John may be accommodating the language of time to describe eternity. Yet there is both a present and partial realization of this healing now, as well as a more complete realization then.

Physical healing is a foretaste of the resurrection of the body. If God has the power to raise from the dead, he has power to heal the sick. For the child of God, the future breaks into the present, in the kingdom of God. We know the kingdom has come because we have tasted the power of the world to come (Heb 6:5). And while divine healing is now possible, then there will be a general resurrection.

Ultimately we are healed from the curse of sin. The symbols of the water of life, tree of life, and its healing leaves, which are continuously available in the eternal state, all suggest that this restoration not only occurs in the instant of the resurrection, but is ongoing and progressive.

REVELATION 22:18-21

The oldest symbol of peace is the olive branch. Noah sent out a dove and it brought back an olive branch, symbolic of the fact that God was no longer angry, but that his wrath had been propitiated. Yet man continued to sin and break God's law. Ultimately, it took the cross to turn away God's wrath.

The cross breaks down all barriers. According to v 14 all who wash their robes [in the blood] have access to the tree of life. All who are washed in the blood of the Lamb are part of the body of Christ. All racial barriers are brought down. The vision of John tells us that people will be saved out of every political grouping, every ethnic unit, every language group, every subculture. When enough enemies start eating from the same tree, they will beat their swords into plowshares and their spears into pruning hooks and they will no longer train for war (Isa 2:4; Mic 4:3). These prophecies by Isaiah and Micah are not speaking of heaven — these are prophecies of the last days, not of eternity. As incredible as this all seems, healing and reconciliation will come through the cross, which is the tree of life.

According to Genesis 2:15 Adam was to work in the Garden of Eden; to till it and guard or preserve it. We will continue to work and serve in heaven for John wrote, "His servants will serve him" (v 3). Adam and Eve worked before the curse. We will work even after the curse has been lifted. There will be no unemployment in heaven. We will serve him "day and night" (Rev 7:15-16).

Ever since the fall of man the creation has been under the curse of sin. The inhabitants of the New Jerusalem will enjoy the blessings of immortality, without any infirmities. They will also enjoy the *beatific vision*, which is seeing God face-to-face, living in the light of God's countenance, serving and reigning forever. This may connect with the Aaronic benediction in Numbers 6:25-27, where the grace of God was depicted as his face shining upon his people (see also 2 Cor 3:18). As God dwells with his people in the New Jerusalem, his presence radiates so much light that the sun is no longer necessary for illumination. The description of God's name on our foreheads alludes to the name of God being on the golden plate which the high priest wore on his forehead (Exod 28:36-38).

The Lord God in v 5 is both the Father and the Son. Both are depicted as on the throne in vv 1, 3 (see also 3:21). This contrast between the blazing light of the New Jerusalem and the *blackest darkness* of the second death (Jude 7) was typified in the ninth plague of Egypt. All the Egyptians had three days of pitch darkness, while the people of Israel lived in light (Exod 10:22-23).

Conclusion 22:6-21

1. The angel's testimony 22:6

John is assured these words are true. This assurance was also given in 19:9; 21:5 and claims equal authority for this book as for the Old Testament prophecies. This verse implies that John held a specific prophetic office and therefore was claiming divine inspiration for his revelation. And the purpose of this inspiration is to insure that what John wrote was trustworthy.

2. Christ's declaration 22:7

In this chapter Jesus promised three times to come quickly (vv 7, 12, 20). And so the book ends just as it begins, with a promise that these events would happen soon or shortly (1:1, 3, 7). Jesus Christ did come in the first century at the day of Pentecost. He also came in judgment to the seven churches, as promised five times in chapters 2-3. He came in vengeance upon the Jewish nation who had rejected him (Luke 21:20-22), and he came to avenge the blood of his believers which had been shed by Roman persecution (6:10). Christ comes to the believer in salvation (3:20). Christ comes for the Christian at death. Christ comes often in judgment and in revival (Acts 3:20). Christ comes whenever believers assemble in his name (Matt 18:20). And he will return physically at the end of the age to raise the dead and judge the world. "This same Jesus will come back in the same way you have seen him go into heaven" (Acts 1:11). Therefore he came in the incarnation, he comes often, and he will come again.

However, when the promise of Christ's coming is qualified to a first century audience with *tachu*, which means *soon* or *shortly*, the subject is not the second advent. John instead is writing about things which occurred in the first century, soon after he wrote.

3. John and the angel 22:8-11

Again John mistakenly worshiped the angel (vv 8-9). The first occasion was in 19:9 where the angel declared, "These are the true words of God." Here John has just heard the voice of Christ and falls down before his angel guide, whom he must have presumed was Christ. In both instances John heard supernatural declarations and was so overwhelmed he directed his worship toward a messenger of God, instead of God. In both cases his motive to worship was right, but it was misdirected. We must resist any attempt to deify human messengers (see Acts 10:25-26; 14:11-18) or even develop superstitious attitudes toward supernatural messengers. God alone is to be the object of our worship and since Christ is consistently portrayed in this book as equal with God, Christ, but not angels, is also worthy of our worship.

Then the angel told John not to seal the message of this book because the time of its fulfillment was near. This reverses the direction given in Daniel 8:26; 12:4, 9. What Daniel saw in the future, John sees in the present. And if the time of the fulfillment is near, it is a mistake to project the fulfillment several centuries later or at some remote period of time.

While the whole period of human life is a probationary state, v 11 describes the end of that probation. Binney wrote, "This verse teaches the unchangeable character, and therefore the fixed, ultimate destiny of all men in the future state after the day of judgment; that the reward of holiness is holiness, and the punishment of sin is sin."[421] God has not predetermined to damn any soul nor has he unconditionally predestined anyone to be saved. He has offered salvation to

---

[421]Binney, *Commentary*, 704.

everyone and those who trust in the work of Christ are saved.

But our initial choice is not necessarily our final answer. Jesus told of a father who had two sons (Matt 21:28-32). When the father told his first son to go and work in the vineyard, his son replied, "I will not." But later he changed his mind and went. The second said all the right words, but he never did go. For him, his initial decision became his final answer, but his brother repented.

However, v 11 warns us that someday that our current condition will become our final decision. There is an awesome sense of finality in this verse. Someday those daily decisions will become our final choice. One day Christ will say to the faithful, "Well done, good and faithful servant! You have been faithful with a few things. I will put you in charge of many things" (Matt 25:21).

But just as this is the hope of the seeker, it is also the warning for the sinner. Time works against him. Like the fresh concrete, his character is setting up. He becomes hardened in his sin. The warning is also to the vile. The Word of God warns us to get rid of all moral filth. The one who dabbles in the realm of that which is vile and impure may excuse himself saying that he can always change. But that which is impure stains his character until he has become vile.

Verse 11 contains four imperatives. The two such verbs regarding unjustness and filthiness are not to be interpreted as divine commands to sin. Instead they are permissive imperatives, usually translated "let him continue in his unrighteousness and filthiness." In other words while they are a command, they also involve the consent of the one commanded. Thus, we see both God's sovereignty and man's responsibility. God allows us to freely choose, but has predestined the consequences of that choice. God has not determined the necessity of their sin, but he has determined the consequences. This is demonstrated in the case of Pharaoh who repeatedly hardened his own heart until God finally confirmed the permanence of that choice. God finally abandoned Ephraim to the consequences of his own choices (Hos 4:17).

Our present tendencies indicate what will likely be our permanent condition. "Whether a tree falls to the south or to the north, in the place where it falls, there will it lie" (Eccl 11:3). This means that whatever is the direction or tendency of our life, we will probably fall in that same direction. Most people will die just like they have lived. It warns those whose lives are leaning out over hell and yet who hope to fall into heaven. If hell is eternal everyone will not ultimately land in heaven. There will be no change in our eternal condition (v 11). When Christ comes, the condition he finds us in becomes our final answer. There will be no second chances nor appeals. "Sow an act — reap a habit: sow a habit — reap a character: sow a character —reap a destiny."

4. Christ's benediction 22:12-16

"My reward is with me and I will give to everyone according to what he has done." The word for *reward* is *wages*, literally "what is due." However, this "due" could be either positive or negative. Beale argued that this must refer to Christ's final coming at the end of the age because this will be the time of the last judgment when each man receives just as his works deserve.

This general judgment will be based upon works. There are forty-two instances in Scripture were we are told we will be judged on the basis of our works.[422] When we are first saved our works are filthy before God (Isa 64:6). Therefore, our faith is imputed to us for righteousness (Rom 4:6). But we are not only justified; we are given the new life of the Holy Spirit and were created in Christ Jesus to do good works (Eph 2:10). We demonstrate true faith by good works (James 2:17-18).

While we are initially saved by faith alone, genuine faith will produce good works. The Greek word used is ἔργον (*ergon*). A frequent theme in Revelation is this final judgement of works or deeds (see 2:2, 5-6, 19, 22-23, 26; 3:1-2, 8, 15; 9:20; 14:13; 16:11; 18:3-6; 20:12-13; 22:12).

Good words do not merit salvation and eternal life, but they are

---

[422] J. B. Smith, *Revelation*, 279.

signs of manifestations of inward grace. Yinger wrote that whether the issue was human or divine evaluation. In both cases it is the value of deeds as manifesting something which stands in the foreground, rather than being a matter of performance. Works are not understood primarily as proof of performance but as a means of knowing and assessing.[423] Faith without works is dead (Jas 2:17-18). And according to John, it is this persevering faith which produces overcomers.

While the Bible affirms that Christ will come again at the end of the age to judge the world, the problem is that v 12 promised this would occur *soon*. However, Beale acknowledged that there is also a sense in which Christ grants heavenly rewards to his people immediately when they die (6:9-11; 14:13) and judges the unrighteous continuously throughout the age (2:22-23).[424] According to Matthew 16:27-28 when Christ came in his glory he would reward each person according to what he had done *and* some to whom Jesus was speaking would live to see that coming. Thus rewards are received in this life, as well as the next. Whenever Christ comes into the heart of a repentant sinner, he brings the gift of salvation. Whenever he comes in judgment, he brings punishment. At the hour of death he brings the consequences described at v 11.

Heaven will be a place of reward. In heaven everyone's cup of joy will be full, but some cups will be larger than others. Our greatest reward will be the privilege of entering the gates of the city and eating from the tree of life (v 14). This tree was removed from the Garden of Eden and is symbolic of eternal life. Paradise will be restored. Christ once more declares, "I am Alpha and Omega" (see 21:6).

Again in v 15 John describes those outside heaven and the list is basically the same as 21:8 except for *dogs*. This term is used in Deuteronomy 23:17-18 for male prostitutes.Wesley wrote that a *dog* was a whoremonger or sodomite. "Such are called *dogs*, Rev 22:15.

---

[423]Yinger, *Paul, Judaism, and Judgment*, 160-161.

[424]Beale, *NIGNT,* 1134.

And it is not improbable they are called so here."[425]

To be *profane* means that a person was placed outside the temple. To be a *prostitute* was to be a stranger or foreigner — to be placed outside the family or nation. To be a *dog* was to be categorized as outside the human race. Therefore, John declares that such *dogs* will also be excluded from heaven. And yet according to 1 Corinthians 6:9-11 it is possible for those who have engaged in this perversion to be washed and ultimately inherit the kingdom of God.

In v 16 the angel gives the testimony of Jesus to *you* which is plural. Morris explained, "The message was not a private one. It was for Christians at large, and so the plural is meaningful."[426] The *you* in v 16 corresponds to the *all* in v 21.

The message delivered is that Jesus is the rightful king, "I am the root and offspring of David." In 5:5 his humanity was emphasized; he was the root of David. Here at v 16 that fact is expanded (see Isa 11:1, 10). *Offspring* is an additional explanation of *root*. But he is both David's son and David's Lord (Matt 22:45). His declaration, "I am the bright Morning Star" is a depiction of hope that a new day is dawning (see Num 24:17).

5. The invitation of the church 22:17

Verse 17 contains three invitations for the thirsty to drink of the water of life. While he does come into our hearts when we are saved, v 17 is not a call for him to come to us, but for us to come to him. Notice that call is for whoever is thirsty to come to Christ. Here John echoes the invitation found in Isaiah 55:1, "Come, all you who are thirsty, come to the waters." Jesus told the woman at the well that whoever drinks the water I give him will never thirst. Indeed, the water I give him will become in him a spring of water welling up to eternal life" (John 4:14).

---

[425]Wesley, *Notes*, 1:654; see also Aune, *WBC*, 52C:1222-1224; 1237; Metzger, *Breaking the Code*, 106.

[426]Morris, *TNTC*, 20:261.

The first call comes from the Spirit. According to John 6:44, no one can come to Christ unless he is drawn by the Father. Some theologians have concluded then that if the Father has predestined you to be saved, he will irresistibly call you by his Spirit and you will be saved. But this calling of the Spirit is not limited to the elect. According to John 12:32, Jesus taught that through the cross all men are drawn to him. But while all are drawn, not all are saved. This call can be accepted or resisted (Acts 2:37-41; 7:51). That is why Jesus taught that comparatively speaking many are called, but few are chosen (Matt 20:16; 22:14). The elect are few, not because God has only chosen a few to be saved but because many resist the call of the Holy Spirit. Yet the necessary grace needed to respond comes with the gospel call.

The bride duplicates the calling of the Holy Spirit. According to 21:9, the bride is the Lamb's wife. Just as Abraham sent Eleazar to find a bride for Isaac, so the Father has sent the Holy Spirit into the world to find a bride for his Son. John the Baptist used this same figure of speech when his followers reported that everyone was following Jesus. John said, "I am not the Christ." Therefore, the bride does not belong to me (John 3:28-29). Jesus is the groom and his bride is the church, all who follow him. See also Ephesians 5:23-32.

Having established the identity of the bride, notice her function. Her message is to coincide with the voice of the Spirit. Those who have got so far from God that they no longer hear the call of the Spirit, should still hear the same call coming from the church. Our message is to those who are thirsty. Come to Christ and he will give you the water of life.

But if the sinner resists both the call of the Spirit and the call of the church, are we to conclude that God never chose them? Or that Jesus Christ did not make atonement for them? There is a third invitation. Let the one who hears the invitation come himself and then on the basis of his experience, let him lift his voice and invite the thirsty to come to Christ. The sinner gains hope from the testimony of one who has overcome.

God could force the sinner to submit and trust, but God has

chosen to limit his power. The invitation "let him come" and "let him take" are both commands, but they are also imperatives of permission, not imperatives of command.

God speaks through his Spirit, his church, and Christian friends, but God will not force anyone to drink the water of life. Notice the condition — the one who is willing [wishes] is commanded to take the free gift. It cannot be alleged that *will* is used here only in the sense of the future tense. "The one who is willing" must receive the free gift of spiritual life.

The unwilling will die of thirst in spite of the availability of water and the fact that they have received three invitations.

6. John's warning and benediction 22:18-21

God's Word is forever settled and permanent. It stands written. The participle *having been written* is perfect passive, meaning that it stands written. When Moses came to the end of the law, he gave this warning, "Do not add to what I command you and do not subtract from it, but keep the commands of the Lord your God that I give you" (Deut 4:2). Again in 12:32, "See that you do all I command you; do not add to it or take away from it." In the wisdom literature, near the end of Proverbs, we find another warning: "Every word of God is flawless [pure, unmixed with error] . . . Do not add to his words, or he will rebuke you and prove you a liar" (30:6).

As we come to the end of prophetic literature, everyone who hears the words of the prophecy of this book is given a third warning: If anyone adds anything to them, God will add to him the plagues described in this book. And if anyone takes words away from this book of prophecy, God will take away from him his share in the tree of life and in the holy city, which are described in this book. Although access to the tree of life and citizenship in the city of God both may be forfeited. Marshall observed, "There is no reason to suppose that these warnings are purely hypothetical, directed against non-existent dangers."[427]

The book of Revelation opened with a pronouncement of blessing upon those who read, and hear, and keep the things that are written (1:3). Likewise, 22:7 ends with a blessing to the one who keeps the words of the prophecy in this book.

It is as though there is a divine seal at the end of the Bible declaring the Word of God perfect and complete. We must not alter his words to make them say what we want them to say.

Scripture is sufficient revelation. God has not told us everything we might want to know, but he has revealed everything we need to know. Sufficiency is implied if nothing can be added nor subtracted from the Word. The old hymn asks, "What more can he say than to you he hath said?"[428] The canon of Scripture is closed.

Scripture is inerrant. God warns us not to tamper with his words because they are perfect. How can you improve upon perfection? In other words, if fallible men edit the perfect revelation of God they only corrupt it. Scripture is authoritative. It comes from God. God promises his blessing on those who reverence his Word. And God warns that our salvation is in jeopardy if we do not respect his Word.

In other words, God's word to us is permanent. Jesus said, Heaven and earth will pass away, but my words will by no means pass away (Matt 24:25). While everything around us changes, God's word stands firm eternally. "Forever, O Lord, Your word is settled in heaven" (Ps 119:89).

In vv 7, 12, 20 Jesus announced that he is coming soon. Deliverance is at hand. He came to the first century in judgment. He comes for each of us at the hour of death. He will come again at the end of the world. Since we do no know when he is coming, we are to be ready.

The response of the church in v 20 is the equivalent of "Your kingdom come" and the Aramaic *maranatha* in 1 Corinthians 16:22. The church lives in the hope of his return, whether it is soon or de-

---

[427]Marshall, *Kept by the Power of God*, 175.

[428]"How Firm a Foundation," (1787).

layed. Liberals assume that the early church expected the second advent in their day and then conclude that Scripture and the early church was mistaken. But the doctrine of the imminent return of Christ is contradicted if Paul expected death, not the rapture (2 Tim 4:6-8), if Peter would die and not be raptured (John 21:18-19), if the Great Commission must be fulfilled before Christ returns, and if there must first be an apostasy (2 Thess 2:1-3). Paul also anticipated future church problems (Acts 20:29).

John closes with a benediction, much like Paul's benedictions. Thus the entire Revelation takes the form of a letter, with the salutation in 1:4 and the closing in 22:21.

Chapters 21-22 Summary

VII. The revelation of the bride of Christ 21-22

- A. The new creation 21:1-8
- B. The new Jerusalem 21:9-14
- C. The walls of the city 21:15-21
- D. The light of the city 21:22-27
- E. The river of life 22:1-5

Conclusion 22:6-21

1. The angel's testimony 22:6
2. Christ's declaration 22:7
3. John and the angel 22:8-11
4. Christ's benediction 22:12-16
5. The invitation of the church 22:17
6. John's warning and benediction 22:18-21

These last two chapters describe the New Jerusalem — the church in both her present and future glory. She invites everyone to share in the present and future blessings of salvation. While her walls keep out sin, her gates are open to all who persevere in faith.

The glory of the church is that God dwells with his people and the hope of the church is that they will dwell with God. Heaven is the gathering place and final destination of the church. John does emphasize that heaven is a *place* (John 14:2). Heaven is a place of sanctity and security. It is a place of holiness and a place of reward. The church has been commissioned to invite whosoever will to come.

BIBLIOGRAPHY

Anderson, Robert. *The Coming Prince.* 1881. Reprint, Grand Rapids: Kregel, 1975.

Arndt, William F, F. Wilbur Gingrich. *A Greek-English Lexicon of the New Testament.* 2nd ed. Walter Bauer's 5th ed. Revised by F. Wilbur Gingrich and Frederick W. Danker. Chicago: University of Chicago, 1979.

Athanasius. *Selected Works and Letters: A Select Library of Nicene and Post-Nicene Fathers of the Christian Church.* Second Series. Vol. 4. Philip Schaff and Henry Wace, eds. 1891. Reprint, Grand Rapids: Eerdmans, 1978. [*NPNF*]

Augustine. *Christian Doctrine: A Select Library of Nicene and Post-Nicene Fathers of the Christian Church.* First Series. Vol. 2. Philip Schaff, ed. 1886. Reprint, Grand Rapids: Eerdmans, 1979. [*NPNF*]

Aune, David E. *Revelation 1-5.* Vol. 52A of *Word Biblical Commentary.* Dallas: Word, 1997. *Revelation 6-16.* Vol. 52B of *Word Biblical Commentary.* Nashville: Thomas Nelson, 1998. *Revelation 17-22.* Vol. 52C of *Word Biblical Commentary.* Nashville: Thomas Nelson, 1998. [*WBC*]

__________. "St. John's Portrait of the Church in the Apocalypse." *The Evangelical Quarterly* 38:3 (July-Sept, 1966) 131-149.

Bahnsen, Greg L. "The Person, Work, and Present Status of Satan." *The Journal of Christian Reconstruction* 1:2 (Winter 1974) 11-43.

__________. *Theonomy in Christian Ethics.* Nutley, NJ: Craig Press, 1979.

Barclay, William. *The Revelation of John.* Revised ed. 2 vols. Philadelphia: Westminster, 1976.

Bass, Clarence B. *Backgrounds to Dispensationalism.* Grand Rapids: Baker, 1960.

Bauckham, Richard. *The Climax of Prophecy.* Edinburgh: T & T Clark, 1993.

Beale, G. K. *The Book of Revelation. The New International Greek Testament Commentary.* I. Howard Marshall and Donald A. Hagner, eds. Grand Rapids: Eerdmans, 1999. [*NIGNT*]

Bell, Albert A, Jr. "The Date of John's Apocalypse: the Evidence of some Roman Historians Reconsidered." *New Testament Studies* 25:1 (Oct 1978) 93-102.

Benson, Joseph. *The Holy Bible, with Notes, All the Marginal Readings, Summaries, and the Date of Every Transaction*, 2nd ed. 5 vols. 1811-1818; Reprint, New York: Carlton & Phillips, 1856.

Binney, Amos and Daniel Steele. *The People's Commentary on the New Testament*. New York: Eaton & Mains, 1878.

Bloesch, Donald G. *Christian Foundations: The Last Things*. Vol 7. Downers Grove, IL: InterVarsity, 2004.

Boyer, Paul. *When Time Shall Be No More: Beliefs in Modern American Culture*. Cambridge, MA: Harvard University Press, 1992.

Bock, Darrell L. ed. *Three Views on the Millennium and Beyond*. Grand Rapids: Zondervan, 1999.

Boettner, Loraine. *The Millennium*. Phillipsburg, NJ: Presbyterian and Reformed, 1957. Revised edition. 1984.

Bright, John. *The Kingdom of God*. Nashville: Abingdon, 1953.

__________. *The Authority of the Old Testament*. Nashville: Abingdon, 1967.

Brown, David. *Christ's Second Coming*. 1876. Reprint, Grand Rapids: Baker, 1983.

Bruce, F. F. *New Testament History*. Garden City, NY: Anchor Books, 1969.

__________. *Revelation* in *The International Bible Commentary*. F. F. Bruce, H. L. Ellison, and G. C. D. Howley, eds. Grand Rapids: Zondervan, 1986.

__________. *The Canon of Scripture*. Downers Grove, IL: InterVarsity, 1988.

Bunyan, John. *The Pilgrim's Progress*. 1678-1684. Reprint, New York: Penguin, 1964.

Caird, G. B. *The Revelation of St. John the Divine. Black's New Testament Commentaries*. Henry Chadwick, ed. 1966. Reprint, Peabody, MA: Hendrickson, 1999.

Carpenter, W. Boyd. *The Revelation of St. John. Ellocott's Commentary on the Whole Bible*. Charles John Ellicott, ed. 8 vols. Reprint, Grand Rapids: Zondervan, 1959.

Carrington, Philip. *The Meaning of Revelation*. London: SPCK, 1931.

Chilton, David. *Days of Vengeance: An Exposition of the Book of Reve-*

lation. Ft. Worth: Dominion Press, 1987.

Clarke, Adam. *The Holy Bible, Containing the Old and New Testaments: the Text Carefully Printed from the Most Correct Copies of the Present Authorized Translations, Including the Marginal Reading and Parallel Texts; with a Commentary and Critical Notes, Designed as a Help to a Better Understanding of the Sacred Writings*. 6 vols. 1811-1825. Reprint, Nashville: Abingdon, 1950.

Clemance, Clement. *The Revelation of St. John the Divine*. Vol. 51 in *The Pulpit Commentary*. Joseph S. Exell and H. D. M. Spence, eds. 52 vols. Reprinted in 23 vols. *Revelation* is Vol. 22 in the reprint. Grand Rapids: Eerdmans, 1950.

Daniell, David. *William Tyndall: A Biography*. New Haven, CY: Yale University, 1994.

Davis, John Jefferson. *Christ's Victorious Kingdom*. Grand Rapids: Baker, 1986.

Delling, Gerhard. "χρόνος." *Theological Dictionary of the New Testament*. Gerhard Friedrich, ed. Grand Rapids: Eerdmans, 1974. 9:581-593.

Duewel, Wesley L. *Touch the World through Prayer*. Grand Rapids: Francis Asbury Press, 1986.

Earle, Ralph. *Word Meanings in the New Testament*. 6 vols. Kansas City: Beacon Hill, 1974-1984.

Edersheim, Alfred. *The Temple*. 1874. Reprint, Grand Rapids: Eerdmans, 1958.

Emery Bob. *An Evening in Ephesus*. Charlottesville, VA: Bench Press, 1998.

Eusebius. *Ecclesiastical History*. AD 325; Reprint, Peabody, MA: Hendrickson, 1998.

Ewing, Ward. *The Power of the Lamb: Revelation's Theology of Liberation for You*. Cambridge, MA: Cowley, 1990.

Farrar, Frederic W. *The Early Days of Christianity*. New York: Cassell, 1884.

Farrer, Austin. *The Revelation of St. John the Divine*. Oxford: Clarendon, 1964.

Field, Benjamin. *A Student's Handbook of Christian Theology*. New York: Methodist Book Concern, 1887.

Fletcher, John. *The Works of the Reverend John Fletcher*. 1833. Reprint,

Salem, OH: Schmul, 1974.

Foxe, John. *The Acts and Monuments of John Foxe*. 1563. Rpt. Stephen Reed Cattley, ed. 8 vols. London: Seeley & Burnside, 1837-1841. This is commonly known as *Foxe's Book of Martyrs*.

France, R. T. *The Gospel According to Matthew: Tyndale New Testament Commentaries*. Leon Morris, ed. Vol. 1. Grand Rapids: Eerdmans, 1985. [*TNTC*]

__________. *Jesus and the Old Testament*. Grand Rapids: Baker, 1971.

Ice, Thomas and Kenneth L. Gentry, Jr. *The Great Tribulation: Past or Future?* Grand Rapids: Kregel, 1999.

Gentry, Kenneth L. Jr. *Before Jerusalem Fell: Dating the Book of Revelation*. Tyler, TX: Institute for Christian Economics, 1989.

__________. *He Shall Have Dominion*. Tyler, TX: Institute for Christian Economics, 1992.

__________. *Perilous Times: A Study in Eschatological Evil*. Texarkana, AR: Covenant Media, 1999.

__________. "A Preterist View of Revelation." C. Marvin Pate, ed. *Four Views on the Book of Revelation*. Grand Rapids: Zondervan, 1998.

__________. *The Divorce of Israel*. 2 vols. Vallecito, CA: Chalcedon Foundation, 2024.

Gregg, Steve, ed. *Revelation: Four Views, A Parallel Commentary, Revised and Updated Edition*. Nashville: Thomas Nelson, 2013.

Head, Peter M. "The Duration of Divine Judgment" in *Eschatology in Bible and Theology*, Brower and Elliott, eds. Downers Grove, IL: InterVarsity, 1997.

Hemer, Colin J. *The Letters to the Seven Churches of Asia*. Grand Rapids: Eerdmans, 2001.

Holford, George Peter. *The Destruction of Jerusalem*. 1805. Revised edition. Nacogdoches, TX: Covenant Media Press, 2001.

John of Damascus. *On the Orthodox Faith: A Select Library of Nicene and Post-Nicene Fathers of the Christian Church*. Second Series. Vol. 9. Philip Schaff and Henry Wace, eds. 1898. Reprint, Grand Rapids: Eerdmans, 1979. [*NPNF*]

Johnson, Alan. *Revelation* in Vol. 12 of *The Expositor's Bible Commentary*. Frank E. Gaebelein, ed. Grand Rapids: Zondervan, 1981. [*XBC*]

Johnson, Dennis E. *Triumph of the Lamb*. Phillipsburg, NJ: Puritan & Reformed, 2001.

Jordan, James B. *The Revelation of Jesus in Revelation 1:12b-16 and its Relation to the Structure of the Book of Revelation*. Niceville, FL: Biblical Horizons, 2003.

__________. *A Brief Reader's Guide to Revelation*. Niceville, FL: Transfiguration Press, 1999.

Josephus, Flavius. *The Complete Works of Josephus*. William Whiston, ed. Reprint, Grand Rapids: Kregel, 1960.

Kasper, Walther, ed. *The Church's Confession of Faith*. San Francisco: Ignatius Press, 1987.

Kelley, Charles H. *The Methodist Commentary on the New Testament*. 1893; Reprint, as *One Volume New Testament Commentary*, Grand Rapids: Baker, 1972.

Kiddle, Martin. *The Revelation of St. John*. London: Hodder & Stoughton, 1940.

Kierkegaard, Søren. *Purity of Heart is to Will One Thing*. Revised ed. Douglas V. Steere, translator. New York : Harper & Brothers, 1948.

Kik, J. Marcellus. *An Eschatology of Victory*. Phillipsburg, NJ: Presbyterian and Reformed, 1971.

Kline, Meredith G. "Double Trouble." *Journal of the Evangelical Theological Society* 32 (1989) 171-179.

Konkel, A. H. "*Sabua*." *New International Dictionary of Old Testament Theology & Exegesis*. Willem A. VanGemeren, ed. Grand Rapids: Zondervan, 1997. 4:20-24.

Ladd, George Eldon. *A Commentary on the Revelation of John*. Grand Rapids: Eerdmans, 1972.

__________. "Historic Premillennialism." The Meaning of the Millennium, Robert G. Clouse, ed. Downers Grove, IL: InterVarsity, 1977.

Lee, Luther. *Elements of Theology*. 1856. 10th edition. Syracuse, NY: Wesleyan Methodist Publishing House, 1888.

Lenski, R. C. H. *The Interpretation of St. John's Revelation*. Minneapolis: Augsburg, 1935.

MacArthur, John, Jr. *The MacArthur New Testament Commentary: Revelation 1-11* and *Revelation 12-22*. Chicago: Moody, 1999, 2000.

Marshall, I. Howard. *Kept by the Power of God*. Revised ed. Carlisle, England: Paternoster, 1995.

Maurer, Christian. "φυλή." *Theological Dictionary of the New Testament*. Gerhard Friedrich, ed. Grand Rapids: Eerdmans, 1974. 9:245-

250.

McClintock, John and James Strong. *Cyclopedia of Biblical, Theological, and Ecclesiastical Literature.* 12 vols. 1867-1887; Reprint, Grand Rapids: Baker, 1981.

McLean, John Andrew. *The Seventieth Week of Daniel 9:27 as a Literary Key for Understanding the Structure of the Apocalypse of John.* Lewiston, NY: Edwin Mellen Press, 1996.

Metzger, Bruce M. *Breaking the Code.* Nashville: Abingdon, 1993.

Michaels, J. Ramsey. *Revelation: The IVP New Testament Commentary Series.* Vol. 20. Grant R. Osborne, ed. Downers Grove, IL: InterVarsity, 1997. [*IVPNTC*]

Morris, Leon. *The Revelation of St. John. Tyndale New Testament Commentaries.* R. V. G. Tasker, ed. Vol. 20. Grand Rapids: Eerdmans, 1969. [*TNTC*]

Mounce, Robert H. *The Book of Revelation.* Revised ed. *The New International Commentary on the New Testament.* Gordon D. Fee, ed. Grand Rapids: Eerdmans, 1998. [*NICNT*]

Mulholland, M. Robert, Jr. *Revelation: Holy Living in an Unholy World.* Grand Rapids: Francis Asbury Press, 1990.

Oden, Thomas C. *The Living God: Systematic Theology: Volume One.* San Francisco: Harper & Row, 1987. *The Word of Life: Systematic Theology: Volume Two.* 1989.

Otto, Rudolf. *The Idea of the Holy.* John W. Harvey, trans. New York: Oxford University, 1958.

Osborne, Grant R. *Revelation. Baker Exegetical Commentary on the New Testament.* Moisés Silva, ed. Grand Rapids: Baker, 2002. [*BECNT*]

Pate, C. Marvin, ed. *Four Views on the Book of Revelation.* Grand Rapids: Zondervan, 1998.

Payne, J. Barton. *Encyclopedia of Biblical Prophecy: The Complete Guide to Scriptural Predictions and Their Fulfillment.* 1973. Reprint, Grand Rapids: Baker, 1980.

Peterson, Eugene H. *Reversed Thunder.* San Francisco: Harper Collins, 1988.

Peterson, Robert A. *Hell on Trial: The Case for Eternal Punishment.* Phillipsburg, NJ: Puritan & Reformed, 1995.

Pinnock, Clark H. "The Conditional View." *Four Views on Hell.* Grand

Rapids: Zondervan, 1996.

Piper, John. *Let the Nations Be Glad*. Grand Rapids: Baker, 1993.

Plummer, Alfred. *The Revelation of St. John the Divine*. Vol. 51 in *The Pulpit Commentary*. Joseph S. Exell and H. D. M. Spence, eds. 52 vols. Reprinted in 23 vols. *Revelation* is Vol. 22 in the reprint. Grand Rapids: Eerdmans, 1950.

Pope, William Burt. *A Compendium of Christian Theology*. 3 Vols. London: Wesleyan Conference Office, 1880.

Ramsay, William M. *The Letters to the Seven Churches of Asia*. 1904. Updated Edition. Mark W. Wilson, ed. Peabody, MA: Hendrickson, 1994.

Reddish, Mitchell G. *Revelation* in *Smyth & Helwys Bible Commentary*. Macon: Smyth & Helwys Publishing, 2001.

Renan. Ernest. *Antichrist*. 1873. William G. Hutchinson, translator and editor. London: Scott, 1899.

Robertson, A. T. *Word Pictures in the New Testament*. 6 vols. Nashville: Broadman, 1930.

Rushdoony, Rousas John. *Thy Kingdom Come: Studies in Daniel and Revelation*. Fairfax, VA: Thoburn, 1978.

Rutherford, Samuel. *Letters*. Edinburgh: Oliphant, Anderston & Ferrier, 1891.

Schaff, Philip. *History of the Christian Church*. 3rd ed. 8 vols. 1890. Reprint, Grand Rapids: Eerdmans, 1995.

Schweizer, Eduard. "σῶμα." *Theological Dictionary of the New Testament*. Gerhard Friedrich, ed. Grand Rapids: Eerdmans, 1971. 7:1024-1094

Scofield, C. I. ed. *The New Scofield Reference Bible*. New York: Oxford, 1967.

Scott, Leland Howard. "Methodist Theology in America in the Nineteenth Century." PhD diss, Yale University, 1954.

Smith, J. B. *A Revelation of Jesus Christ*. Scottdale, PA: Herald Press, 1961.

Smith, Wilbur M. *Revelation* in the *Wycliffe Bible Commentary*. Everett F. Harrison, ed. Chicago: Moody, 1962.

Staples, Rob L. *Words of Faith*. Kansas City: Beacon Hill, 2001.

Steele, Daniel. "Why I Am Not a Premillennialist." *The Methodist Review* 93 (May 1911) 405-415.

Southerland, Dan. *Transitioning: Leading Your Church Through Change*. Grand Rapids: Zondervan, 1999.

Sproul, R. C. *The Last Days According to Jesus*. Grand Rapids: Baker, 1998.

Stuart, Moses. A Commentary on the Apocalypse. 2 vols. 1845. Reprint, Eugene, OR: Wipf and Stock, 2001.

Sutcliffe, Joseph. *A Commentary on the Old and New Testament.* 2 vols. 1834. Reprint, Salem, OH: Allegheny, 2000.

Sweet, J. P. M. *Revelation*. Philadelphia: Westminster, 1979.

Swete, Henry Barclay. *The Apocalypse of St. John*. 3rd ed. London: MacMillan, 1909.

Tenney, Merrill C, ed. *Zondervan Pictorial Encyclopedia of the Bible.* 5 vols. Grand Rapids: Zondervan, 1975.

__________. *Interpreting Revelation*. Grand Rapids: Eerdmans, 1957.

Tennyson, Alfred. *Idylls of the King*. London: Henry S. King and Co, 1875.

Terry, Milton S. *The Prophecies of Daniel Expounded*. New York: Hunt & Eaton, 1893.

__________. *Biblical Hermeneutics*. 2nd ed. 1885. Reprint, Grand Rapids: Zondervan, 1974.

__________. *Biblical Apocalyptics*. 1898. Reprint, Grand Rapids: Baker, 1988.

Tong, William. *Matthew Henry's Commentary on the Whole Bible.* "*Revelation*" in volume 6. 1706-1721. Reprint, McLean, VA: MacDonald, 1985.

Tozer, A. W. *Jesus is Victor!* Camp Hill, PA: Christian Publications, 1989.

__________. *The Tozer Pulpit*. 2 vols. Gerald B. Smith, ed. Camp Hill, PA: Christian Publications, 1994.

Wall, Robert W. *Revelation* in *New International Biblical Commentary.* W. Ward Gasque, ed. Peabody, MA: Henderson, 1991. [*NIBC*]

Walvoord, John F. *The Revelation of Jesus Christ*. Chicago: Moody, 1966.

Wesley, John. *Explanatory Notes Upon the New Testament.* 1754. Reprint, Salem, OH: Schmul, 1976.

__________. *Explanatory Notes Upon the Old Testament.* 3 vols. 1765. Reprint, Salem, OH: Schmul, 1975.

_________. *The Bicentennial Edition of the Works of John Wesley.* Randy Maddox, ed. 26 vols. to date. Nashville: Abingdon, 1976-.

Whedon, Daniel D. *Commentary on the New Testament.* 5 vols. 1860-1880. Reprint, Salem, OH: Schmul, 1977.

Wiley, H. Orton. *The Harps of God and Other Sermons*. Kansas City: Beacon Hill, 1971.

Wilson, Dwight. *Armageddon Now!* 1977. Reprint, Tyler, TX: Institute for Christian Economics, 1991.

Wilson, J. Christian. "The Problem of the Domitianic Dating of Revelation." *New Testament Studies* 39:4 (Oct 1993) 587-605.

Woodrow, Ralph. *His Truth is Marching On*. Riverside, CA: Ralph Woodrow Evangelistic Association, 1977.

Wright, N. T. *Jesus and the Victory of God.* Minneapolis: Fortress, 1996.

_________. *Surprised by Hope*. Grand Rapids: Zondervan, 2008.

Yinger, Kent L. *Paul, Judaism, and Judgment According to Deeds*. New York: Cambridge University Press, 1999.

Young, E. J. *The Prophecy of Daniel.* 1949. Reprint, Edinburgh: Banner of Truth, 1972.

Yun, Brother with Paul Hattaway. *The Heavenly Man*. Carlisle, UK: Piquant, 2003.

Zahn, Theodor. *Introduction to the New Testament.* Trans. John Moore Trout, et al, 3 vols. Edinburgh: T & T Clark, 1909.

www.ingramcontent.com/pod-product-compliance
Lightning Source LLC
LaVergne TN
LVHW010638110826
845149LV00014B/2871

* 9 7 9 8 9 9 5 7 5 8 9 0 7 *